Ken Guindon has written a well-documented acc   ...ological foray into the liturgical churches that is both relevant and insightful. His impeccable scholarship and convincing argumentation demands the attention of everyone enamored with Catholicism or Orthodoxy. This is a book that needed to be written, and we should be grateful that one so competent and intelligent has done just that.

More than a mental exercise or academic investigation, the substance of this book stems from the crucible of personal experience. Sharing personal lessons from his cross-cultural immersion into sacerdotalism, he attacks no straw men, but carefully and candidly documents ecclesiastical distinctions long recognized, but frequently overlooked.

Like David returning from the Philistines, the author has returned to the evangelical fold with a greater appreciation of the gospel. More pioneer than prodigal, the author "came to his senses" with a reaffirmation of faith that is both inspiring and sobering. We welcome him back with honor and kudos for a sensitive critique of Orthodoxy and Catholicism that is both transparent and courageous.

—**Stephen Brown**
Professor of Bible and History,
Shasta Bible College and Graduate School

Because of a number of recent accounts of evangelicals joining the Roman Catholic or the Eastern Orthodox Church, this is an important and much-needed book. Through the examination of church history, theology and Scripture, Ken Guindon shares his spiritual journey and explains why he returned to evangelical Christianity. His study is fair-minded and well-written, and provides a sound defense for his decision.

—**Edmond C. Gruss,**
Professor Emeritus, The Master's College

This is a very pertinent book for our time when many prize church history and personal experience above Biblical truth in their search for spiritual vitality. Like many today who find a shallowness of doctrine and life in many contemporary evangelical churches, the author tells of his search for genuine Christianity in the Roman Catholic and Orthodox churches whose ancient roots are said to signal authentic Christianity. Although acknowledging enjoyable aspects of the worship atmosphere and recognizing the presence of godly believers, the author explains why these churches did not satisfy his search. Utilizing church history and Biblical theology, many teachings and practices of the Orthodox and Catholic churches are shown to be foreign to the New Testament and contrary to the complete graciousness of salvation—many of them having arisen much later in accommodation to surrounding influences. Written with a loving heart, this work is worth reading by everyone interested in authentic Christianity and is particularly helpful for anyone who is tempted to think that age and claims to infallibility are criteria of the true church.

—**Robert L. Saucy**
Former Distinguished Professor of Systematic Theology,
Talbot School of Theology

The author describes his goal in writing this tome as twofold: to explain why evangelicals are leaving their faith for "highly ceremonial worship," even adopting contrary doctrines to do so; and to "present a short 'apologia' for biblical faith." That is a worthy aim, and the author does a good job reaching his objective, with the book divided pretty well into his double theme—the latter taking a slight edge. His "unrelenting goal is to help outsiders to grasp the issues that are leading evangelicals to become members of these ancient churches." He correctly notes, "A person's way of life will be based upon one of two clear-cut principles: either the Word of God or the word of men." Tradition clearly falls into the latter category.

Guindon sums up succinctly, based on his own experience, why evangelicals are attracted to Roman and Orthodox bodies, offering four positives and two negatives. His chapters on baptism, worship, and sacerdotalism were especially good, we thought. He is convinced one of the major problems in all this relates to confusion between salvation and sanctification. And we liked his observation that someone said, "The Protestant trusts Christ to save him; the Catholic [or Orthodox] trusts Christ to help him save himself." We have always felt this to be true.

Guindon's own summary of his work is, "One faith is the true faith and has no temples, no priests, no material sacrifices. God saves us and our works add nothing to His work."

We were very impressed with this careful, scholarly work. *High Church Heresy* is a good book deserving a wide circulation. It is a delight to endorse it.

—**Robert L. Sumner**
Editor, *The Biblical Evangelist*

HIGH CHURCH HERESY

Exposing **Resurgent** Catholicism and Orthodoxy

KENNETH R. GUINDON

Regular Baptist Books
Arlington Heights, Illinois

High Church Heresy: Exposing Resurgent Catholicism and Orthodoxy
© 2015 • Regular Baptist Press • Arlington Heights, Illinois
www.RegularBaptistPress.org • 1-800-727-4440
RBP5152 • ISBN: 978-1-62940-216-1

Contents

Dedication

To the memory of Dr. Harold L. Fickett Jr., former pastor of First Baptist Church, Van Nuys, California, for his confidence, trust, and mentoring, and to the memory of Major Ian Thomas of England, founder of the Capernwray Missionary Fellowship of Torchbearers. And to a longtime witness of my spiritual journey, Dr. Edmond C. Gruss of Newhall, California, who still takes time to listen and give encouragement.

Acknowledgments

Special thanks to Dr. David Nicholas of Redding, California, who suggested I write this book and then took time from his busy schedule as president of Shasta Bible College and Graduate School to write the foreword. My thanks to Dr. Edmond C. Gruss, who encouraged me in my writing. To all those who read the manuscript and offered advice, such as Tim Knickerbocker and Larry McDonald, I remain indebted.

For all who graciously endorsed my book, I beg the Lord of Glory to bless them and their families. None of them are responsible for any weaknesses or errors. I accept full responsibility for the opinions expressed herein.

I thank God most of all for my wife, Monique, who ministers faithfully to me in innumerable ways and has enabled me to devote time to my studies and writing.

Foreword

IN A DAY WHEN SO MANY EVANGELICALS are attracted to and intrigued by the liturgy, formality, and ritual of Eastern Orthodoxy and Roman Catholicism, Ken Guindon has done Biblical Christianity an incredible service. Saved and discipled in an evangelical church, his sincere but misguided quest for authentic Christianity led him on a nineteen-year pilgrimage into the theological depths of both Orthodoxy and Catholicism. Thankfully, he has returned to *sola scriptura*, convinced that ultimate truth is found only in God's infallible, inerrant Word. God has now enabled and equipped him to focus the light of Scripture on the historical influences and the incremental changes that moved the simplicity of early Christian worship and practice toward a legalistic hierarchy and the sacramental practices that today characterize both the Roman Catholic and Eastern Orthodox churches.

An understanding of the history and heritage of authentic Biblical Christianity has always been important throughout the history of the church. Today, however, such an understanding is not only important, but mandatory. Winds of change and pragmatism are now sweeping across the fundamental/evangelical landscape. Coupled with the surrounding cultural influences of ethical relativism, situation ethics, and the deliberate deconstruction of our moral and ethical values by the secular progressives, these winds of change have sent many sincere believers on a frantic search for either relevance or some kind of historic spiritual security.

Some say the answer is found in making the gospel more palatable to unbelievers and Christ less offensive to the culture. This is the cry

5

of the so-called seeker sensitive movement, which seems to overlook the apostle Paul's inspired observation in Romans 3:11, "There is none that seeketh after God." Also ignored is the "offence of the cross" (Gal. 5:11; 1 Pet. 2:7, 8) and Paul's axiom that "the preaching of the cross is to them that perish foolishness; but unto us which are saved it is the power of God" (1 Cor. 1:18). Thus, the mention of sin and its spiritual consequences, they say, must be minimized, and those who are too outspoken in their condemnation of lifestyles and religious beliefs contrary to Biblical precepts and principles, marginalized. The heritage of past spiritual blessing must be erased and eradicated to make way for new approaches to doing church that will help us to finally get orthodoxy right. As Brian McLaren, a leading spokesperson for the Emerging Church movement, recently stated in *Christianity Today*, "I don't think we've got the gospel right yet. . . . I don't think the liberals have it right. But I don't think we have it right either. None of us has arrived at orthodoxy." John MacArthur, in his book *The Truth War,* identifies the problem well: "In the Emerging Church movement, truth (to whatever degree such a concept is even recognized) is assumed to be inherently hazy, indistinct, and uncertain—perhaps even ultimately unknowable."

Others, longing for the security of the past, have decided to return to the "orthodoxy" of either Roman Catholicism or the Eastern Orthodox Church. Surprisingly, an increasing number of former evangelicals have embraced the writings of the church fathers, the tradition of the church, and in some cases even the apocryphal books as tantamount in importance to the inspired, inerrant Word of God canonized in Holy Scripture. They somehow long for the liturgy and legalism, the smell of incense, the sacraments and the "security" that comes from returning to the "mother church." To them, God's inspired, inerrant Word is not enough, and they seem to overlook all the implications of 2 Timothy 3:16 where Paul tells us that all Scripture is inspired by God (God-breathed) and profitable for teaching, for reproof, for correction, for training in righteousness so that the man of God may be thoroughly equipped for every good work.

For them, Scripture is not enough. It is not sufficient. They want the mediating services of the priest, although 1 Timothy 2:5 instructs, "There is . . . one mediator between God and men, the man Christ Jesus." They want to revel in sacerdotalism, confining God in bread and wine, keeping Him in a gilded box, or holding Him up in a monstrance for adoration despite the fact that Scripture clearly states in Acts 17:24 and 25, "[The] God that made the world and all things therein, seeing that he is Lord of heaven and earth, dwelleth not in temples made with hands; neither is worshipped with men's hands, as though he needed any thing." All this goes along with praying to Mary and the saints, works-based salvation, and adherence to the syncretistic canons of the church, which historically have blended Christianity with pagan religious practices, producing a composite religion with which all can identify, to the point of even recognizing the Islamic religion as legitimate.

This book deserves the attention of all Bible-believing Christians, not just evangelical scholars. It not only explains why evangelicals are attracted to both Orthodoxy and Catholicism but it speaks the truth in love concerning the heresies and even apostate beliefs inherent within these two religious systems. Ken Guindon is uniquely equipped to expose the subtlety of sacramentalism, the lure of liturgy and legalism, the perniciousness of pragmatism, the peril of praying to the saints, the mistakes and misunderstandings of Mariolatry, the ritual of the Rosary, the ineffectiveness of infant baptism, the truth about tradition, and the sabotage of salvation by both Roman Catholicism and the Eastern Orthodox Church by the addition of works to the clear teaching of Scripture that salvation is by grace through faith alone (Rom. 3:27, 28).

David R. Nicholas, ThD
President, Professor of Theology
Shasta Bible College and Graduate School
Redding, California

Introduction

FOR THE LAST FIFTY YEARS OR SO, a new drumbeat has been heard in the West. Evangelicals[1] have been joining either the Roman Catholic Church, the Eastern Orthodox Church, or some other formalistic liturgical church. Thomas Howard (after a stint with Anglicanism) chose Roman Catholicism and later wrote a book with the striking title *Evangelical Is Not Enough*. Former Presbyterian Pastor Scott Hahn, a professor at Franciscan University of Steubenville in Ohio, can be seen on EWTN, a Roman Catholic television network. Also on EWTN is former Presbyterian minister Marcus Grodi, with his *The Journey Home* TV program and his ministry to help evangelical ministers considering joining the Catholic church. The latest surprise has been the "return" of Frank Beckwith, president (2007) of the Evangelical Theological Society, to the Roman Catholic Church of his youth. On the Eastern Orthodox[2] side of the equation one finds Frank Schaeffer, the son of Presbyterian theologian and philosopher Francis Schaeffer; Peter Gillquist; Gordon Walker; Jack Sparks; and their companions who were key people in Campus Crusade for Christ. A number of the latter are now Orthodox priests. Many of those marching eastward were once Anglican, Lutheran, Presbyterian, Baptist, or Pentecostal ministers. Their spiritual journeys have already been told in books and magazines, so it is pointless to detail them here. The following pages present an analysis of the reasons for such conversions to ancient liturgical churches and then my own "Journey Home" back to the evangelical

1. The term "evangelical" as used in this book refers to a born-again Christian who believes the Bible to be the inspired Word of God. Due to a lot of confusion today, "evangelical" has come to mean almost anyone who attends any kind of "Christian" church. We do not address the latter meaning here.

2. Throughout this book, the term "Orthodox" will refer to those churches popularly known as "Eastern Orthodox."

faith. This book should definitely strengthen your personal faith in Jesus Christ, Who saves us completely by grace through faith. Christian pastors and counselors will also discover helpful chapters with information on historical questions, the church fathers, repetitive prayer, the worship of images, and sacramentalism.

In recent decades a definite trend toward *churchianity* has developed within evangelical churches, moving even toward Eastern practices like meditation and yoga. The use of candles, robes, and repetitious responses is seen more frequently in American churches today. New thinking, new methods, and new names such as "missional church" or "emergent church" seek to renew the church's focus. This trend is often a sign of a more cosmetic activism, marking a return to forms of worship as seen in ancient temples and religions. We are seeing a return to pre-Reformation times, when huge cathedrals were packed with people who superstitiously sought salvation in the practice of sacraments, the worship of saints, and the purchase of indulgences to shorten their time in purgatory. Those poor people simply trusted the faith they had inherited from their fathers.

The Pope Mobile and Pope Appeal

The resurgence of the traditional faiths can be seen in recent World Youth Day celebrations, held yearly by international and American Catholic dioceses. World Youth Day was instituted by Pope John Paul II in 1985 and first held in 1986. In 1995, the closing Mass in the Philippines set a world record, with five million in attendance. Pope Francis broke that record in 2015 with six million in attendance in Brazil. These huge gatherings have been held in Vatican City, Rome, Argentina, Brazil, Australia, Spain, Poland, France, the USA, and Canada, inspiring a resurgence of Catholicism. Many are boarding the "pope mobile" and Catholic bandwagon to join the parade. Parish signs and TV ads have held a Catholic "come home" campaign to urge former Catholics to return to their church.

In the meantime, popes, patriarchs, and bishops are frequently seen on television as they issue statements on fraternal relations with Muslims, Jews, and Protestants, and issue documents detailing the need for ecological care of Earth's resources. These leaders meet together in

Jerusalem and elsewhere, appealing for world peace.

And the pope's appeal is on the rise. Pope Francis, the latest pope, endeavors to live modestly in a small apartment. He speaks out on women's rights, divorce, and homosexuality, gaining the attention of university students as well as social media. Popes and bishops now have their own blogs, Facebook pages, and Twitter accounts. They are shaking off the opinion people formerly held that they were old-fashioned and deserved to be marginalized. Youth are taking notice to some extent, and many former Catholics are returning to the church of their parents as a possible source of stability and peace in troubled times.

Magnetic Pull

The Orthodox (OC) and Roman Catholic (RCC) Churches contend that they have faithfully preserved the apostolic faith as taught in both the Scriptures and tradition. Their apologists reference the church fathers in support of their teachings on the Eucharist and baptism. Due to a growing uneasiness with denominationalism and the arbitrariness of so many pastors, people are seeking the "true" church Christ organized around His twelve apostles.

Faced with the conflicting opinions of so many churches and denominations, people today might surmise that they can find faithful guides to Christ's teachings in the apostolic fathers. After all, were they not the apostles' direct spiritual successors? Having received the promise of the Holy Spirit, would not Christ's church accurately preserve and transmit the deposit of faith? Was not the noted Anglican patristic scholar J. N. D. Kelly to be trusted when he wrote,

> In the eyes of both of them [Cyril and Theodoret] the authority of
> the Fathers consisted precisely in the fact that they had so faith-
> fully and fully expounded the real intention of the Bible writers.
> What they found impressive was that so many famous and saintly
> teachers, venerated in the whole Church were unanimous in their
> interpretation of Scripture and in their statement of the doctrines
> set forth, or at any rate implied, in it.[3]

3. J. N. D. Kelly, *Early Christian Doctrines*, 2nd ed. (New York: HarperCollins, 1960, 1978; San Francisco:

In my own search for the visible church of Christ, such reasoning led me to leave the safe harbor of the Scriptures for the stormy waters of church history.

In 1986, I read Dr. Nicolas Wiseman's *Conférences sur les doctrines et les pratiques les plus importantes de l'Eglise Catholique.*[4] I began to think that the church fathers and church councils should be trusted. I asked myself, did Christians as far back as Justin Martyr and Ignatius look at the bread and wine as types[5] or symbols, that is, as a simple memorial of Christ's death on the cross? Or did they believe that the bread and the wine were transformed into the actual body and blood of Christ during the liturgy? On the other hand, could it be that these early apologists were unduly influenced by their background and their cultural environment (Platonism, Hellenism, or Judaism)? As immediate successors to the apostles, did they faithfully transmit Christ's teachings like a sacred treasure to be protected? Did they believe that regeneration took place in the baptismal waters? It appeared that they did, and this led me to believe that the Roman Catholic Church was founded by our Lord Jesus Christ. At that moment I knew practically nothing about the Orthodox Church, so it was not an option.

Another question occupied my mind at that point: What happened to Christianity during the twenty to fifty years after the apostles established churches in the Diaspora? My reading in the church fathers gradually led me to the conviction that the Catholic church may have grown out of the apostolic church, like an acorn becoming an oak tree. Did a Judaizing spirit permeate the atmosphere in which the newly founded Christian churches (*ecclesias*) were established? Did the insidious gnostic currents of the Mediterranean basin inspire monasticism? What about platonic and neo-Platonic ideas everywhere in vogue?

Prince Press edition, 2003), 49. Citations refer to the Prince Press edition.

4. Nicolas Wiseman, *Conférences sur les doctrines et les pratiques les plus importantes de l'Eglise Catholique,* trans. Alfred Nettement (Paris: Beaujouan et Jourdan, 1839). Dr. Wiseman was also a cardinal in the Catholic church. The spine of the book has the intriguing title *Conférences sur le Protestantisme* ["Conferences on Protestantism"] stamped on it. This is what motivated my purchase from a used-book store in Perpignan, France, where I was living at the time.

5. Of realities in Heaven (reminiscent of Platonism).

Did these affect the development of Christian theology or spirituality in any way? How can one account for the evident differences between primitive Christianity with its simple style of worship and the elaborate ceremonies of the post-Nicene period?

The ancient churches (RCC, OC) proudly argue from history and practice (tradition), citing the fathers from the second century onward. Should we accept such authorities as compatible with the gospel found in the Word of God? What about our Lord's warning in the Parable of the Sower? Jesus said that while the sower slept, the enemy would come and sow the field with weeds (Matt. 13). The separation of the tares, or weeds, from the true wheat will take place at the end of the age when the sower (Christ) returns for the harvest. These tares would begin to appear as early as the apostles' days, according to Paul's prediction in Acts 20:28 and 29: "Be on guard for yourselves and for all the flock, among whom the Holy Spirit has appointed you as overseers, to shepherd the church of God, which He purchased with His own blood. I know that after my departure savage wolves will come in among you, not sparing the flock" (HCSB).

The apostle Paul warned the church at Thessalonica that the apostasy was not just on the horizon; it was already raising its ugly head: "For the mystery of lawlessness *is already* at work; only He who now restrains will do so until He is taken out of the way" (2 Thess. 2:7, italics added). To Timothy, his child in the faith, Paul prophesied, "The time will come when they will not endure sound doctrine, but after their own lusts shall they heap to themselves teachers, having itching ears, and they shall turn away their ears from the truth, and shall be turned unto fables" (2 Tim. 4:3, 4).

The Assurance of the Gospel

This book attempts to answer several questions: Should Christians look to the church fathers, to the Scriptures alone, or to both as sure guides when considering sacramentalism and salvation? Does the Orthodox Church really teach that ecclesiastical rules and observances must be obeyed for one to be a faithful Christian? Consequently, have the ancient churches confused salvation and sanctification? Most importantly, do these practices and church rules undermine the authentic Christian gospel? Do these ancient churches teach that salvation is *in* and *through* the church? Another important but subsidiary question is, What is worship, and in reality is there a difference between the worship offered to God and that offered to saints? My goal is to provide church leaders, pastors, evangelists, and interested laypeople with a handy reference book on this timely topic.

I quote the church fathers, but not because I consider any of them to be an infallible guide to a correct interpretation of Scripture. One may find the church fathers informative at times, but no one should overemphasize them. A Christian trusts the triune God, Who speaks through His Word found in the canon of the inspired Holy Scriptures. But over time, apostolic teaching began to be interpreted in new ways, and the church fathers, as well as the ecumenical councils, came to be considered by many as *infallible*.

All the possible questions and issues that come to mind in a review of the Scriptures and the church fathers cannot be addressed here, so my goal is twofold: (1) to make people aware of the reasons some evangelicals have opted out of Protestant churches for a more ceremonial worship and have adopted doctrines contrary to evangelical teaching, and (2) to present an *apologia* for a Biblical faith.

The subject matter obliges us to look at church history, patristics, and exegesis of the Holy Scriptures because it is important for evangelicals to understand why people are attracted to either the Catholic or the Orthodox faith. How many of these converts revert later in life to the evangelical faith? Certain individuals may be tempted to consider this book an attack upon their cherished beliefs, but that would be a mistake. My sole purpose is to lay before the public the Scriptural and historical reasons for my return to a truly Biblical faith. Love for Christ and His message motivates my writing. I do not wish to criticize or denigrate anyone because I have chosen to examine his church's teachings. I do love and appreciate my Catholic and Orthodox friends. Thousands of Orthodox believers preferred martyrdom under the Islamic yoke rather than renounce the name of Christ for Muhammad. Both Catholics and Orthodox have founded important charitable works, such as orphanages and hospitals, at home and abroad; such zeal for Christ and neighbor is worthy of respect.

I have spent much of the last fifteen years reading, meditating, and reflecting on my spiritual experience in Orthodoxy. Uneasiness and dissatisfaction constantly afflicted me, causing me to remember when I was truly "resting in Christ" (Matt. 11:28–30; Heb. 4:3). On September 23, 2001, having witnessed a TV broadcast of the massive interfaith service held at Yankee Stadium in New York City to commemorate the events of 9/11, I was shocked to see the participation of Archbishop Demetrios of the Greek Orthodox Archdiocese (benediction prayer) and to note the attendance of my own metropolitan and head of the Orthodox Church in America (Theodosius). Why this concern? Because the canons of the Orthodox Church prohibit Orthodox clergy from participating in joint prayers with other religions. The Orthodox Church sees itself as unique, *the* Lord's Body. That day in September saw Baptists, Catholics, Orthodox, Sikhs, Buddhists, Hindus, Jews, and Muslims praying together for our country. The visual effect communicated that all religions are equal and that people worship the same God because there is only one God. This led me to break communion with my priest, parish, and church and to move to Florida to support a fiercely anti-ecumenical (old calendarist[6]) Orthodox Church with a very small presence in our country. Still, I did not find peace of mind or heart. I had been reading the Bible, and something constantly nagged and pulled at me. For a short time I visited several evangelical churches but did not feel at home there as I once had. Eventually, I returned to the Orthodox Church and became a member of the Russian Orthodox Church outside Russia (known also by the acronym ROCOR, a fairly anti-ecumenical group, present in many countries). I thought I had found a shelter and resting place for my wife and me.

---

6. Today's Orthodox Churches are divided into "Old Calendarists," who follow the Julian calendar, and "New Calendarists," who follow the Gregorian calendar, which they like to call the "Revised Julian Calendar." Ecumenism and the church calendar have been the cause of a lot of dissension in the Orthodox Church, some groups breaking away from the main bodies. The place of the Oriental Orthodox Churches is another issue and is the result of a schism dating back to the fourth century. These churches are not under consideration here.

The Roman Catholic and Orthodox Churches share similar ideas on the sacraments and salvation, although some differences do exist. During the last thirty years or so, representatives from these churches have been meeting to discuss issues such as the addition to the Creed by Roman Catholics of the *filioque* clause, baptism, and the role of the pope. The Western (Roman) and the Eastern (Orthodox) churches are agreeing that they share the same priesthood and sacraments. (Many Orthodox reject this; nevertheless, it is widely admitted today.) A great many Orthodox clergymen consider other churches to be either schismatic and/or heretical. However, these issues do not concern us here.

Self-justification has no real value, and I am writing only to make others aware that I have chosen to stand on the same ground as the apostle Paul: God is "the justifier of the one who has faith" (Rom. 3:26). Having been an active member of the Roman Catholic and the Orthodox Churches for about twenty-five of my adult years, I believe I understand their belief systems well enough to compare them fairly with the faith taught in the Holy Scriptures. These pages will answer numerous questions concerning the ancient churches and the reasons they draw so many evangelicals into their fold.

Throughout this book I have endeavored to maintain the primacy of Scripture. The so-called church fathers *never* claimed infallibility for their writings. It may seem logical to suppose that the earliest witnesses to the apostolic faith would be more trustworthy witnesses than those who succeeded them centuries later, but that may not be the case as we shall see later. But keep in mind, Christ promised us that the gates of Hell would not prevail against His church!

PART 1

CHAPTER 1

Tradition, Scripture, and the Church Fathers

VERYONE IS FAMILIAR with the request to "please put that in writing." It is considered the best way to avoid misunderstandings that arise when memories have dimmed. Similarly, contracts, deeds, and wills are recorded and notarized to avoid long contests in court. The Bible, too, is a written document, even, one might say, a contract that has been confirmed and notarized by God's Son, Jesus Christ. Although the prophets of both Testaments said much that is not recorded in the Bible, in the written Word we have all the essential and necessary truths for our salvation (1 Pet. 1:10–12, 23; 2:2). So in matters that involve our faith, our fellowship with God, and our fellowman, should not God's written Word take precedence?

Numerous teachings of the ancient churches are not found in the Word of God. People are not saved by a knowledge of church traditions such as purgatory, the immaculate conception of Mary, papal infallibility, or fasting for a certain number of days and hours before taking Communion, but they are saved by means of the gospel message that Jesus Christ is the Savior of the world (John 4:42). The purpose of Scripture is to provide the history of salvation from creation to the Second Coming of Christ and the accomplishment of God's purposes. Tradition does not add anything of importance to the content of the gospel. People will be saved without knowing whether Jesus had brothers and sisters or whether Peter was the head of the apostolic band and the first pope.

The Old Testament was the Bible of the apostolic church, and its members scrutinized it for types and prophecies of the Messiah. They found in the New Testament about three hundred Old Testament references and allusions. And the Holy Spirit led them to find the true meaning of the Torah and other parts of the Old Testament that predicted the Messiah (Luke 24:25–27; 2 Cor. 3:14–16; Rev. 19:10). Can we say that like the Bible, Tradition[1] is a two-edged sword (Heb. 4:12)? Is Tradition inspired? If the answer is no, why do some people fight to hold onto Tradition or traditions? The apostle Paul tells us that all Scripture is inspired, that is, God-breathed (2 Tim. 3:16). The book of Revelation in particular informs us that it is "the testimony of Jesus" and "the faith of Jesus" (Rev. 12:17; 19:10; 14:12). Who can say this about traditions, since they are based on people's memories and stories?

Issues of Authority

What is the definitive and final authority in Christ's church? This question, along with what is the means of salvation, takes precedence over every other point of controversy. Roman Catholic and Orthodox church members trust their church leadership for guidance, for constituting the definitive and final authority.

Some in the church, however, questioned that authority. They wanted to purge the church of its extra-Biblical superstitions (traditions). Saints, purgatory, penances, and indulgences weighed heavily upon people and kept the simple multitudes from experiencing the peace that comes from knowing Jesus Christ as Savior and mediator. Thus the Reformation was born. The Reformers did not, however, envision building another church, but thought only of cleansing the one into which they had been born. Reformation preachers invited men and women to focus on Christ, His grace, and the Scriptures alone (therefore the five "solas"[2]). Their struggle brought many benefits, but

---

1. "Tradition" is generally capitalized in this book when it refers to a source of dogma received in the ancient churches.

2. The five solas are *sola scriptura*, "Scripture alone"; *sola fide*, "faith alone"; *sola gratia*, "grace alone"; *solo Christo*, "Christ alone"; *soli Deo Gloria*, "to the glory of God alone."

it also produced its own problems. While preachers sought to instruct the masses in the truths of Scripture, the focus moved away from worship and to the preacher and preaching. Worship became limited to the singing of psalms and hymns and listening to the best preacher a church could secure; in a word, worship became mostly an intellectual experience.[3]

To grapple with the issues that lead evangelicals to become members of ancient churches, the relationship between Tradition and Scripture remains critical. Are they both equally reliable sources for Christian faith? Evangelicals also need to come to grips with the "church fathers." How should we evaluate them in relation to the Holy Scriptures?

The Word *Tradition* in the New Testament

What do the Scriptures teach about tradition, and what do the ancient liturgical churches teach on the subject? *Parádosis* is the Greek noun generally translated "tradition" or "traditions" in our Bibles. It basically means "to hand down" or "hand over," "to transmit." By extrapolation it may refer to doctrine or teaching. Interestingly, the Darby Version, which is a very literal translation, says "doctrines" at Galatians 1:14, with a footnote reading "traditions." We know that the oral preaching of the gospel was eventually committed to writing. The apostle Paul, in his first letter to the Corinthians, refers to his gospel preaching concerning Christ, "Moreover, brethren, I declare to you the gospel which I preached to you, which also you received and in which you stand, by which also you are saved. . . . For I delivered [*paradidomai*] to you first of all that which I also received: that Christ died for our sins according to the Scriptures" (15:1–3). We also have his oral teaching ("the traditions," HCSB) on the Lord's Supper written down: "Now I praise you because you remember me in all things and keep the traditions [KJV, "ordinances"] just as

3. R. C. Sproul, *A Taste of Heaven* (Orlando: Reformation Trust, 2006), 20, 150. Dr. Sproul comments on page 150, "When God prescribed worship in the Old Testament, the whole person was involved." See also Joseph A. Pipa Jr., ed. *The Worship of God* (Taylors, SC: Mentor, 2005), 36–37, and chapter 9 in Michael Horton's *A Better Way* (Grand Rapids: Baker Books, 2003), 158–59.

I delivered them to you" (1 Cor. 11:2, HCSB). Interestingly, *parádosis* occurs twice here: once as a noun and once as a verb.

Another positive reference is 2 Thessalonians 2:15: "Therefore, brethren, stand fast and hold the traditions which you were taught, whether by word or our epistle" (cf. 3:6). We believe that there can be no difference between Paul's "word" and his "epistle." *Parádosis* occurs in thirteen New Testament verses. Eight of these occurrences are found in a negative context in the Gospels, where Jesus condemned the Jews who preferred their traditions to the spiritual and sincere practice of Judaism. Knowing how much weight both the Roman Catholic and the Orthodox churches place on Tradition, we would expect to find more positive references than the few we have in the New Testament. Scriptural support for the ancient churches' reliance on Tradition appears to be rather slim, if it exists at all.

In 1 Peter 1:18, "tradition" is compounded with another word and translated as "tradition from your fathers." Albert Barnes commented on this phrase: "*Received by tradition from your fathers. The mode of worship which had been handed down from father to son. The worship of idols depends on no better reason than that it is that which has been practised in ancient times; and it is kept up now in all lands, in a great degree, only by the fact that it has had the sanction of the venerated men of other generations.*"[4] Since images were honored as representatives of gods, not always as the gods themselves, these statements would apply to any discussion about image worship (see chapter 9).

Tradition should always be examined to determine whether it is in harmony with God's commandments.

Issues of Authority Lead to Evangelical Conversions to Orthodoxy

Originally Protestants separated from the Roman church mainly because of the defective teaching in the medieval church, but also

---

4. Albert Barnes, *Barnes' Notes on the New Testament*, ed. Ingram Cobbin (Grand Rapids: Kregel, 1962), 1403.

because of the low moral life of many clergymen. Still, the issue of what constitutes the final authority for God's people was uppermost in all the intramural debates. The two ways of looking at the differences have been succinctly summarized in *The Teaching of the Catholic Church*, edited by the famous Jesuit Karl Rahner: "God could have addressed the Word of his revelation to individuals independently of any human community or authority. This was the idea of the Reformers. But he could also have *entrusted his truth to a human community* and set up a responsible guardian for its presentation. This is what Christ did."[5]

This is clearly a straw man argument because it is not true even on the surface of it. The fact that Jesus chose, trained, and then sent out the twelve apostles with authority to preach and to found and build up churches is accepted by everyone within Christianity; consequently, the assertion above is false (Matt. 28:18–20). The Reformers never rejected authority. The entire argument with the Catholic church revolved around the issue of the proper authority *in* the church. The Roman Catholics referred to the popes, the ecumenical councils, and the bishops as the source of authority for all interpretations of Tradition and Scripture. The Reformers held up the Holy Scriptures alone as the supreme authority in the church; nevertheless, let us continue for the moment.

It is always better to go directly to the sources to interview informed spokespeople rather than outsiders to learn what a group believes. This will be our procedure as we lay a foundation for the discussion of Scripture and Tradition.

Orthodox priest Anthony M. Coniaris describes the importance of a ministry having a historical connection to the apostles:

> What do we mean when we use the word "church?" Look at the tremendous variety of groups that call themselves churches. In fact, anyone can [now] establish a church for himself. . . . But are they truly churches? Were they founded by Jesus and the

---

5. Josef Neuner and Heinrich Roos, *The Teaching of the Catholic Church as Contained in Her Documents*, ed. Karl Rahner, trans. Geoffrey Stevens (Staten Island: Alba House, 1967), 53.

Apostles? What kind of historical connection do they have with the apostles. . . . We Orthodox Christians mean by Church the Body through which Jesus is present in the world today. It was founded by Christ through the Apostles and has maintained a living, historical connection with the Apostles through the ordination of clergy. The fact that the bishop who ordains an Orthodox priest today can trace his ordination historically all the way back to the Apostles and through them to Christ is a guarantee that the Orthodox Church was not founded by someone called Joe Smith a few centuries ago but by Christ Himself and traces its existence back to Jesus.[6]

Are we correct to conclude that his statement, "a living, historical connection with the Apostles," is another way of speaking of "Holy Tradition" in the Orthodox church? Actually, this idea is called *successionism*, which supposedly guarantees Tradition.[7]

How does the Orthodox church view itself, and how do recent converts view their new church and the denominations they left? Frank Schaeffer wrote a three-hundred-page tome that sets out to prove that, in spite of being the son of the famous evangelical Francis Schaeffer, he discovered evangelicalism to be a religion in which each person is free to follow his own opinions, his personal conscience. Schaeffer takes aim at the multitude of evangelical groups and also the Catholic church, when he writes, "The Church has never seen itself as a chaos of spiritual individualism, let alone as a maelstrom of twenty-three thousand denominations battling for turf, each armed with its own subjective reading of Scripture and its self-invented 'traditions.' Nor has the historical Church seen itself as under a dictator or 'infallible' pope."[8]

He speaks out against what he calls the "American Protestant frenzy for self-realization," which, he says, "built to a fever pitch in the eighteenth and nineteenth centuries [when] whole new frontier

---

6. Anthony M. Coniaris, *Introducing the Orthodox Church* (Minneapolis: Light and Life Pub. Co., 1982), 1, quoted in Frank Schaeffer, *Dancing Alone: The Quest for Orthodox Faith in the Age of False Religion* (Brookline, MA: Holy Cross Orthodox Press, 1994), 149.

7. See the appendix for a further discussion of succession.

8. Frank Schaeffer, *Dancing Alone* (Brookline, MA: Holy Cross Orthodox Press, 1994), 149.

cults, sects and religions were invented practically out of thin air."[9]

He certainly earns points for colorful writing, with descriptions such as these: "With Christian religion reduced to the level of a sectarian squabble in America," "the utopian, Protestant-Enlightenment sickness," and "Americans seem to believe in their Puritan-utopian-millennial enlightened, self-proclaimed goodness, in being converted to see the light, in having some sort of special call or covenant that sets them apart from the normal rules of history."[10]

From the beginning of his book, Schaeffer demonstrates the importance of Tradition in the Orthodox mind as he describes his rationale for leaving his family's Reformed faith:

> A day came when it became clear to me that if I was to believe the history books I was reading, and the writings of the Fathers of the Church, then I had to choose between the Protestant world view and the Holy Tradition. What was obvious was that they were not one and the same. . . .

> It seemed to me that we Protestants had deliberately avoided the study of the historical Church and concentrated on endless theological debates. Perhaps theological theories are easier to manipulate than history.[11]

Another writer who left evangelicalism describes the "pilgrimage" of evangelicals, ministers, and congregations to the Orthodox church. Written by Peter E. Gillquist, *Becoming Orthodox* relates the exodus of a number of leaders from the Campus Crusade for Christ ministry. These people were seeking answers, and sincerely so. They wanted to find the New Testament church. Gordon Walker (a former Baptist minister, now an Orthodox priest) says, "For the life of me, I cannot tell you the details of *where* that New Testament Church *went*."[12] What happened to the New Testament church is a huge question that has caused the shipwreck of many in the ship called

---

9. Ibid., 123.

10. Ibid., 133, 136, 11.

11. Ibid., 18.

12. Peter E. Gillquist, *Becoming Orthodox*, rev. ed. (Ben Lomond, CA: Conciliar, 1992), 24.

"denominationalism." Evangelical church members need better education in their faith if they are to refute the confusion that is causing many to lose their way.

Gillquist, who became an Orthodox priest, discloses another reason that led him and his companions to distrust their evangelical experience.

> The second reason I trust the Holy Spirit to lead the Church and preserve her traditions is the way He gave us the Holy Scriptures. Not only were the Scriptures written under the inspiration of the Holy Spirit, the books were gathered together under the inspiration of the Spirit.
>
> . . . Though a visible consensus regarding most of the New Testament books existed for years beforehand, it was not until the Synod of Carthage, which met in A.D. 397, that we find the final list of the biblical canon as we know it today.
>
> This is the point. If we can trust the Holy Spirit to guide the Church in discerning the books to be included in the canon of Scripture, then we can trust that He has led the Church in her other decisions as well! And remember—how did the Church know which books were doctrinally sound and thus to be included in the canon? On the basis of the doctrines passed down through holy tradition!
>
> There is no way to take the Scriptures and trash tradition. They come to us as a package.[13]

We see clearly how Orthodox Christians view other churches, even the Roman Catholic Church, when Gillquist opines,

> Saddled even more with late tradition is the Protestant movement. Whereas Rome generally added to the faith, Protestantism has subtracted from it. . . .
>
> Mary has become a no-name; holy communion, a quarterly memorial; authority and discipline in the Church, a memory;

---

13. Ibid., 65–66.

doctrine, a matter of personal interpretation, constantly coming up for renegotiation.[14]

Vladimir Lossky provides a short definition of tradition in the Orthodox faith: "Tradition is the life of the Holy Spirit in the Church."[15] Expanding further on this, Bishop Ware writes, "[Tradition] means the books of the Bible; it means the Creed; it means the decrees of the Ecumenical Councils and the writings of the Fathers; it means the Canons, the Service Books, the Holy Icons—in fact, the whole system of doctrine, Church government, worship, spirituality and art which Orthodoxy has articulated over the ages."[16]

It is important to also take account of the attitudes of the ultra-conservative Orthodox who are not part of mainstream Orthodoxy. Schisms have occurred due to recent trends in ecumenism and modernism, which the hardliners reject as being a betrayal of the true faith. An educated but inflexible spokesman, Father Michael Azkoul, PhD, was a member of several Orthodox churches in the United States before he left them because of their modernist tendencies and ecumenism. He explains what his party believes:

> Tradition, which exists only within the Church, contains everything she must profess. Whatever is necessary to believe for salvation is found in her. . . . The sacred content of Tradition is changed neither by what the Fathers have written, nor by the customs of the local Church, nor by the composition of Creeds by the universal Church. These are all witnesses to the immutable Tradition which they expound and defend.[17]

Again, the opinion that the Orthodox church is *the* true church shines through when Azkoul explains that "in a word, the Catholic Church has one Faith, while all else is heretical perversion."[18] This

14. Ibid., 68.

15. Vladimir Lossky, *In the Image and Likeness of God* (Crestwood, NY: St. Vladimir's Seminary, 1974), 152, quoted in Timothy Ware, *The Orthodox Church*, 2nd rev. ed. (London: Penguin Books, 1993), 198.

16. Timothy Ware, *The Orthodox Church*, 2nd rev. ed. (London: Penguin Books, 1993), 195–96.

17. Michael Azkoul, *Once Delivered to the Saints* (Seattle: Saint Nectarios Press, 2000), 25.

18. Ibid., 31.

teaching is held by many bishops, priests, and laypeople, and by many of the monks of the influential monastic peninsula of Mount Athos, Greece.

Elder Cleopa of Romania, now deceased, is very much loved and respected for his steadfastness as a Christian during the time the Communists controlled his country. He stated that Tradition "is unerring," then added, "The Church lived the truth of the Gospel even before anything was committed to writing, having lived with the Holy Tradition from the outset. . . . It carries the same weight as Holy Scripture."[19]

Finally, a reference from an authority in Greece:

> The Church teaches and interprets those divine truths brought out in Holy Scripture and Sacred Tradition. Scripture and Tradition, then, are equally valid, possess equal dogmatic authority, and are equal in value as sources of dogmatic truth. The Church's teaching shows that the Scriptures are in complete harmony with Apostolic Tradition.
>
> Thus, Sacred Tradition is both older and richer than the Scriptures. . . . Thus, as we have said, the Scriptures embody but a small portion of Sacred Tradition, and consequently need to be interpreted and fulfilled in the light of Sacred Tradition.[20]

These quotations acquaint us with the Orthodox church's teaching expressed by its saints, articulate theologians, and the evangelicals who have converted to it. According to them, "Holy Tradition" is equal in weight with the Holy Scriptures, preceded the Scriptures, is more complete than the Scriptures, and is equal to the Scriptures as a source of dogma. Thus someone could reasonably pay as much or more attention to Tradition than to the Scriptures if never questioning Tradition.

---

19. Elder Cleopa, *The Truth of Our Faith*, trans. and ed. Peter Alban Heers (Thessalonica, Greece: Uncut Mountain, 2000), 55.

20. John Karmiris, *A Synopsis of the Dogmatic Theology of the Orthodox Catholic Church*, trans. George Dimopoulos (Scranton: Christian Orthodox Edition, 1973), 5–6.

No wonder a chasm exists between true evangelical Bible believers and Orthodoxy or Roman Catholicism. How is dialogue possible under such circumstances? According to the nineteenth-century Roman Catholic scholar Nicolas Wiseman, the question of what constitutes the rule of faith for Christians is "the heart of the controversy that divides the two religions."[21] Because the ancient churches constantly refer to the church fathers as proper interpreters of the Scriptures and ancient church beliefs, we look next at a sampling of the church fathers on Scripture and Tradition.

The Church Fathers on Scripture and Tradition

Made a cardinal shortly before his death, Yves M.-J. Congar, a famous Dominican scholar, led in the revival of patristic studies in the Catholic church. Congar presents several propositions from an earlier writer and summarizes them this way:

> In early Christianity there was no *problem* about Scripture and Tradition. Moreover, for the Apostolic Fathers and the apologists, Scripture is the Old Testament whose meaning, it was taken as evident, was entirely christological. The dominant idea was that of faith and of the Church's preaching or "kerygma". It was in the Church's preaching and by the faith that welcomed it that the content of Scripture (that is, the mystery of Jesus Christ the Saviour) was understood. . . . [Here, he summarizes Irenaeus's views.] Scripture and Tradition have the same content, but under two different aspects and in two states. . . .
>
> In the earliest Fathers, no distinction was made, from the point of view of content, between an *oral* tradition and what is transmitted to us in Scripture, though Tertullian and Origen were well aware that there were things held and practiced in the Church for which Scripture provides no express testimony. This awareness was more distinct and more clearly expressed in the fourth century.[22]

---

21. Nicolas Wiseman, *Conférences sur les doctrines et les pratiques les plus importantes de l'Eglise Catholique*, trans. Alfred Nettement (Paris: Beaujouan et Jourdan, 1839), 1:82–85.

22. Yves M.-J. Congar, *Tradition and Traditions*, trans. Michael Naseby and Thomas Rainborough (New York: Macmillan, 1967; San Diego: Basilica, 1997), 377–78. Citations refer to the Basilica edition.

This is what one would expect if any fidelity existed at all in the early years after the church's birth. Teachings orally taught and transmitted would be based upon the content of the gospel and perhaps some oral instructions to presbyters[23] and people. Tradition would certainly not transmit new doctrines or myths never taught by Christ or His apostles. This traditional gospel teaching, preserved by faithful bishops, served as a bulwark against gnostic groups that claimed a special knowledge *(gnosis)* for their speculative teachings. As time passed, the distinction between Scripture and Tradition became ever more pronounced. The church was distancing itself from the apostolic faith as it evolved due to influences from within and without. Professor Norman Cantor remarks,

> From one point of view, then, the church thus developed away from pure, apostolic Christianity. On the other hand, it may be claimed that only thus could the church progress, adapting itself to a changing world, to new people and new ideas.
>
> Like the empire, the church worked out a strict system of hierarchy based on levels reminiscent of the Platonic concept of the Chain of Being, the continuous hierarchy between pure matter and pure idea. In the Christian church, obedience was due from priest up to bishop, from bishop to archbishop, and from archbishop up to the pope (father) in the West and the patriarchs in the East. Borrowing Platonic philosophy and the Roman system of government, the church developed the Christian priesthood, with its priests set apart from ordinary men and women.[24]

During the early centuries there were groups such as Gnostics, Sabellians, Montanists, Manichaeans, and Arians, and all these parties cited the Scriptures. Orthodox, that is, true Christians were obliged to ask, What is the correct principle of interpretation? During the first and second centuries the term "Scriptures" *primarily* meant

---

23. A presbyters was an official in the early Christian church who served in directing the congregation.

24. Norman F. Cantor, *The Civilization of the Middle Ages* (New York: Harper Perennial, 1994), 37, 39.

the Old Testament. The New Testament writings were still in the process of being copied and circulated in different languages throughout the empire.

What did earlier church writers believe? Irenaeus, in his famous book *Against Heresies*, stood firm against the gnostic sects and refuted their idle chatter about secret knowledge, which they claimed to possess. The Gnostics emphasized the role of a secret tradition by which teachings not contained in the written Word were passed on. Refuting them, Irenaeus wrote, "We have learned from none others the plan of our salvation, than from those through whom the Gospel has come down to us, which they did at one time proclaim in public, and, at a later period, by the will of God, handed down to us in the Scriptures, to be the ground and pillar of our faith."[25] There can be no doubt that Irenaeus acknowledged the Holy Scriptures as the ground and pillar of Christian faith; further, the church was responsible to only teach publicly the facts of salvation to the world.

Another ancient testimony to Scripture is provided by Tertullian, who, although not a church father, is an important witness to the faith as practiced in North Africa.

> Let us be content with saying that Christ died, the Son of the Father; and *let this suffice*, because the Scriptures have told us so much. For even the apostle, to his declaration—which he makes not without feeling the weight of it—that "Christ died," immediately adds, "according to the Scriptures," [1 Cor. 15:3] in order that he may alleviate the harshness of the statement by the authority of the Scriptures, and so remove offence from the reader.[26]

25. Irenaeus of Lyons, "Irenæus Against Heresies," 3.1.1, in *The Apostolic Fathers with Justin Martyr and Irenaeus*, ed. Alexander Roberts, James Donaldson, and A. Cleveland Coxe, vol. 1, The Ante-Nicene Fathers (Buffalo, NY: Christian Literature Company, 1885), 414. An interesting discussion on the role of Scripture and Tradition is found in chapter 5 in *Bible, Church, Tradition*, vol. 1 of Collected Works of Fr. Georges Florovsky (Belmont, MA: Nordland, 1972). Also quoted in "The Function of Tradition in the Ancient Church," *Commentary on the Gospel of Saint Luke*, by Cyril Patriarch of Alexandria, trans. R. Payne Smith (Studion Publishers, 1983).

26. Tertullian, "Against Praxeas," *Latin Christianity*, vol. 3 of The Ante-Nicene Fathers (Buffalo, NY: Christian Literature Company, 1885), 625.

Generations later, Athanasius wrote to Macarius, "For although the sacred and inspired Scriptures are sufficient to declare the truth."[27] And John Chrysostom in his *Epistle to the Colossians* would advise,

> *Tarry not, I entreat, for another to teach thee; thou hast the oracles of God.* No man teacheth thee as they; for he indeed oft grudgeth much for vainglory's sake and envy. Hearken, I entreat you, all ye that are careful for this life, and procure books that will be medicines for the soul. If ye will not any other, yet get you at least the New Testament, the Apostolic Epistles, the Acts, the Gospels, for your constant teachers. If grief befall thee, *dive into them as into a chest of medicines*; take thence comfort of thy trouble, be it loss, or death, or bereavement of relations; or rather dive not into them merely, but take them wholly to thee; keep them in thy mind.

> *This is the cause of all evils, not knowing the Scriptures.*[28]

It is important to acknowledge that the church fathers recognized the determinative role that the Holy Scriptures played in the refutation of heresies in their church councils. In this way, *right* doctrine was defended. This is the origin of the word *orthodox*, which is formed from *orthos*[29] ("right") and *doxa* ("glory" or "worship").

A little later, the respected bishop and church father Cyprian of Carthage wrote,

> Nor ought custom, which had crept in among some, to prevent the truth from prevailing and conquering; for custom without truth is the antiquity of error. . . . This truth Christ showed to us in His Gospel, and said, "I am the truth" [John 14:6]. Wherefore, if we are

---

27. Athanasius of Alexandria, "Against the Heathen," 1.3, in *St. Athanasius: Select Works and Letters*, ed. Philip Schaff and Henry Wace, trans. Archibald T. Robertson, vol. 4, A Select Library of the Nicene and Post-Nicene Fathers of the Christian Church, Second Series (New York: Christian Literature Company, 1892), 4.

28. John Chrysostom, "Homilies of St. John Chrysostom, Archbishop of Constantinople, on the Epistle of St. Paul the Apostle to the Colossians," homily 9, in *Saint Chrysostom: Homilies on Galatians, Ephesians, Philippians, Colossians, Thessalonians, Timothy, Titus, and Philemon*, ed. Philip Schaff, trans. J. Ashworth and John Albert Broadus, vol. 13, A Select Library of the Nicene and Post-Nicene Fathers of the Christian Church, First Series (New York: Christian Literature Company, 1889), 300–301.

29. The New Testament uses it four times, where it is translated "plain" and "rightly."

in Christ, and have Christ in us, if we abide in the truth, and the truth abides in us, let us keep fast those things which are true.[30]

In an effort to avoid tediousness, only one more testimony will be cited, this time from Hippolytus:

> There is, brethren, one God, the knowledge of whom we gain from the Holy Scriptures, and from no other source. For just as a man, if he wishes to be skilled in the wisdom of this world, will find himself unable to get at it in any other way than by mastering the dogmas of philosophers, so all of us who wish to practise piety will be unable to learn its practice from any other quarter than the oracles of God. Whatever things, then, the Holy Scriptures declare, at these let us look; and whatsoever things they teach, these let us learn; and as the Father wills our belief to be, let us believe; and as He wills the Son to be glorified, let us glorify Him; and as He wills the Holy Spirit to be bestowed, let us receive Him. Not according to our own will, nor according to our own mind, nor yet as using violently those things which are given by God, but even as He has chosen to teach them by the Holy Scriptures, so let us discern them.[31]

These numerous quotations provide a glimpse into the earlier church fathers' attitude toward the Word of God.[32] This should suffice for fair-minded readers.

Does Tradition Always Conflict with the Word of God?

The Jewish leaders kept certain customs they claimed to have received from Moses. They resisted Jesus, charging Him with trying to change their customs (Acts 6:14; Matt. 15:1–15). That was foolishness on their part. There is nothing wrong with tradition as long as it is not

---

30. Cyprian of Carthage, "The Epistles of Cyprian," 73.9, in *Fathers of the Third Century: Hippolytus, Cyprian, Novatian, Appendix*, ed. Alexander Roberts, James Donaldson, and A. Cleveland Coxe, trans. Robert Ernest Wallis, vol. 5, The Ante-Nicene Fathers (Buffalo, NY: Christian Literature Company, 1886), 389. Cyprian disagrees with Steven, bishop of Rome, concerning the baptism of heretics.

31. Hippolytus, "Against the Heresy of One Noetus," *Fathers of the Third Century: Hippolytus, Cyprian, Caius, Novation*, vol. 5 of Ante-Nicene Fathers, 227.

32. Keith Mathison, "The Early Church," *The Shape of Sola Scriptura* (Moscow, ID: Canon Press, 2001). Also, Yves M.-J. Congar's *Tradition and Traditions* includes many references to the church fathers.

harmful or a distortion of anything that Christ or His apostles laid down as necessary to belief or practice. For example, suits and ties are a traditional manner of dressing for church but are not harmful in any way. To respect such a tradition is a matter of taste, culture, and choice. It does not go against any Biblical principle to respect this style of dressing, but to insist upon our tradition or tastes in a hot and humid climate, such as in Louisiana and Florida or Asia and Africa, could be considered a lack of respect for the inhabitants of those places.

Socrates Scholasticus (ca. AD 440), an early church historian, gave an interesting account of the liberty that the apostles allowed to the churches, and he spoke of various customs that existed in the early church, as well as speaking of the dispute over the date for celebrating Easter.

> The aim of the apostles was not to appoint festival days, but to teach a righteous life and piety. And it seems to me that just as many other customs have been established in individual localities according to usage. So also the feast of Easter came to be observed in each place according to the individual peculiarities of the peoples inasmuch as none of the apostles legislated on the matter. And that the observance originated not by legislation, but as a custom the facts themselves indicate.[33]

Scholasticus was still able to breathe a refreshing air of spiritual liberty, which was rapidly disappearing due to the sacralization and consolidation of Christianity as a state religion.

In his *Ecclesiastical History* (ca. AD 300–325), Eusebius writes about Papias, who is said to have known the presbyter John (the apostle?). This is very important if we are to understand how easily erroneous traditions crept into the church and later came to be thought of as ancient apostolic traditions. Eusebius was only two hundred years removed from Papias when he wrote,

---

33. Socrates Scholasticus, "The Ecclesiastical History, by Socrates Scholasticus," 5.22, in *Socrates, Sozomenus: Church Histories*, ed. Philip Schaff and Henry Wace, trans. A. C. Zenos, vol. 2, A Select Library of the Nicene and Post-Nicene Fathers of the Christian Church, Second Series (New York: Christian Literature Company, 1890), 130.

The same writer gives also other accounts which he says came to him through *unwritten tradition*, certain strange parables and teachings of the Saviour, and some other more *mythical things*. To these belong his statement that there will be a period of some thousand years after the resurrection of the dead, and that the kingdom of Christ will be set up in material form on this very earth. I suppose he got these ideas through a misunderstanding of the apostolic accounts, not perceiving that the things said by them were spoken mystically in figures. For he appears to have been of very limited understanding, as one can see from his discourses. But it was due to him that so many of the Church Fathers after him adopted a like opinion, urging in their own support the antiquity of the man; as for instance Irenaeus and any one else that may have proclaimed similar views.[34]

In all this, let us listen to the advice of our beloved apostle Paul: "Test all things; hold fast what is good" (1 Thess. 5:21).

Whom Should We Believe?

The church father Basil of Caesarea said, "Let God-inspired Scripture decide between us; and on whichever side be found doctrines in harmony with the word of God, in favour of that side will be cast the vote of truth."[35] Yet the Roman Catholic claim to be "the Mother of the Bible" easily gives the impression that the church believes in its superiority over the Bible. Catholicism assumes that because the Bible belongs to Rome, the church can permit or not permit the laity to read the Bible and that she alone determines the correct interpretation of the Scriptures.

Such ideas are the cause of the church's many deviations from the apostolic faith. Of course, Catholics reiterate the claim that

---

34. Eusebius of Caesaria, "The Church History of Eusebius," 3.39.11–13, in *Eusebius: Church History, Life of Constantine the Great, and Oration in Praise of Constantine*, ed. Philip Schaff and Henry Wace, trans. Arthur Cushman McGiffert, vol. 1, A Select Library of the Nicene and Post-Nicene Fathers of the Christian Church, Second Series (New York: Christian Literature Company, 1890), 172. My italics.

35. Basil of Caesarea, "Letters," 189.3, in *St. Basil: Letters and Select Works*, ed. Philip Schaff and Henry Wace, trans. Blomfield Jackson, vol. 8, A Select Library of the Nicene and Post-Nicene Fathers of the Christian Church, Second Series (New York: Christian Literature Company, 1895), 229.

development is natural to any living organism, that these developments are natural, a growth to maturity of the seed of faith. Rome teaches that she is the only authorized interpreter of the Bible because she is infallibly guided and indwelt by the Holy Spirit. The Orthodox church claims as much for herself.

Rebelling against the burdens and superstitions of the Middle Ages, Europe's peoples sought relief in the Reformation cry of "Christ alone, Scripture alone!" But the Roman church bitterly resisted calls for ecclesiastical reforms. The result was a splintering and breaking up of the European church-state union that had existed since Charlemagne's time. In any case, every Christian should examine his religious ideas by applying the rule of faith that church fathers Basil and Irenaeus acknowledged: the Holy Scriptures.

The argument from antiquity is not always as strong as it may appear at first. The fact that an idea is ancient does not make it right. Scholars who engage in textual criticism are well aware of this as they sort through ancient manuscript copies and classify the variants they encounter. Although a variant may be ancient, it may have been written by a heretic or have entered the textual history due to a gloss (a comment or explanation placed in the margin of a manuscript).

Why We Reject Tradition with a Capital T

The acceptance of church traditions as part of the "deposit of faith" has proven to be a source of bondage. In many cases, Tradition conflicts with the Word of God. The matter of blind obedience to men is the result of esteeming leaders as more than they are. The laws they impose upon people who should be enjoying freedom in Christ have caused many heartaches, as good, sincere men and women strive to obey church laws, or in order to be accepted, they blindly follow what their parents practiced. The apostle Paul addressed this matter in several of his letters:

"Stand fast therefore in the liberty by which Christ has made us free, and do not be entangled again with a yoke of bondage" (Gal. 5:1).

"But now after you have known God, or rather are known by God, how is it that you turn again to the weak and beggarly elements, to which you desire again to be in bondage? You observe days and months and seasons and years. I am afraid for you, lest I have labored for you in vain" (Gal. 4:9–11).

"So let no one judge you in food or in drink, or regarding a festival or a new moon or sabbaths, which are a shadow of things to come, but the substance is of Christ. Let no one cheat you of your reward, taking delight in false humility and worship of angels, intruding into those things which he has not seen, vainly puffed up by his fleshly mind" (Col. 2:16–18).

It is an arduous task to study church history and the church fathers to verify the teachings of the ancient churches, to determine whether they are or are not apostolic in origin. Hopefully this work will help sincere individuals who are troubled or feel under pressure from relatives and friends who seek to persuade them to "get with it, stay in the church Jesus Christ founded." Surprisingly, even professional historians admit the difficulty of ascertaining what is accurate fact from the early centuries of church history. Jaroslav Pelikan, professor emeritus of church history, concludes,

> Yet the task of reconstructing it [apostolic doctrine] from the existing documents is a complex one. . . .
>
> Another set of problems in the study of the state of Christian doctrine in the second and third centuries is raised by the literary and historical analysis of the documents. The manuscript tradition of the epistles of Ignatius contains two and even three recensions of his works, varying not only in length and style but also in doctrinal content. . . . Similarly, the garbled transmission of the manuscripts of Cyprian's *Unity of the Church* has raised questions about his doctrine of the primacy of Peter. . . .
>
> These literary problems, which could be multiplied almost endlessly through these two centuries and well beyond them, jeopardize any history of the early development of Christian

doctrine that proceeds from one thinker to the next, tracing origins, influences, borrowings, and divergences.[36]

Is this not reason enough to look to the Holy Scriptures for guidance as we seek to live as Christians filled with the Holy Spirit?

By What Authority?

Evangelicals often hear an objection proffered by the ancient churches' apologists: "An infallible Bible needs an infallible interpreter." This simply means that the Roman or the Orthodox church is such an interpreter. Paul's statement that the "church of the living God [is] the pillar and ground of the truth" is cited in support of this teaching. Theologian Keith Mathison replies to such an argument based on 1 Timothy 3:15:

> The words he [the apostle Paul] uses describe a structural foundation. . . .
>
> It is also important to note that the Church is not identical to the truth (John 17:17). Jesus is the truth (John 14:6), and the Word of God is truth (John 17:17), but the Church is not identical to the truth. She is the pillar and ground of truth in the sense that she is called to uphold and proclaim the truth, but she is distinguished from the truth she upholds. This is important because 1 Timothy 3:15 is often used by Roman Catholic apologists to support an ecclesiology which either subordinates Scripture to the Church or else puts the Church on an equal level of authority with the Scripture. . . . The Church is the place where the truth may be found, but it is the truth which has the ultimate authority.[37]

Mathison quotes a Roman Catholic apologist who argued that "if Scripture is infallible, then its cause, the Church, must be infallible." Mathison puts that argument to rest with this comment: "But if that is the case, then an infallible Old Testament requires an infallible Israel.

---

36. Jaroslav Pelikan, *The Emergence of the Catholic Tradition (100–600)*, vol. 1 of The Christian Tradition: A History of the Development of Doctrine (Chicago: University of Chicago Press, 1975), 121–22.
37. Mathison, *The Shape of Sola Scriptura*, 204.

... The infallibility of both Testaments is due to the inspiration of the infallible Holy Spirit."[38]

Many Orthodox theologians consider the church fathers to be infallible guides whenever they are agreed on any particular point. I believe that the church fathers are important as a source of information about what the church taught at a particular point in time. Not everything in their writings should be rejected, but not everything should be accepted. Discernment is needed. I also believe the church fathers were men who loved Christ. They were closer in time to the apostles and to the language of the Bible, and we should acknowledge our indebtedness to them for the structure they gave to the Christian faith as they responded to philosophical and heretical attacks on Christian doctrine. Sometimes their advice on spirituality may be helpful, but too often their monasticism and methods reek of a gnostic antipathy for the physical body. This is known as warfare against fleshly passions, which they were striving to master. For this reason, such writings should be avoided.

It is evident that any dialogue between the ancient churches and the evangelical churches turns on one point: *authority*. Cardinal Wiseman stated as much in the 1830s in his public lectures that were later published as *Conferences on Protestantism*. Regarding authority, we invite our traditionalist friends to consider one more statement from church father John Chrysostom, who advised his listeners to be wary of others.

> For how is it not absurd that in respect to money, indeed, we do not trust to others, but refer this to figures and calculation; but in calculating upon facts we are lightly drawn aside by the notions of others; and that too, though we possess an exact balance, and square and rules for all things, the declaration of the divine laws? *Wherefore I exhort and entreat you all, disregard what this man and that man thinks about these things, and inquire from the Scriptures all these things; and having learnt what are the true riches, let us pursue after them* that

---

38. Ibid., 293–94.

we may obtain also the eternal good things; which may we all obtain, through the grace and love towards men of our Lord Jesus Christ, with Whom, to the Father and the Holy Spirit, be glory, might, and honor, now and ever, and world without end. Amen.[39]

Would that we all could always adhere to such good advice!

If issues must be decided by both the Word of God *and* Tradition, we should all join an ancient liturgical church. But if infallible truth is found *only* in the inspired Word of God, we must look to God's Word for infallible guidance. Consequently, *sola scriptura* is not an empty slogan. Christians should reject the liturgical churches' claims to occupy the historical ground because their history does not go far enough back, that is, to the apostolic era! Their "gospel" cannot be considered good news; it is *another* gospel (Gal. 1). This is why we invite the members of liturgical churches to seek a church that teaches *Christ alone, faith alone, grace alone,* and *Scripture alone.* A number of essential matters will be taken up when we survey the culture and philosophies of the time of Christ. The church grew up in a hostile world, where Platonism, gnosticism, and mystery religions offered alternative ways of viewing life and the hereafter. It is important to uncover the influences that such an environment may have had on Christianity, its worship, and the celebration of the sacraments.

---

39. John Chrysostom, "Homilies of St. John Chrysostom, Archbishop of Constantinople, on the Second Epistle of St. Paul the Apostle to the Corinthians," homily 13, in *Saint Chrysostom: Homilies on the Epistles of Paul to the Corinthians,* ed. Philip Schaff, trans. J. Ashworth and Talbot B. Chambers, vol. 12, A Select Library of the Nicene and Post-Nicene Fathers of the Christian Church, First Series (New York: Christian Literature Company, 1889), 346. My italics.

CHAPTER 2

Historical Issues

A STUDY OF THE NEW TESTAMENT along with a reading of church history reveals that changes took place within the church shortly after the apostles passed away. From today's vantage point, one can detect the way in which powerful forces and influences within and without the church brought about a rapid transformation. There is a tremendous difference between the simplicity of the apostolic preaching of faith in Christ, the kingdom of God, baptism and the Lord's Supper, and the post-apostolic period, when a hierarchical body, a priesthood, and sacred mysteries were taking root. For example, compare the simplicity of the phrase "breaking of bread" in the book of Acts with the exalted language used by John Chrysostom in the fourth century. He speaks of the Eucharist as the "holy mysteries," the "secret mysteries," even the "dread mysteries." In his *First Instruction to Catechumens,* he says, "For he who is about to approach these holy and dread mysteries must be awake and alert, must be clean from all cares of this life."[1] Regarding this early period in church history, J. N. D. Kelly makes the following observation: "[T]he difference of atmosphere becomes immediately apparent as one crosses from the apostolic to the post-apostolic age. . . . By the sixth century, both in East and West, the reign of

---

1. John Chrysostom, "Instructions to Catechumens," 1.2, in *Saint Chrysostom: On the Priesthood, Ascetic Treatises, Select Homilies and Letters, Homilies on the Statues,* ed. Philip Schaff, trans. W. R. W. Stephens and T. P. Brandram, vol. 9, A Select Library of the Nicene and Post-Nicene Fathers of the Christian Church, First Series (New York: Christian Literature Company, 1889), 160.

formalism and scholasticism was well under way."[2]

The problem facing evangelical Christians is how to account for this evolution in the church and its celebration of the sacraments. Distinguished Professor Emeritus Jaroslav Pelikan of Yale University believes that "the relation of Christian doctrine to Jewish and to pagan thought is a subject worthy of investigation for its own sake. The very legitimacy of the development of Christian dogma has been challenged on the ground of its supposed hellenization of the primitive message; the contrast between Greek and Hebrew ways of thought has been used to explain the distinctiveness of Christian doctrine. These are only modern versions of an ancient debate."[3]

This book is not an attempt to resolve all the issues that a student of church history may confront, because they fall mostly within the domain of specialists. My objective is simply to provide enough information to enable readers to make sound judgments. At a minimum, readers need to be aware that missionaries to the Gentiles spoke to people with existing prejudices and expectations, people who lived in a "twilight world of pagan syncretism, magic, and astrology. Even the apparently exclusive religion of Judaism had been welcomed into the loose amalgam of polytheism by identifying the God of the Jews with Dionysus or . . . with Saturn.[4]

Providing a number of quotations from recognized scholarship is meaningful because these matters outweigh personal opinions. A survey of history reveals how the church's liturgy evolved and how its doctrines were defined through discussions, even heated debates, in ecumenical councils. To what extent did the world's philosophies and religious ideas penetrate the hearts and minds of early Christian

---

2. J. N. D. Kelly, "The Background," *Early Christian Doctrines*, 2nd ed. (New York: HarperCollins, 1960; Prince Press, 2003), 3. Presbyterian theologian Paul K. Jewett says, "It must not be forgotten, however, that the earliest ages of Christian history are marked not only by rapid expansion, but also by rapid change. For example, the very Episcopal office these bishops held was unknown in the year A.D. 100: in the apostolic age there were no monarchical bishops." Paul K. Jewett, *Infant Baptism and the Covenant of Grace* (Grand Rapids: Eerdmans, 1978), 19.

3. Pelikan, *The Emergence of the Catholic Tradition (100–600)*, 1:12.

4. Henry Chadwick, *The Early Church*, vol. 1, The Penguin History of the Church (New York: Penguin Books, 1993), 33.

writers? This chapter hopes to demonstrate that powerful forces were at work and did indeed influence early Christian worship and beliefs.

Greek Philosophy

The Mediterranean world was a religious world consumed by questions about the gods and how to placate them. People wanted to know more about life, death, the future, and especially how to live a successful life. They were just as human and troubled as mankind is today. People believed that the pursuit of knowledge was necessary and good and that ignorance was evil.

Philosophy is the school of thought that seeks answers to life's great questions and endeavors to teach others how to live a good life and how to obtain or know virtue, justice, and truth. The ancient schools of thought many considered to be important are those of Socrates, Plato, Aristotle, and Plotinus, whose philosophy is known as Neoplatonism. Many Christian converts grew up with these philosophies; the question is, did their studies color their Christian thinking to some extent? Christians like Justin the Philosopher, Clement of Alexandria, and Augustine the bishop of Hippo were converted philosophers. Origen of Alexandria, a disciple of Clement, is considered the greatest of the early Christian philosophers and theologians. William McNeill, professor emeritus of history at the University of Chicago, describes Origen's influence: "In his defense of Christianity against philosophical attacks, Origen grafted onto Christian tradition much of the vocabulary and some of the concepts of pagan philosophy."[5]

Catholic priest Tomas Spidlik tells us,

> Christianity had its roots in a Judaic world already in contact with Hellenism and no doubt already partly Hellenized. To oversimplify, we may say that primitive Christianity grew on the eastern shores of the Mediterranean basin and in a Greek (and, soon, a greco-roman) setting.

---

5. William H. McNeill, *History of Western Civilization*, 6th ed. (Chicago: University of Chicago Press, 1986), 183.

> In such a cultural and spiritual climate, the Fathers were exposed in the schools above all to philosophic doctrines which, more than anything else, created the atmosphere in which they lived: an eclectic philosophy, some sort of philosophic-religious *koiné*, a mixture of popularized Stoicism, Pythagoreanism, Middle Platonism, and later Neoplatonism. When compared to that of the classical era, this type of philosophy presents a character of its own, a specifically moral and religious orientation.[6]

Christian missionaries were not speaking in a vacuum. They evangelized and converted people who had grown up with the opinions of their day. Would the converts' former ideas eventually surface to sabotage their new faith? In praise of philosophy, theologians tell us that philosophy provided a vocabulary and thought structure that enabled Christian bishops to give clarity to doctrines like the Trinity, the Person of Christ, and the soul. Although this may be true, one has a right to wonder to what extent the pagan philosophies and religious ideas about the world and its gods and about forms and matter may possibly have influenced doctrines and worship in the early church.

Samuel Vargas Montoya, professor of philosophy in the University La Salle in Mexico City, writing on the period immediately preceding the Christian era, states that "in the fusion of Greek thought with the oriental religions, the *mystical* and *religious* factor achieved superiority from the beginning, and so the integration of philosophy was more a theosophical system than philosophical."[7]

Two examples immediately come to mind. The first one has to do with the Eucharist. Explaining Plato's teaching about "Forms," Kelly says, "In fact, the latter, the world of Becoming, is modeled on the world of Forms, and particulars only are what they are in so far as the Forms are participated in, or copied, by them."[8] Could this not have

---

6. Tomas Spidlik, *The Spirituality of the Christian East,* trans. Anthony P. Gythiel (Kalamazoo, MI: Cistercian Publications, 1986), 9. John Chryssavgis has an excellent discussion of the evolution of Christian thought in "Dependence and Divorce: Patristic Theology, Hellenistic Philosophy, and Scholastic Thought," chapter 5 in *The Way of the Fathers,* Analecta Vlatadon 62 (Thessaloniki, Greece: Patriarchal Institute for Patristic Studies, 1998).

7. Samuel Vargas Montoya, *Historia de las Doctrinas Filosóficas,* 14th ed. (Mexico City: Editorial Porrúa, 1992), 153. Author's translation.

8. Kelly, 16–17. See also page 212, where Kelly discusses symbols in the ancient world and says that

given rise to the teaching that in reality, the emblems (particulars) are what they are (the body and blood of Christ) because they participate in (share), or are copies of the reality, that is, the Forms? Aristotle took this idea a little further (it seems to me he made it clearer): Being types of realities in Heaven, the Eucharistic emblems are not just signs, but are the body and blood of Jesus Christ.

The second example is one I have noticed a number of times in both philosophy and Hinduism. Helpful as always, Kelly gives us a brief outline of Neoplatonism.[9] First he tells us that this system incorporated Aristotelian, Stoic, and even Oriental elements and is best exemplified by Plotinus.[10] The three stages of ascent toward union with "the One" finally end in "mystical union with the One." To an Eastern Orthodox Christian, this is very reminiscent of goals set before Orthodox monks and even ordinary believers. In Orthodoxy, these stages of spiritual progress are purification, illumination, and theosis (deification), that is, union with God. The *Catholic Encyclopedia* has an article on Clement of Alexandria, who was Origen's teacher. Concerning possible influences on Clement, the writer says,

> Some scholars see in the chief writings of Clement, the "Exhortation", "The Tutor", the "Miscellanies", a great trilogy representing a graduated initiation into the Christian life—belief, discipline, knowledge—three states corresponding to the three degrees of the neo-Platonic mysteries—purification, initiation, and vision. Some such underlying conception was doubtless before the mind of Clement, but it can hardly be said to have been realized. He was too unsystematic.[11]

Orthodox and Catholic scholars are well aware of these similarities but will claim that this is exactly what they are—similarities. However, as said before, nothing takes place in a vacuum, and the Christianity taught in the New Testament has nothing in common with

in some sense they are the thing symbolized.

9. Ibid., 20–22.

10. Ibid., 20.

11. Francis P. Havey, "Clement of Alexandria," *The Catholic Encyclopedia* (New York: Robert Appleton Company, 1913), 4:46. Articles from *The Catholic Encyclopedia* may be viewed online at www.newadvent.org.

such spiritual movements as monasticism and a mystical struggle for "union with God." The Holy Spirit places a believer in the Body of Christ, and the person is said to be "in Christ." A Christian is *in Christ* and Christ is *in us* (Col. 1:2, 27). Only people with a penchant for philosophy or who are influenced by the world would seek to complicate simple truth. This is why the apostle Paul wrote, "Beware lest any man spoil you through philosophy and vain deceit, after the tradition of men, after the rudiments of the world, and not after Christ" (Col. 2:8).

Gnosticism

What is gnosticism? Where does it come from? Many books have been written on this intriguing topic, and it has provoked many a scholarly debate. In short we can say gnosticism is a system that emphasizes the importance of knowledge *(gnosis)* for salvation. It is a speculative religious philosophy that is Asian in origin. It is theosophic and blends elements from Hellenism, Zoroastrianism, Judaism, and ascetic ideas originating in Hinduism and Buddhism together with Christianity, teaching that God is far removed from this material world and its creation.

Matter being inherently evil, the whole idea that God became man is gross according to gnostic thinking. Salvation being through knowledge means liberation, regeneration, and escape from the material world. Dr. Hans Jonas, in his book *The Gnostic Religion*, explains,

> The goal of gnostic striving is the release of the "inner man" from the bonds of the world and his return to his native realm of light.
>
> Equipped with this *gnosis*, the soul after death travels upwards, leaving behind at each sphere the psychical "vestment" contributed by it: thus the spirit stripped of all foreign accretions reaches the God beyond the world and becomes reunited with the divine substance.[12]

Wilhelm Bousset, who traced gnosticism to Babylonian and Persian sources, says that "gnosticism is first of all a pre-Christian

---

12. Hans Jonas, *The Gnostic Religion,* 2nd rev. ed. (Boston: Beacon Press, 1963), 44–45.

movement which had roots in itself."[13] There were many types of gnosticism, which is why it either confuses or intrigues people. Simon Magus, Cerenthus, Basilides, Saturninus, Marcion, Isidorus, Carpocrates, Valentinus, and Heracleon are all famous names in the list of gnostic heretics. Hans Jonas says that the church fathers regarded Simon Magus as the father of all heresy and that Manichaeism was the most important product of gnosticism.[14] Augustine was once a devotee of Manichaeism. In its "Christian" variety, gnosticism became a dangerous heresy threatening the early church, and Manichaeism became a widely adopted alternative to Christianity.

Having surveyed the various religious inroads made on Greek philosophy, we may wonder what religious influences gnosticism suffered in the period when Christianity was expanding. Elaine Pagels informs us that there were even Buddhist influences on gnosticism: "Trade routes between the Greco-Roman world and the Far East were opening up at the time when gnosticism flourished (AD 80–200); for generations, Buddhist missionaries had been proselytizing in Alexandria. We note, too, that Hippolytus, who was a Greek-speaking Christian in Rome (ca. 225), knew of the Indian Brahmins—and includes this tradition among the sources of heresy."[15]

To satisfy any curiosity or doubts, the reference from Hippolytus (AD 170–236) is reproduced below.

> But there is also with the Indians a sect composed of those philosophizing among the Brachmans. They spend a contented existence, abstain both from living creatures and all cooked food, being satisfied with fruits; and not gathering these from the trees, but carrying off those that have fallen to the earth. They subsist upon them, drinking the water of the river Tazabena. But they pass their life naked, affirming that the body

---

13. Wilhelm Bousset, *Kyrios Christos* (Göttingen, 1913; English trans., 1970), quoted in Elaine Pagels, *The Gnostic Gospels* (New York: Random House, 1979; Vintage Books, 1989), 3. Citations refer to the Vintage edition.

14. Jonas, *The Gnostic Religion*, 103, 208.

15. Elaine Pagels, *The Gnostic Gospels* (New York: Random House, 1979; Vintage Books, 1989), xxi. Citations refer to the Vintage edition.

has been constituted a covering to the soul by the Deity. These affirm that God is light, not such as one sees, nor such as the sun and fire; but to them the Deity is discourse, not that which finds expression in articulate sounds, but that of the knowledge through which the secret mysteries of nature are perceived by the wise. And this light which they say is discourse, their God, they assert that the Brachmans only know on account of their alone rejecting all vanity of opinion which is the soul's ultimate covering. These despise death, and always in their own peculiar language call God by the name which we have mentioned previously, and they send up hymns (to him). But neither are there women among them, nor do they beget children. But they who aim at a life similar to these, after they have crossed over to the country on the opposite side of the river, continue to reside there, returning no more; and these also are called Brachmans. But they do not pass their life similarly, for there are also in the place women, of whom those that dwell there are born, and in turn beget children. And this discourse which they name God they assert to be corporeal, and enveloped in a body outside himself, just as if one were wearing a sheep's skin, but that on divesting himself of body that he would appear clear to the eye. But the Brachmans say that there is a conflict in the body that surrounds them, (and they consider that the body is for them full of conflicts); in opposition to which, as if marshaled for battle against enemies, they contend, as we have already explained. And they say that all men are captive to their own congenital struggles, viz., sensuality and inchastity, gluttony, anger, joy, sorrow, concupiscence, and such like. And he who has reared a trophy over these, alone goes to God; wherefore the Brachmans deify Dandamis, to whom Alexander the Macedonian paid a visit, as one who had proved victorious in the bodily conflict. But they bear down on Calanus as having profanely withdrawn from their philosophy. But the Brachmans, putting off the body, like fishes jumping out of water into the pure air, behold the sun.[16]

---

16. Hippolytus of Rome, "The Refutation of All Heresies," 1.21, in *Fathers of the Third Century: Hippolytus, Cyprian, Novatian, Appendix*, The Ante-Nicene Fathers, 5:21–22.

Henry Chadwick describes the various gnostic sects, their origins, and the challenge gnosticism posed to the early church, including the following:

> Both these types of heresy, at Corinth and Colossae, belong to the general category commonly labeled 'Gnosticism', a phenomenon which became an immense problem and threat to the Church as the personal authority of the first generation of Christian leaders receded into the past. Gnosticism is a generic term used primarily to refer to theosophical adaptations of Christianity propagated by a dozen or more rival sects which broke with the early church between A.D. 80 and 150. The word is often used in a much wider and vaguer sense to describe an imprecise, syncretistic religiosity diffused widely in the Levantine world, and existing independently and prior to Christianity. Behind this double usage of the word there lies a complicated controversy—whether and in what sense Gnosticism existed before Christianity. . . . There is no dispute that many of the raw materials of Gnosticism, drawn from Platonism, Hellenized Zoroastrianism, and Judaism, were present before Christianity. . . .
>
> The majority of the sects demanded an ascetic life with rules for the mortification of the flesh and a special prohibition on marriage (or at least on procreation), so that the divine soul might be liberated from the bonds of sense and bodily appetite and assisted to turn itself towards higher things.[17]

William Jones, a nineteenth-century author, also wrote about these ascetic practices. His description of gnosticism and philosophies during the time of Christ sounds familiar: "The body, on the contrary, as the source of every depraved appetite, was, according to them, to be reduced and brought into subjection by hunger, thirst, and every other species of mortification, and neither to be supported by flesh or wine, nor indulged in any of those gratifications to which it is naturally prone."[18]

---

17. Chadwick, 34–36. One of the best explanations and descriptions of gnosticism can be found in *The Early Church*. This small Penguin paperback edition is well worth acquiring.

18. William Jones, *The History of the Christian Church from the Birth of Christ to the XVIII Century*

All the above surely has some relationship not only with itself, but with the practices of the monks who sought refuge from the world by fleeing to the desert. The Christian ascetics practiced vegetarianism, held long vigils in prayers, abstained from fleshly intercourse (marriage), and strived for mystical union with the Deity. There were parallels to this in the thinking and practices of certain Christians in Egypt and Asia. No doubt the monks were pious, but they were far removed from the Christianity we read about in the New Testament. Comparing various false religions with Christianity, Indian evangelist Paul Pillai, in a fascinating book, writes,

> They emphasise that man is what he does. But the Gospel of Christ comes from a diametrically opposite premise, which is that action reflects what the man is. It is not the doing that determines, rather it is the being that provides the basis for doing. No man is saved by doing anything. Every one is saved by being. Doing is only the spontaneous reaction of being. The being matures by personal faith in the universal Redeemer who makes everything new. If any man be in Christ he becomes a new creature.[19]

Judaism

Wondering how the priesthood developed in the liturgical churches, a number of questions come to mind. If all Christians are priests and Jesus is their high priest, and if the law with its sacrifices is fulfilled in Christ, why are bishops and priests offering a sacrifice in these ancient churches? Although I intend to return to these questions more in depth, a simple summary of how the Jews in the first century met to pray and receive instruction in their faith will be beneficial here.

The apostle Paul encountered Jewish followers of the law in their meeting places. This was a convenient place to inform them that the long-awaited Messiah had come. Two verses from the book of Acts are

(London: n.p., 1826; Gallatin, TN: Church History Research and Archives, 1983), 1:34.

19. K. V. Paul Pillai, *India's Search for the Unknown Christ,* 3d ed. (New Delhi: Indian Inland Mission, 1984), 25.

typical: "And he went into the synagogue and spoke boldly for three months, reasoning and persuading concerning the things of the kingdom of God" and "Then Crispus, the ruler of the synagogue, believed on the Lord with all his household. And many of the Corinthians, hearing, believed and were baptized" (Acts 19:8; 18:8).

We turn our attention to Judaism and its meeting places because logically, if the first Christian converts were Jews, everything they knew and everything they did would be inspired out of Jewish habits and traditions. W. H. C. Frend, a New Testament scholar, describes the first Christian assemblies and their activities: "In this period churches were still regarded as synagogues, whose members prayed three times a day and fasted twice a week like Jews, only they chose Wednesday and Friday to commemorate Christ's arrest and crucifixion and not the normal Jewish Monday and Thursday. . . . Within individual congregations they continued to think, argue, and act like their Jewish counterparts."[20]

We know that Hebrew Christians still considered themselves Jews; the only difference was they had accepted Jesus of Nazareth as Israel's Messiah, the fulfillment of their cherished hopes. Perhaps the only two questions left unanswered were, Would Messiah Yeshoua ["Jesus" in Hebrew] now restore the messianic Kingdom to Israel? And was the Mosaic law still obligatory for Christians?

The *International Standard Bible Encyclopedia* describes the Jewish synagogue as a meeting place for prayer and reading of the holy books. We can easily imagine the first Jewish converts following a simple order of worship before the priesthood crept back into the church. The Greek word *sunagoge* means "gathering" and is used in Acts 13:43 and Luke 7:5 in reference to the Jewish place of worship inside and outside Israel. When Christians began meeting, they used synagogues as the model for their meeting places.

> That the synagogue was, in the time of our Lord, one of the most important religious institutions of the Jews is clear from the fact

20. W. H. C. Frend, *The Rise of Christianity* (Philadelphia: Fortress Press, 1984), 121–22.

that it was thought to have been instituted by Moses. . . . It must have come into being during the Babylonian exile. At that time the more devout Jews, far from their native land, having no sanctuary or altar, no doubt felt drawn from time to time, especially on Sabbath and feast days, to gather round those who were specially pious and God-fearing, in order to listen to the word of God and engage in some kind of worship. That such meetings were not uncommon is made probable by Ezekiel 14:1; 20:1. This would furnish a basis for the institution of the synagogue. After the exile the synagogue remained and even developed as a counterpoise to the absolute sacerdotalism of the temple, and must have been felt absolutely necessary for the Jews of the Dispersion. Though at first it was meant only for the exposition of the Law, it was natural that in the course of time prayers and preaching should be added to the service. Thus these meetings, which at first were only held on Sabbaths and feast days, came also to be held on other days, and at the same hours with the services in the temple. The essential aim, however, of the synagogue was not prayer, but instruction in the Law for all classes of the people.

In Palestine the synagogues were scattered all over the country, all the larger towns having one or more. . . . In Jerusalem, in spite of the fact that the Temple was there, there were many synagogues, and all parts of the Diaspora were represented by particular synagogues (Acts 6:9). Also in heathen lands, wherever there was a certain number of Jews, they had their own synagogue.[21]

The customs of the Orthodox churches vary from country to country and may differ depending on whether a particular church is more or less traditional. A brochure on my desk reads, "Orthodox Christians have maintained the custom of standing during divine services since apostolic times." In the more traditional churches, the women stand on the left side of the church building and the men on the right side facing the altar. The people stand for the liturgies and offices, but benches or seats are found along the walls for the elderly or the

---

21. Paul Levertoff, "Synagogue," *International Standard Bible Encyclopedia*, gen. ed. James Orr (Chicago: The Howard-Severance Company, 1915), 5:2878.

infirm. In the United States, one may notice that frequently this does not hold true, because many church buildings have rows of pews. The traditional Orthodox are proud to inform us they have inherited their style of worship from apostolic traditions.

So what have scholars discovered about whether people stood or sat for services in the synagogues, or whether the women were separated from the men? I have personally visited the catacombs in Rome and seen the paintings on the walls depicting a person standing with arms extended in prayer. Does that prove that the first Christians stood for two to three hours as sometimes occurs in long Orthodox liturgies? If so, who has seen the Orthodox congregation standing with their hands extended at the shoulders (as in the painting) to show they are traditional in prayer? In fact, if visitors walked in on such a scene, they might think they had happened upon a charismatic or Pentecostal meeting, not an Orthodox one. It is true that Augustine has mentioned in *De Civitate Dei* (book II, chap. 28) that there was a separation of the sexes in the church building; but that was in the fourth century. Could James 2:2 and 3 be pertinent here? "For if there should come into your assembly a man with gold rings, in fine apparel, and there should also come in a poor man in filthy clothes, and you pay attention to the one wearing the fine clothes and say to him, '*You sit here* in a good place,' and say to the poor man, 'You stand there,' or, '*Sit here* at my footstool'" (italics added).

I have not found any Biblical support for such Orthodox traditions. In any case, whether people stood, sat, or kneeled, or whether women stood or sat apart from the men on the opposite side of the building is not really important; more significant questions require our attention. People can be faithful to details in any tradition and still come up far short in essential matters. This is commonly called "majoring on the minors." The fact is that people may have stood because movable chairs such as those sold today were not available. Maybe they used benches?

Several more quotations from the *International Standard Bible Encyclopedia* may be helpful: "The question whether women in the ancient period were separated in worship remains in dispute. Ancient synagogues had a series of stone benches along the walls."[22] "The antiquity of the custom of separating the women from the men is a matter of debate among scholars."[23] "Leadership rotated among influential and educated members in each community rather than being imposed by some overarching institution or system."[24] "The elders . . . were the mainstays of the synagogues; from them the head of the synagogue was chosen."[25]

Clericalization

This brings us to the matter of the move from elders to priests. Jaroslav Pelikan, writing on the priesthood in the first century church, states,

> The growth of the cultic, hierarchical and ethical structures of Christianity led to the Christianization of many features of Judaism. While much of that growth does not belong directly to the history of the development of doctrine, it is important because of this "re-Judaization" of Christianity. Justin argued that one of the differences between the old covenant and the new was that the priesthood had been superseded and "we [the church as a whole] are the true high-priestly race of God." In the New Testament itself the concept of "priest" referred either to the Levites of the Old Testament, now made obsolete, or to Christ or to the entire church—not to the ordained ministry of the church. But Clement, who was also the first to use the term "layman [λαικός]," already spoke of "priests" and of "the high priest" and significantly related these terms to the Levitical priesthood; a similar parallel occurred in the *Didache* and in Hippolytus.[26]

Pelikan's statement is an accurate reflection of the state of things in the first century. The church founded by Jesus Christ did not have

---

22. W. S. LaSor and T. C. Eskenazi, "Synagogue," *International Standard Bible Encyclopedia*, rev. ed., gen. ed. Geoffrey W. Bromily (Grand Rapids: Eerdmans, 1988), 4:679.

23. Ibid., 4:680.

24. Ibid., 4:681.

25. Ibid.

26. Jaroslav Pelikan, *The Emergence of the Catholic Tradition (100–600)*, 1:25–26.

a special class of priests such as existed under the Mosaic law. All Christians were priests (1 Pet. 2:9). Note Pelikan's use of the word "re-Judaization"; this took place in the century after Peter's writing. Frend states that such a change was taking place within the Christian synagogue or ecclesia (assembly/church) and that a movement toward the monarchial rule was gaining momentum. He writes, "By the end of the century, however, there had been a marked move away from the collegial system of church government."[27]

Roman Catholic priest and church historian Thomas Bokenkotter agrees with the preceding sketch and goes so far as to say,

> At first the Christian presbyter or elder avoided any resemblance to the pagan or Jewish priests and, in fact, even deliberately refused to be called a priest. He saw his primary function as the ministry of the Word. The ritualistic features of his sacramental ministry were kept in a low key. Even as late as the fifth century, John Chrysostom still stressed preaching as the main task of the Christian minister. But the image of the Christian presbyter gradually took on a sacral character.[28]

Need I say more? Hopefully, this chapter will satisfy most readers. Church organization, bishops and priests, the papacy, and patriarchs are not part of the apostolic tradition but came about because of a doctrinal shift along with a gradual hierarchical development during the early centuries of the church's history.

Asceticism

We know that early Christians were in frequent contact with Gnostics in Alexandria, Rome, and Asia. We have uncovered the roots of the ascetic practices and the spirituality of Eastern Orthodoxy and Roman Catholicism, and we find they are similar to various non-Christian movements. Pelikan, who entered the Orthodox church toward the end of his life, says, "Christian asceticism certainly

---

27. Frend, *The Rise of Christianity*, 140.
28. Thomas Bokenkotter, *A Concise History of the Catholic Church*, rev. ed. (1977; New York: Doubleday, 2004), 53–54.

predated Christianity. The world early Christianity entered was experiencing a series of vigorous movements dedicated to the denial of the
claims of the physical life and to the cultivation of the disciplines of
self-restraint in relation to food, drink, bodily comfort, and above all
sexuality."[29]

Admittedly, similarity does not make any spirituality heretical in
and of itself, but if Orthodox Christians are told that such practices
are necessary for their spiritual progress, that purification, illumination, and theosis are goals for all Orthodox people, are we not
justified in concluding that these practices pervert the simple gospel
message of salvation and justification by faith in the finished work of
Jesus Christ? When church leaders seek to impose ascetic practices
on people whose only desire is to know Christ in His plenitude and
to experience His magnificent liberating truth, those church leaders
need to be exposed in love. In fact, it is a Christian duty to denounce
such practices as corruptions of the purity of the gospel (Gal. 1:8).
Surely no one desires to speak ill of others or to denigrate them, but
error needs exposure to the light (John 3:19–21).

Older, More Familiar Ways

We now have before us a clear picture of the world into which
Christianity was born and the culture the church encountered. There
seems to be no doubt that once the foundation stones of the church
were no longer there to guide her and persecution was relaxed, the
newly baptized brought their old ideas with them. Little by little the
church assumed older, more familiar ways.

Biblical Christianity deals with realities that are spiritual and
therefore difficult for infants in the faith. Paul himself realized how
difficult it was to explain the faith to certain Corinthian believers who
had not yet grown to maturity. He wrote, "Brothers, I was not able to
speak to you as spiritual people but as people of the flesh, as babies
in Christ" (HCSB). The Old Testament contains many patterns, types,

---

29. Jaroslav Pelikan, *Mary through the Centuries* (New Haven, CT: Yale University, 1996), 114. See
pages 114–116 on dualism and on platonic ideas.

and figures that find their fulfillment in Christ Jesus and His death on the cross. There is a significant difference between the Jewish Old Testament system and the New Testament church established by Christ. We shall delve into this more when we compare the good news of salvation with the *salvation process* imposed by the ancient liturgical churches. Hopefully this chapter has provided an understanding of the world and the atmosphere in which Christianity evangelized and spread around the Mediterranean. The next chapter on the sacraments will provide a foundation for comparing the Old and the New Testament systems of worship.

Sacramental Teaching in Ancient Churches

*S*ACRAMENT is not a common word, and most people connect it with the Roman Catholic, Episcopalian, or Lutheran church. Apart from Anglicans, Presbyterians, Lutherans, and the like, most evangelicals (independent churches and Baptists) call their observances (baptism and the Lord's Supper) *ordinances*. They understand something different from what the Roman and the Orthodox churches teach.

Tertullian from Carthage, North Africa, was a pagan lawyer before becoming a Christian. He is said to have been the first Christian writer to use the word *sacrament*. Originally, a sacrament was the oath of fidelity a Roman soldier swore to his superior.

In view of what chapter 2 says about the possible influence of philosophy on early Christianity, it is interesting to note that Augustine is said to have used principles of Greek philosophy to explain the meaning of sacraments. "A sacrament, he says, is a sign of a sacred thing."[1] In and of itself, this definition does not appear erroneous. Yet this is not all that the Orthodox and the Catholic churches teach about the sacraments.

The Number of Sacraments

Most evangelical churches celebrate only two ordinances: baptism

---

1. Russell Shaw, ed., *Our Sunday Visitor's Encyclopedia of Catholic Doctrine* (Huntington, IN: Our Sunday Visitor, 1997), 588–89.

and the Lord's Supper. The Council of Trent, however, addressed the number and affirmed seven sacraments:

Trent, Canon 1

If anyone says that the sacraments of the New Law were not all instituted by our Lord Jesus Christ, or that there are more or less than seven, namely, baptism, confirmation, Eucharist, penance, extreme unction, order and matrimony, or that any one of these seven is not truly and intrinsically a sacrament, let him be anathema.

Let us turn now to the Eastern Orthodox Church. Originally, the Western and the Eastern churches were united in the same faith. The separation occurred during the eleventh century over issues of church government (the papacy) and the addition of an article to the Nicene Creed by the Roman church concerning the procession of the Holy Spirit. Thomas Hopko explains the Orthodox church's viewpoint as follows:

The sacraments in the Orthodox Church are officially called the "holy mysteries." Usually seven sacraments are counted: baptism, chrismation (or confirmation), holy eucharist, penance, matrimony, holy orders and the unction of the sick.

The practice of counting the sacraments was adopted in the Orthodox Church from the Roman Catholics. It is not an ancient practice of the Church and, in many ways, it tends to be misleading since it appears that there are just seven specific rites which are "sacraments" and that all other aspects of the life of the Church are essentially different from these particular actions. The more ancient and traditional practice of the Orthodox Church is to consider everything which is in and of the Church as sacramental or mystical.[2]

While the early church fathers made several lists of the canonical books to refute heretics' claims for their own writings, they never enumerated seven sacraments in the church. This in itself is evidence

---

2. Thomas Hopko, *The Orthodox Faith* (Syosset, NY: Orthodox Church in America, 1972), 2:25.

that the practice of listing seven sacraments was a later development.

Roman Catholic and Orthodox Views of the Sacraments

The *Catechism of the Catholic Church*[3] contains the latest and most authoritative explanation of the Catholic church's teachings. In this section, several paragraphs are quoted verbatim to avoid accusations of misrepresentation due to ignorance or bias. The paragraph number as listed in the catechism follows each quotation.

> The sacraments are efficacious signs of grace, instituted by Christ and entrusted to the Church, by which divine life is dispensed to us. The visible rites by which the sacraments are celebrated signify and make present the graces proper to each sacrament. (1131)

> ... The seven sacraments are the signs and instruments by which the Holy Spirit spreads the grace of Christ the head throughout the Church which is his Body. The Church, then, both contains and communicates the invisible grace she signifies. It is in this analogical sense, that the Church is called a "sacrament." (774)

We understand this to mean that the Catholic Church considers the sacraments the means by which God dispenses His grace or, in the Catholic view, His presence, work, and favor. The church is considered the indispensable storehouse of the grace necessary for salvation. Do sacraments effect, or bring about, what they signify? The Roman and Orthodox churches think so.

Roman Catholic

Statements defining the Catholic position are readily available, but evangelicals should find interesting those crafted specifically to counter the Reformers' teachings and to explain Catholic doctrine. An anathema[4] was pronounced on all who rejected Rome's teachings. The canons and anathemas promulgated during the Council of

---

3. *Catechism of the Catholic Church*, 2nd ed. (New York: Doubleday, 1997). This second edition includes modifications from the *editio typical*, or official source text.

4. In Catholic thought, an anathema is a curse, a delivering up to Satan, equivalent to being damned. A long explanation from the *Catholic Encyclopedia* can be found at www.newadvent.org.

Trent (1545–1563) have never been repudiated. The following is from the section on the sacraments.

Canon 6
If anyone says that the sacraments of the New Law do not contain the grace which they signify, or that they do not confer that grace on those who place no obstacles in its way, as though they were only outward signs of grace or justice received through faith and certain marks of Christian profession, whereby among men believers are distinguished from unbelievers, let him be anathema.

Canon 8
If anyone says that by the sacraments of the New Law grace is not conferred *ex opere operato*, but that faith alone in the divine promise is sufficient to obtain grace, let him be anathema.

Note first of all that these canons affirm the church's position that the sacraments confer grace, that they are not just signs.[5] Second, they are said to be efficacious in and of themselves. In canon 9, the Council of Trent declares that certain sacraments leave an "indelible mark" on the soul: "If anyone says that in three sacraments, namely, baptism, confirmation and order, there is not imprinted on the soul a character, that is, a certain spiritual and indelible mark, by reason of which they cannot be repeated, let him be anathema."

Concerning the first of the sacraments, the *Catechism of the Catholic Church* states, "Baptism imprints on the soul an indelible spiritual sign, [called] the character, which consecrates the baptized person for Christian worship. Because of the character Baptism cannot be repeated (cf. DS 1609 and DS 1624)" (1280).

Orthodox

The differences between the Roman Catholic Church and the Eastern Orthodox Church are often explained this way: The Orthodox

---

5. Compare *Catechism of the Catholic Church*, par. 1279, "The fruit of Baptism, or baptismal grace, is a rich reality that includes forgiveness of original sin and all personal sins, birth into the new life by which man becomes an adoptive son of the Father, a member of Christ and a temple of the Holy Spirit. By this very fact the person baptized is incorporated into the Church, the Body of Christ, and made a sharer in the priesthood of Christ."

church never experienced a scholastic and a reformation period as did the Catholic church. The Orthodox church resists defining "mysteries" in a juridical or legalistic manner, as the church in the West does. For this reason *transubstantiation* is not a word widely used in the Orthodox church, except where Catholic theology had some influence due to politics or to Orthodox leaders who studied abroad. The Orthodox church does not have a single monarchial head or government as the Catholic Church does, nor does it possess a universal catechism similar to the *Catechism of the Catholic Church.*

An excellent explanation of the Eastern Orthodox view of sacraments has been given by the Greek Orthodox theologian John Karmiris. He writes,

> Justifying and sanctifying Divine Grace which abides in the Church is administered by the Church to the people by means of the Holy Mysteries, which are divinely instituted ceremonies that deliver, by visible means, mysteriously transmitted invisible Grace.
>
> Thus it is that the sacraments, when they are worthily received, become instruments, means of transmission, of Divine Grace.[6]
>
> In no way is the efficacy of the sacrament contingent *upon the faith or moral qualifications of either celebrant or recipient* [Karmiris's footnote 4 quotes John Chrysostom and other Fathers on this], yet every magical and mechanical action is excluded in the performance of the sacrament. . . . Furthermore, the Orthodox Catholic Church believes that Divine Grace is not dispensed outside of the True Church.[7]

It is important that evangelicals understand this last statement by an eminent Orthodox church theologian. According to him, grace is not dispensed outside the "True Church" (his church). Second, the sacraments are effective in and of themselves, and faith is not a requirement. This undoubtedly refers to the baptism and participation in communion of babies and young children. Third, the

6. John Karmiris, *A Synopsis of the Dogmatic Theology of the Orthodox Catholic Church*, trans. George Dimopoulos (Scranton: Christian Orthodox Edition, 1973), 100.

7. Ibid., 101 (my italics).

sacraments are "instruments" or "means" of grace.

The words *Divine Grace* are spelled with capital letters because in the Orthodox church grace is considered an uncreated "energy," a "power" that proceeds from God but is not separate from God; therefore grace is divine. Vladimir Lossky, a famous theologian in the Orthodox church in France, quotes church father Basil the Great, who explained the difference between God in His essence and God in His energies. To understand the sacraments and grace in the Orthodox church, one has to be aware that deification, or divinization, is the goal of an Orthodox Christian. We will look at this subject later, but a brief quotation from Lossky should suffice for now: "In the same way, St. Basil talks of the role of the energies in *manifesting,* opposing them to the unknowable essence: 'It is by His energies'—he says—'that we say we know our God; we do not assert that we can come near to the essence itself, for His energies descend to us, but His essence remains unapproachable.'"[8]

Traditional Roman Catholic Church theology differs from the Orthodox teaching on grace. Roman Catholic theologian Ludwig Ott says, "Sanctifying Grace is a created supernatural gift really distinct from God."[9] The Orthodox church denies that grace is created, because the church considers grace as being God acting in His powers or energies. To remain within the limits of this chapter, we will take up this important topic again in chapter 13.

Baptism

The Roman Catholic View

The Catholic church claims to be the universal (catholic) church, the mother of all churches, and clothed with apostolic authority, especially that of Peter, the head of the apostles, whose successor the pope claims to be.[10] The pope is considered the vicegerent of Christ who rules the church in company with the bishops, who are consid-

---

8. Lossky, *The Mystical Theology of the Eastern Church,* 71–72.
9. Ludwig Ott, *Fundamentals of Catholic Dogma* (1955; rep., Rockford, IL: Tan Books, 1960), 254.
10. *Catechism of the Catholic Church,* 669–70.

ered successors of the apostles. With such authority the church says,

> Holy Baptism is the basis of the whole Christian life, the gateway
> to life in the Spirit *(vitae spiritualis ianua),* and the door which
> gives access to the other sacraments. Through Baptism we are
> freed from sin and reborn as sons of God; we become members
> of Christ, are incorporated into the Church and made sharers in
> her mission: "Baptism is the sacrament of regeneration through
> water in the word." (1213)

> Incorporated into Christ by Baptism, the person baptized is
> configured to Christ. Baptism seals the Christian with the indel-
> ible spiritual mark (*character*) of his belonging to Christ. No sin
> can erase this mark, even if sin prevents Baptism from bearing
> the fruits of salvation. Given once for all, Baptism cannot be
> repeated. (1272)

In the section on baptism, the Catholic church solemnly proclaimed at the Council of Trent,

Canon 3
If anyone says that in the Roman Church, which is the mother
and mistress of all churches, there is not the true doctrine concerning the sacrament of baptism, let him be anathema.

Canon 5
If anyone says that baptism is optional, that is, not necessary for
salvation, let him be anathema.

The Eastern Orthodox View

In the Orthodox church baptism begins with the catechumen
(baptismal candidate) standing in the narthex at the entrance to the
sanctuary. The priest asks the candidate three times if he renounces
Satan, to which he replies, "I renounce Satan." Then he turns away
from the altar and spits on Satan. After turning again in the direction of the altar, he is asked three times if he accepts Christ, to which
he replies each time, "I accept Christ." Then he is asked to kneel and
make a prostration, touching the floor with his forehead. He arises,

professes the church's creed, and is anointed with chrism (consecrated oil used in Greek and Latin churches especially in baptism, chrismation, confirmation, and ordination) on various points of his body. Then the catechumen is immersed three times in the names of the persons of the Trinity.

The Eucharist

The Roman Catholic View

The *Catechism of the Catholic Church* states the Roman Catholic belief concerning the Eucharist: "The Eucharistic presence of Christ begins at the moment of the consecration and endures as long as the Eucharistic species subsist. Christ is present whole and entire in each of the species and whole and entire in each of their parts, in such a way that the breaking of the bread does not divide Christ." (1377)

The Eastern Orthodox View

Thomas Hopko, a priest and former professor at Saint Vladimir's Seminary in New York, explains,

> The sacrament of the eucharist is also called **holy communion** since it is the mystical communion of men with God, with each other, and with all men and all things in him through Christ and the Spirit. The eucharistic liturgy is celebrated in the Church every Sunday, the Day of the Lord, as well as on feast days. Except in monasteries, it is rarely celebrated daily. Holy Communion is forbidden to all Orthodox Christians on the week days of Great Lent except in the special communion of the Liturgy of the Pre-sanctified Gifts . . . because of its joyful and resurrectional character. The eucharist is always given to all members of the Church, including infants who are baptized and confirmed. It is always given in both forms—bread and wine. It is strictly understood as being the real presence of Christ, his true Body and Blood mystically present in the bread and wine which are offered to the Father in his name and consecrated by the divine Spirit of God.[11]

---

11. Thomas Hopko, *The Orthodox Faith*, 2:35.

Alexander Schmemann, a well-known writer from the same seminary, wrote,

> The purpose of the eucharist lies not in the change of the bread and wine, but in our partaking of Christ, who has become our food, our life, the manifestation of the Church as the body of Christ.
>
> This is why the holy gifts themselves never became in the Orthodox East an object of special reverence, contemplation and adoration, and likewise an object of special theological "problematics": how, when, in what manner their change is accomplished. The eucharist—and this means the changing of the holy gifts—is a mystery that cannot be revealed and explained in the categories of "this world"—time, essence, causality, etc. It is revealed only to faith: "I believe also that this is truly Thine own precious Blood." Nothing is explained, nothing is defined, nothing has changed in "this world."[12]

One may ask why, in the Russian tradition, do those attending a Divine Liturgy during the week make a complete prostration at the moment the priest calls down the Holy Spirit over the bread and the wine? (In the Greek Church the people kneel.) Canonically, prostrations, even kneeling, on the part of the people are not permitted on Sundays because this day is a little *Pascha* (Easter), a day of resurrection and joy. This canon is not followed in the rubrics (explanations or instructions) for the parishes of the Greek Archdiocese in the US. On Sundays, only the priest makes a prostration, and in the Greek Orthodox church, the people kneel at this point.

Reformed Teaching on the Lord's Supper

Benjamin Warfield, who taught at Princeton Seminary at the end of the nineteenth century, was an articulate spokesman on Biblical theology. He wrote an article titled "The Fundamental Significance of the Lord's Supper." In this article, he says that "all who partake of this bread and wine, the appointed symbols of his body and blood,

---

12. Alexander Schmemann, *The Eucharist, Sacrament of the Kingdom,* trans. Paul Kachur (Crestwood, NY: St. Vladimir's Seminary, 1988), 226.

therefore, are symbolically partaking of the victim offered on the altar of the cross, and are by this act professing themselves offerers of the sacrifice and seeking to become beneficiaries of it."[13]

Admittedly, Warfield could be subject to misunderstanding. Actually, he is pointing out the relationship between the Passover meal and the Lord's Supper and Christians' participation in a sacrificial meal that is the essence of the Passover. I believe he speaks this way because Christians are a spiritual priesthood. Only a few lines later, Warfield writes, "As we eat these in their symbols, we are—certainly not repeating his sacrifice, nor yet prolonging it—but continuing that solemn festival upon it instituted by Christ, by which we testify our 'participation in the altar' and claim our part in the benefits bought by the offering immolated on it."

Contrast this now with the Orthodox and Catholic churches' dogma that the communicants participate in the same sacrifice of the cross, which is continually offered on their altars.

As the following chart makes clear, both the figurative language of John 6:40 and the straightforward language of John 6:54 describe the same phenomenon: salvation by grace through faith in Jesus Christ. Therefore, the sacramental views of the Lord's Supper cannot really be substantiated by an appeal to John 6:40.[14]

John 6:40	John 6:54
Everyone who	Whoever
looks to the Son	eats my flesh
And	and
believes in him	drinks my blood
shall have eternal life,	has eternal life,
And	and
I will raise him up	I will raise him up
at the last day.	at the last day.

13. Benjamin Warfield, "The Fundamental Significance of the Lord's Supper," *The Bible Student* 3, no. 2 (February 1901): 82, quoted in Keith A. Mathison, *Given for You, Reclaiming Calvin's Doctrine of the Lord's Supper* (Phillipsburg, NJ: P&R, 2002), 170. See also pages 167–70.

14. This chart can be found at http://jamesgmccarthy.com. The chart is contained in a tract, "The Mass: From Mystery to Meaning," by James G. McCarthy, a former Roman Catholic. His tract is a penetrating discussion of the Roman Catholic doctrine of the Lord's Supper.

Following the Passover meal, which the Jews understood well enough because of its yearly celebration, Jesus instituted the Lord's Supper as the fulfillment of the Passover in Himself as the foretold, slaughtered Lamb of God. Just as the Jews kept the Passover in remembrance of the blood shed and splattered on the lintels of their doors, followed by their exodus (freedom from bondage) from Egypt, Christians are called to remember and celebrate what God has done for them in giving His Son, Jesus Christ, as a sacrifice for us. We are called to live in faith in His redeeming death, knowing how much God loves us (John 3:16). The Lord's Supper is no more, no less than this, in spite of the ancient churches, which read too much into the words of institution. They seem to ignore the fact that Christ's flesh is in Heaven at the right hand of God, whereas He is present in His divinity through the Holy Spirit in us and in the church. Are we blessed when we celebrate this meal? Indeed we are, because we commune with our Lord, and our faith in His death on our behalf is strengthened by our remembrance of Him.

Are the Sacraments Magical?

In Catholicism it is possible for an apostate priest to "confect" the Eucharist and for a Muslim or nonbeliever to baptize someone in an emergency. This fact could easily lead one to believe that there is something magical about the pouring of water on someone's head if the correct formula is used.[15] The Roman Catholic Church teaches there is a difference between a *valid* sacrament and an *illicit* sacrament. A sacrament may be valid but illicit. For example, a priest separated from the church by schism may celebrate the Eucharist because he has received ordination, and a valid transubstantiation will take place. This transubstantiation is, however, considered illicit; therefore it is not lawful for a faithful Roman Catholic to attend a Mass led by such a priest and to take the Eucharist from him.

Such is not the case in the Orthodox church, where the priest must be in communion with a canonical bishop who has received his

---

15. See paragraph 1247 of *Catechism of the Catholic Church.*

episcopacy in direct line from the apostles and also professes right (*orthodox*) doctrines. The Orthodox believe the priest must be a legitimate priest in order to celebrate the sacraments; in other words, he cannot be a heretic.

This idea of succession (even certain Baptists espouse it) rests on flimsy ground historically and is detrimental to the church. In 1409, three popes claimed the papacy at the same time. After the French Revolution, the government appointed bishops without regard for Rome's wishes. In a word, those who hold to succession have to admit there have been many claimants and impostors.

A Sacrament, a Reformed Definition

John Calvin is one of the best known men of the Reformation. His *Institutes of the Christian Religion* is a formidable compendium of knowledge and logic on matters of theology and faith. Calvin covered a vast array of ideas in these books. When something occurs to me, I find that Calvin has probably already discussed it. In the *Institutes*, he writes, "One may call [a sacrament] a testimony of divine grace toward us, confirmed by an outward sign, with mutual attestation of our piety toward him."[16] Calvin points out the obvious error concerning sacraments being received without faith or concerning people who imagine the sacraments produce some effect of their own, as if they were magical: "There are those who attach to the sacraments some sort of secret powers with which one nowhere reads that God has endowed them. . . . But what is a sacrament received apart from faith but the most certain ruin of the church? For nothing ought to be expected from it apart from the promise, but the promise no less threatens wrath to unbelievers than offers grace to believers."[17]

Finally, Calvin explains God's intended purpose in the administration of the sacraments: "Therefore, let it be regarded as a settled principle that the sacraments have the same office as the Word of God:

---

16. John Calvin, *Institutes of the Christian Religion*, vol. 2, bk. 4 in The Library of Christian Classics, ed. John T. McNeill, trans. F. L. Battles, 2 vols. (Louisville: Westminster John Knox Press, 1960), 1277.

17. Ibid., 1289.

to offer and set forth Christ to us, and in him the treasures of heavenly grace. But they avail and profit nothing unless received in faith."[18]

Remember, opinions of famous theologians, past and present, are cited only because they are respected men in the areas we are investigating, but above all our appeal is to the inspired Word of God.

Fruits of Church-State Union and the Controversies over Baptism

A short study of how the transformation of apostolic Christianity took place will help us better grasp what happened to the Scriptural doctrine of baptism. The abandonment of apostolic teachings bore negative fruits that were not becoming to the church's testimony. The magical-sacramental belief was the first harmful fruit, and it led to a division between the laity and the clergy, who performed the sacraments for the benefit of the simple who became attendees seeking salvation in the church. After Christianity was legalized, the state involved itself in the church's affairs, lending her not only financial but also political support. This was extremely detrimental, because then the chiefs of state sought support from the church. The church desired kings and emperors favorable to her, and the state sought out popes, patriarchs, and bishops who would support the state's political ambitions.

History informs us that forced baptisms, whether of Jews or of conquered peoples, occurred in the West. In some cases people lined up by the hundreds, even by the thousands, behind a tribal chief or king, and the missionaries baptized a multitude of unconverted pagans. Faith, that golden jewel, was lost over the centuries as the baptism of babies, tribes, and nations became the rule. As early as the end of the fourth century, all Roman citizens had to adhere to Christianity as the state religion. Membership in the church was esteemed a civic obligation and a guarantee of salvation. In 391, imperial laws were promulgated against heretics and against the re-baptism of a member of the Catholic religion. Catholic priest and historian

18. Ibid., 1292.

Newman Eberhardt provides us an example of an early Roman Catholic decision in Spain: "During the latter part of the seventh century the Councils of Toledo required that baptism be administered within thirty days of birth. Whereas previously the sacrament had normally been conferred only by the bishop in the Paschal and Pentecostal seasons, now priests administered it at need in the parish churches. Since immersion continued to be a general custom, a baptistry appeared attached to the parish church."[19]

Under Charlemagne, baptism was compulsory in Saxony, and death was the penalty for refusal. People were required to bring their children to the fonts for baptism to become members of the state religion. Everyone had to obediently follow the emperor's version of the universal (*catholic*) religion. Particularly in the East, if the emperor was a semi-Arian or a Monophysite,[20] he endeavored to install patriarchs and bishops in line with his convictions. If the emperor was an iconoclast,[21] the people would be ordered to destroy icons. All dissenters were persecuted and obliged to follow his wishes. A patriarch or bishop who refused was banned or imprisoned. Disobedience was considered a sign of heresy. The conduct of the masses and the educated leaders who considered themselves Christians was often greatly different from that of the scattered, persecuted, apostolic followers of "the way." How different from the primitive believers who preferred death rather than betray their Lord and Savior. Their spilled blood was the strongest testimony to their faith, and it motivated thousands of others to become Christians.

State religion sought to impose religious unity by suppressing ideas considered deviant or heretical; uniformity in the empire was highly esteemed. In the fifth century, the Nestorian churches separated from Orthodoxy because they rejected the decrees of the Council of Ephesus. Religious ideology split the church, and the Eastern (now

---

19. Newman C. Eberhardt, *A Summary of Catholic History*, 2 vols. (St. Louis: B. Herder, 1961), 1:439.

20. Semi-Arianism was a heresy that held Jesus to be *like* God the Father, but not equal to Him. Monophysitism held that the Divine Logos took human flesh with the result that there was one nature: Christ. The human nature was divine.

21. A person who criticizes or opposes widely accepted beliefs and practices.

called "Oriental") churches fanned out into Persia and India and even
to faraway China. The separation of Egypt, including Sudan and Ethio-
pia, from the Roman emperor's religious and political control was to a
certain degree due to the enforcement of the decrees of the Ecumenical
Council of Chalcedon in 451. In Palestine and Egypt, Christians battled
Christians in the streets. Philip Hughes describes the carnage.

> Once again the troops had to fight the mob and the monks
> before the formalities could be gone through and the new bishop
> elected. Still the fighting in the streets continued, the troops
> were driven into the great temple of the old religion—the Sera-
> peion—and held there until with the buildings they perished in
> the flames. The imperial government must evidently fight for its
> own existence. All Egypt was placed under military law and the
> pro-Dioscoros bishops everywhere deposed. So a certain exter-
> nal order was at last obtained. It lasted for an uneasy five years.[22]

Due to such hot religious and political fervor, the Oriental Orthodox Churches and the Coptic Church in Egypt came into existence.

In Europe, independent groups continued to spring up over the
centuries in spite of Rome's close supervision. Some of these groups
were truly heretical and deviant. Others were more evangelical and
tried to live what they considered to be the apostolic life. During the
Reformation period, baptism once again became a source of disputes
and executions, because the law obliged subjects to follow their lord
or king. This practice would be known later as *cujus regio ejus religio,*
when in Germany each region had its own ruler and religion. To be
out of step with one's lord was treasonous and could be punishable
by death. It is remarkable that Catholics and Protestants together persecuted those in Anabaptist movements. Anabaptism was considered
an ancient heresy because re-baptism (whence the name ana-baptist)
was considered a rejection of the established order and therefore a
threat to be extinguished. In Catholic kingdoms, Anabaptists were

---

22. Philip Hughes, "The Traditional Faith and the Imperial Policies," in *A History of the Church to the Eve of the Reformation,* 3 vols. All three volumes can be read online or downloaded from www.ewtn.com/library/chistory/hughhist.txt.

burned at the stake, and in Protestant lands they were drowned in rivers and lakes or beheaded. That baptism became a serious issue can be seen from the fact that during the 1500s Anabaptists were whipped, branded, imprisoned, banished, or executed.

It is time to shine the light of the Holy Scriptures on baptism. The Bible has more to say about baptism than the Lord's Supper due to so many accounts narrated in the book of Acts. Consequently, this study will focus on baptism because we have sufficiently examined the ancient churches' doctrine of the Eucharist, and also because the intent of both ordinances is the same: to serve as signs and confessions of Christian faith.

CHAPTER 4

Baptism in the Early Church—Part 1

IN 1873, A MANUSCRIPT, dated circa AD 1056, was discovered in Constantinople. It is commonly known as the *Didache*, that is, "the Teaching." Its Latin name is *Codex Constantinopolitanus*. Outside the New Testament, the *Didache* gives us the clearest view of the Christian liturgy during the period around the close of the first century.

The *Didache:* The Teaching of the Twelve Apostles

The original title was *Doctrinae Apostolorum*, or "Doctrine of the Apostles," but it is also known as the "Doctrine of the Lord taught to the nations by the Twelve Apostles." Today the manuscript is located in Jerusalem. Most scholars think it was written about AD 120, although others believe it could have been written as early as AD 50–70. Henry Chadwick favors a date between AD 70 and 110.[1]

The *Didache* is a religious manual containing instructions on the two ways: the way of life and the way of death. It also contains a description of baptism and the Eucharist, as well as some liturgical instructions. The document is also supposed to give instructions that originated with the apostles. Actually, it has nothing to do with the twelve apostles, but only with apostles in general. Athanasius

---

1. Henry Chadwick, *The Early Church*, 1:46–47.

mentions it as being used in Egypt to instruct catechumens. Concerning baptism, we read in the *Didache*:

> Regarding baptism, baptize thus. After giving the foregoing instructions, Baptize in the name of the Father, and of the Son, and of the Holy Spirit in running water. But if you have no running water, baptize in any other; and, if you cannot in cold water, then in warm. But, if the one is lacking, pour the other three times on the head in the name of the Father, and Son, and Holy Spirit. But, before the baptism, let the one who baptizes and the one to be baptized, fast, and any others who are able to do so. And you shall require the person being baptized to fast for one or two days.

> But let no one eat or drink of the Eucharist with you except for those baptized in the name of the Lord, for it was in reference to this that the Lord said: "Do not give that which is holy to dogs."[2]

The document tells us that candidates for baptism were to first be instructed, and then they were to fast for a day or two in preparation for their baptism. This bit of information reveals two important things: the converts were capable of learning and expressing their new faith, and they believed the gospel. The *Didache* and Justin Martyr also inform us that baptism[3] was required in the early church before one could partake of the Eucharist. We conclude that the Eucharist was limited to believers in Christ and members of the ecclesia.

My passion for history motivated me to read the early church fathers, and like many potential converts, I was astonished how "Catholic" it all sounded. Baptismal regeneration, the Eucharist, transubstantiation, and the authority of bishops appeared to be part of the woof and warp of the apostolic fathers and the later church fathers.

---

2. Quoting sections 7 and 9. The complete text may be found in Jack N. Sparks, ed., *The Apostolic Fathers* (Nashville: 1978; repr., Minneapolis: Light and Life, n.d.), 307–19. My text is from personal notes, which explains any differences in style.

3. "But we, after we have thus washed him who has been convinced and has assented to our teaching, bring him to the place where those who are called brethren are assembled, in order that we may offer hearty prayers in common for ourselves and for the baptized [illuminated] person, and for all others in every place." Justin Martyr, "The First Apology of Justin," 65, in *The Apostolic Fathers with Justin Martyr and Irenaeus*, The Ante-Nicene Fathers, 1:185.

Justin Martyr's Views on Christian Baptism

Justin Martyr (ca. AD 155) provides a classic description of baptism and relates the preparation for it. Those to be baptized were converts who had repented and had asked for forgiveness of the sins of their past life.

> I will also relate the manner in which we dedicated ourselves to God *when we had been made new through Christ*; lest, if we omit this, we seem to be unfair in the explanation we are making. *As many as are persuaded and believe that what we teach and say is true, and undertake to be able to live accordingly, are instructed to pray and to entreat God with fasting, for the remission of their sins that are past, we praying and fasting with them.* Then they are brought by us where there is water, and are regenerated in the same manner in which we were ourselves regenerated. For, in the name of God, the Father and Lord of the universe, and of our Saviour Jesus Christ, and of the Holy Spirit, they then receive the washing with water. For Christ also said, "Except ye be born again, ye shall not enter into the kingdom of heaven." Now, that it is impossible for those who have once been born to enter into their mothers' wombs, is manifest to all. And how those who have sinned and repent shall escape their sins, is declared by Esaias the prophet, as I wrote above; he thus speaks: "Wash you, make you clean; put away the evil of your doings from your souls; learn to do well; judge the fatherless, and plead for the widow: and come and let us reason together, saith the Lord. And though your sins be as scarlet, I will make them white like wool; and though they be as crimson, I will make them white as snow. But if ye refuse and rebel, the sword shall devour you: for the mouth of the Lord hath spoken it."
>
> And for this [rite] we have learned from the apostles this reason. Since at our birth we were born without our own knowledge or choice, by our parents coming together, and were brought up in bad habits and wicked training; in order that we may not remain the children of necessity and of ignorance, *but may become the children of choice and knowledge*, and may obtain in the water the remission of sins formerly committed, there is pronounced

over him who chooses to be born again, and *has repented of his sins*, the name of God the Father and Lord of the universe; he who leads to the laver the person that is to be washed calling him by this name alone. For no one can utter the name of the ineffable God; and if any one dare to say that there is a name, he raves with a hopeless madness. And this washing is called illumination, because *they who learn these things are illuminated in their understandings.* And in the name of Jesus Christ, who was crucified under Pontius Pilate, and in the name of the Holy Ghost, who through the prophets foretold all things about Jesus, he who is illuminated is washed.[4]

Up to this point in time, whenever I came across such references in my investigations, I asked myself, "How can I know for sure that these early writings have not been altered?" Or, "It just proves you can't trust anything outside the Bible." Due to a challenge (which I accepted) to read the Apostolic Fathers, my attitude began to gradually change until finally I decided to return to the Roman Catholic Church in which I had grown up. Although several questions remained unanswered, I put them aside because of my decision to "trust the church."

A Brief Scriptural Response

The highly respected New Testament scholar F. F. Bruce, in his commentary *The Epistle to the Hebrews*, refers to Justin Martyr and his use of the term *enlightened.*

It is tempting to understand the verb here in the sense of baptism—a sense which it bore among Christians in Rome in the middle of the second century. [footnote 39: "Justin (First Apology, 61:12f.; 65:1) uses the verb φωτίζω and the noun φωτισμός to describe baptism, and does so in a way which indicates that this was a current usage among the Christians of his acquaintance."] The use of "enlightenment" in the sense of baptism need not be a borrowing from the language of the mysteries; it is quite in line with New Testament teaching. [See footnote 40.] At any rate, the

---

4. Justin Martyr, "The First Apology of Justin," 61, in *The Apostolic Fathers with Justin Martyr and Irenaeus,* The Ante-Nicene Fathers, 1:183 (my italics).

enlightenment here is something which has taken place once for all—like baptism itself, which is unrepeatable for the simple reason that its repetition would contradict its whole significance.[5]

Bruce dates this description to "the middle of the second century." This is approximately one hundred years after the apostle Paul. During this period, a gradual growth in church organization and practice had been taking place. It is obvious that if a person requested and submitted to baptism, he or she had *already* heard the gospel preached and had been *enlightened,* or convinced that Christ is the Messiah, the Redeemer of souls. In that case, how can anyone deny that baptism signifies what has *already* occurred in someone's heart and mind? This enlightenment is obviously the work of the Holy Spirit in one's soul or spirit (or mind, Greek *nous*); these words are closely connected in meaning and appear at times to refer to the same thing, that is, the heart, the understanding, or the inner man.

It is easy to conclude, therefore, that the inner transformation is symbolized by the outward washing with water. Our Lord taught that "no one can come to Me unless the Father who sent Me draws him" (John 6:44). This is a holy and mysterious work of grace in a sinner's heart, be he the worst sinner or the most sanctimonious church leader. Consequently, the inner illumination occurs invisibly, and others are made aware of it when the new convert steps forward publicly to request baptism, thereby identifying himself with Christ's disciples.

Even our Lord was baptized at His own request, and in doing so He left us an example. He was not baptized because He was guilty of sin, but because He was going to bear the sins of mankind on the cross. Jesus identified Himself with the people who came to the River Jordan, where John was baptizing those who confessed their sinfulness. "Then Jesus came from Galilee to John at the Jordan, to be baptized by him. But John tried to stop Him, saying, 'I need to be baptized by You, and yet You come to me?' Jesus answered him, 'Allow it for now, because this is the way for us to fulfill all righteousness.' Then he allowed Him to be baptized" (Matt. 3:13–15, HCSB).

5 F. F. Bruce, *The Epistle to the Hebrews* (Grand Rapids: Eerdmans, 1964), 120.

> The next day John saw Jesus coming toward him and said, "Here is the Lamb of God, who takes away the sin of the world! This is the One I told you about: 'After me comes a man who has surpassed me, because He existed before me.' I didn't know Him, but I came baptizing with water so He might be revealed to Israel."
>
> And John testified, "I watched the Spirit descending from heaven like a dove, and He rested on Him. I didn't know Him, but He who sent me to baptize with water told me, 'The One you see the Spirit descending and resting on—He is the One who baptizes with the Holy Spirit.' I have seen and testified that He is the Son of God!" (John 1:29–34, HCSB; cf. Acts 1:5, 8)

Baptism is a public declaration of faith in Christ. When a new believer is baptized, he identifies himself with Christ, signifying that he is united with Him in His death, burial, and resurrection (see Romans 6).

In John 1, we read that Jesus baptizes His people with the Holy Spirit. Here is a simple but very important fact: men baptize with water, but God baptizes with the Holy Spirit. A baptism with the Holy Spirit occurred at Pentecost when the disciples were gathered together in Jerusalem waiting for the Spirit's coming, as foretold (Luke 24:49). Since Pentecost, a baptism in the Holy Spirit takes place for each believer. The Holy Spirit incorporates the believer into the church, Christ's Body (1 Cor. 12:13). The timing and manner of this will be evident from a consideration of the following Scriptures. Then, under the heading "Historically Speaking," we will learn just how far people drifted away from this truth as men imagined they were carrying out what only God can do.

The next five Scripture passages will, I hope, satisfy anyone that the invisible regeneration of a soul by the Holy Spirit is *portrayed* in the act of baptism; water (the sign of the sacrament) aptly signifies what takes place in a new Christian. Any idea that water baptism confers sonship or adoption upon anyone, whether a child or an adult, should be rejected (Gal. 4:5, 6). Baptism is an obligation required of a new believer because it fulfills the Lord's command to make disciples who follow and imitate Him. Jesus commanded His disciples to go forth unto all nations, to teach them and to baptize them in the name of the Father and the Son and the Holy Spirit (Matt. 28:19, 20). The first baby step a new believer takes is to seek baptism from the church.[6] In Acts 2, we read, "Those who gladly received his word were baptized; and that day about three thousand souls were added to them" (v. 41; cf. 18:8).

Here are the passages that describe the Holy Spirit's work symbolized by water baptism (other, more controversial passages, will be considered in chapter 5):

> "And such were some of you. But you were washed, but you were sanctified, but you were justified in the name of the Lord Jesus and by the Spirit of our God" (1 Cor. 6:11).

> "For by one Spirit we were all baptized into one body—whether Jews or Greeks, whether slaves or free—and have all been made to drink into one Spirit" (1 Cor. 12:13).

> "Husbands, love your wives, just as Christ also loved the church and gave Himself for her, that He might sanctify and cleanse her with the washing of water by the word, that He might present her to Himself a glorious church, not having spot or wrinkle or any such thing, but that she should be holy and without blemish" (Eph. 5:25–27).

> "Not by works of righteousness which we have done, but according to his mercy he saved us, by the washing of regeneration and renewing of the Holy Ghost, which he shed on us abundantly through Jesus Christ our Saviour; that being justified by his grace, we should be made heirs according to the hope of eternal life" (Titus 3:5–7).

---

6. Faith and regeneration are personal between God and an individual. Baptism, administered in a church context, indicates a church's reception of a new believer who desires to follow Christ and be united to the local church (Acts 2:41, 47). Afterward, the newly baptized believer and the church body (the local assembly of believers), united as one flock, celebrate the Lord's Supper together. This is the second church ordinance whereby the means of salvation (Christ's offering of His body and blood for us) are continually remembered (Gr. *anamnesis*, "relived"), the church being gathered for worship of its Head in Heaven.

"Baptism, which corresponds to this, now saves you (not the removal of the filth of the flesh, but the pledge of a good conscience toward God) through the resurrection of Jesus Christ" (1 Pet. 3:21, HCSB).

Historically Speaking

The reader needs to bear in mind that 100 percent certainty about what the early church fathers had in mind is not always possible because we are so far removed from them in time. We also need to remember that our language, culture, and world outlook are very different from theirs. Orthodox and Catholic apologists will reply that the church fathers' writings were constantly followed and interpreted by bishops who were part of a continuous tradition. They will assure us that we have nothing to fear; laypeople should trust the church and obey her like a mother. This subject will be taken up again in chapter 12.

How far these early teachers, bishops or church fathers, eventually strayed from Scriptural teaching is demonstrated by the power bishops were believed to possess. Whereas the apostle Paul preached salvation and forgiveness of sins through the blood of Christ (Eph. 1:7), the *Apostolic Constitutions* indicate that men quickly usurped a power that was not theirs.[7]

> XXXIII. For if the divine oracle says, concerning our parents according to the flesh, "Honor thy father and thy mother, that it may be well with thee;" and, "He that curseth his father or his mother, let him die the death;" how much more should the word exhort you to honor your spiritual parents, and to love them as your benefactors and ambassadors with God, *who have regenerated you by water*, and endued you with the fullness of the Holy Spirit, who have fed you with the word as with milk, who have nourished you with doctrine, who have confirmed you by their admonitions, who have imparted to you the saving body and precious blood of Christ, *who have loosed you from your sins*, who have made you partakers of the holy and sacred eucharist,

---

7. The section of the document quoted here has been dated to the second half of the third century.

who have admitted you to be partakers and fellow-heirs of the promise of God! Reverence these, and honor them with all kinds of honor; for they have obtained from God the power of life and death, in their judging of sinners, and condemning them to the death of eternal fire, as also of loosing returning sinners from their sins, and of restoring them to a new life.[8]

Gregory Nazianzen, a pious church father of the fourth century, in his *Oration 40 on Holy Baptism*, spoke of baptism as a covenant with God, an illumination, the clothing of immortality, the laver of regeneration. He could not say enough about it and its power.

With the passing of time, the Roman Catholic Church eased and simplified its practices of fasting and the celebration of the sacraments, especially since the Second Vatican Council. For instance, the baptismal ceremony has been greatly abbreviated. In spite of many calls for changes in the liturgical languages, fasting, the calendar, and modes of dress, the Orthodox church has retained her ancient practices. For example, the Orthodox church dips the baptismal candidates three times in water, just as Tertullian related in his letter "Against Praxeas."

After His resurrection He promises in a pledge to His disciples that He will send them the promise of His Father; and lastly, He commands them to baptize into the Father and the Son and the Holy Ghost, not into a unipersonal God. And indeed it is not once only, but three times, that we are immersed into the Three Persons, at each several mention of Their names.[9]

Such respect for ancient practices made a strong impression upon me personally. Deceived by their ancient claims, I lost the freedom

---

8. Alexander Roberts, James Donaldson, and A. Cleveland Coxe, eds., "Constitutions of the Holy Apostles," 2.33, in *Fathers of the Third and Fourth Centuries: Lactantius, Venantius, Asterius, Victorinus, Dionysius, Apostolic Teaching and Constitutions, Homily, and Liturgies*, trans. James Donaldson, vol. 7, The Ante-Nicene Fathers (Buffalo, NY: Christian Literature Company, 1886), 412 (my italics).

9. Tertullian, "Against Praxeas," 26, in *Latin Christianity: Its Founder, Tertullian*, ed. Alexander Roberts, James Donaldson, and A. Cleveland Coxe, trans. Peter Holmes, vol. 3, The Ante-Nicene Fathers (Buffalo, NY: Christian Literature Company, 1885), 623. For a good description of the early baptismal ceremony, see Henry Chadwick, *The Early Church*, 260.

I had enjoyed because of the gospel. I could not believe the early church could have deviated to such an extent because of Christ's promise to her (Matt. 28:20).

The ancient churches' claims are answered best by explaining that traditions, customs, and liturgical forms were evolving during the early centuries of church history. Doctrinal developments were also taking place.[10] As Christians studied the Old Testament prophecies searching for support for Christian doctrines, they also looked to their experience in Judaism for patterns and forms of worship; and, perhaps, certain philosophical ideas influenced their thinking. Chapter 5 may prove helpful for readers who desire a more in-depth study of baptism.

---

10. Matters never imagined in the first century were discussed and debated in local synods, ecumenical councils, and ecclesiastical writings for centuries. Image worship and the place/role of Mary and the saints are two examples of this.

Baptism in the Early Church—Part 2

P EOPLE GENERALLY KNOW that the New Testament speaks about more than one kind of baptism. There is John's baptism "unto repentance," "divers baptisms" or Jewish ablutions/washings, Holy Spirit baptism, baptism in fire (some think this is the same as Holy Spirit baptism, but others think it refers to the destruction of Jerusalem), Christian baptism, and baptism in blood (which by identification with Christ may refer to death as a Christian martyr, Mark 10:38, 39). John Calvin taught that John's baptism is the same as Christian baptism. The common view, however, is that they differ in purpose. The limits of this study do not permit me to cover all these types of baptisms. Let it simply be noted that John's baptism was a baptism that called upon the Jewish nation to repent and admit their sinfulness by a washing (baptism) in or with water. The people would demonstrate humility if they accepted such a baptism, admitting their need of conversion. They would thus acknowledge their need for a Messiah. Acts 19:4 records, "Paul said, 'John baptized with a baptism of repentance, telling the people that they should believe in the One who would come after him, that is, in Jesus'" (HCSB). In this case, did baptism give the Jews repentance, or were they demonstrating their repentance by requesting John the Baptizer to baptize them?

Baptism—A Sign

Baptism is a witness to all: to the church body and to those outside the church. The church accepts the new Christian's credible profession of faith, while notice is given to the world that the baptismal candidate rejects the world's claims on him. The new Christian is still "in the world," but not "of the world," as was true of his new Master, Jesus Christ (John 17:14–17). Through the new birth, the person becomes a new creature and is now in Christ (2 Cor. 5:17), a child of God (Gal. 4:5–7), an heir of God, and a joint heir with Christ (Rom. 8:17). Baptism signifies ("sign"-ifies; baptism is a sign of) a person's identification and union with Christ, his burial and resurrection with Christ to walk in "newness of life" (Rom. 6:3–13). For all these reasons, baptism is a sign of the promised new life: "You must be born again" (John 3:7) and of having been washed, made holy, and justified (1 Cor. 6:11). Furthermore, it is the pledge or request for a good conscience before God (1 Pet. 3:21). Baptism also grants entrance into God's church and brings privileges and responsibilities in the church.

Baptism is not to be taken lightly. How could anyone who claims to be a Christian belittle its significance? In the apostolic church, baptism not only meant a person had accepted the gospel message that Christ is Savior and Lord and that he had experienced a change of life or heart, but it was the door into the local ecclesia, or church. Henceforth, the world would view the new convert as a "Christian," a disciple of Jesus the Messiah (Acts 11:26), and one who belonged to "the Way" (Acts 9:2; 19:9; 22:4; 24:14).

Baptism—A Controversy

A verse from Mark's Gospel is evidence of the importance of baptism in the primitive church (16:16). We read that Jesus said, "He who believes and is baptized will be saved; but he who does not believe will be condemned." Oh, how much ink has flowed from discussions and arguments over these words! Many scholars claim that this portion of Mark was not part of the original Greek text, but was added later by another hand. Modern Bibles usually include it but with a note that this passage is absent in the earliest manuscripts that textual scholars accept as key witnesses to the original Greek text. The longer ending of Mark has few sources before the third century that attest to any kind of antiquity. In any case, this passage has been used to support the teaching that baptism is necessary for salvation.

Leaving the textual matter here, the question is, What does the passage teach as the bottom line? First of all, does it not teach the necessity of faith, then the importance of a new believer following through by receiving baptism? Why? Because Jesus said, "He who believes," and also, "He who does not believe will be condemned." The emphasis is clearly upon faith, and the proof of a living faith is a person's desire to be baptized and become a member of a local church. Acceptance of the discipline and ministry of the church's leadership follows baptism. Any other course of action would not give evidence of a real conversion. Mark 16 may possibly explain why and how the new converts slipped from the "sign" of faith and new birth to a mystical or magical view of the church ordinances, believing them to be necessary to salvation, with the visible act or sign outweighing the inward, invisible action of God. Not only do the ancient churches and a number of the major denominations differ on the meaning and efficacy of sacraments, but they are divided over how baptism should be administered, whether by one immersion or three, or by pouring water three times on the head of an adult or a baby.

The Requirement for a Scriptural Baptism

Before we jump into the deep, we need to get our feet wet. Listen to our Lord's words to His disciples when after His resurrection He foretold the work they would carry out: "And that repentance and remission of sins should be preached in His name to all nations, beginning at Jerusalem" (Luke 24:47, cf. 5:32). Notice how repentance and forgiveness of sins are linked. The book of Acts constitutes the historical account. That book describes the apostle Peter preaching a gospel message to vast crowds assembled in Jerusalem for the Feast of Pentecost. Convicted of their sin, members of the crowd asked what they needed to do. Peter told the crowd, "Repent, and let every one of you be baptized in the name of Jesus Christ for the remission of sins; and you shall receive the gift of the Holy Spirit" (Acts 2:38).

Again, note that repentance and remission (forgiveness) of sins are linked. Keep in mind that the people who gathered for the feast were Jews and Jewish proselytes who came from all over the empire. They were familiar with the many lustrations and purifications a Jew was constrained to perform to be ceremonially clean. The twofold question is, Does baptism produce repentance and remission of sins, or does it signify or testify that these godly operations on the heart have already taken place? We might also ask, What would a refusal to be baptized indicate about conversion and repentance?

Eis in Relation to Baptism

When interpreting the Holy Scriptures we must never isolate a verse from its immediate context. Examining the context in the second chapter of Acts, we note, first, the good news was preached; next, the people were told that to be forgiven, they needed repentance and faith; and, third, "they were cut to the heart" (v. 37). Those who were convicted of sin were told to demonstrate it by receiving baptism in the name of Jesus Christ. Verse 41 describes this: "Then those who gladly received his word were baptized." The phrase "baptized . . . for the remission of sins" in Acts 2:38 has caused difficulty for many readers. What could "for the remission of sins" mean? Does baptism remit sins? The ancient churches answer yes. The Bible teaches that the blood of Jesus Christ alone washes sin(s) away (John 1:29; Heb. 9:14; Rev. 7:14).

To ascertain which English word or phrase harmonizes best with the general interpretation of the subject throughout the New Testament, we will need to examine various translations of a Greek word, εἰς. A lot of ink has been spilled over the little preposition εἰς (*eis*, often translated *in, into, respecting,* or *for*). Several Greek scholars, like J. R. Mantey and A. T. Robertson for example, believe *on account of* or *because of* would be preferable in these passages about baptism.[1] Other scholars do not agree. You will have to decide if such a translation as *because of* or *on account of* will suffice and, more importantly, if it will harmonize with the general New Testament teaching on faith and baptism.

As stated above, scholars have debated whether the Greek preposition εἰς (*eis*, here translated *for*) could also be rendered in English as *because of*. Such a translation does remove the ambiguity in Acts 2:38, because repentance and faith are the usual requirements for baptism. This fits neatly with the circumstances of Peter's preaching and then his listeners' reaction. Baptism is definitely a visible testimony that God forgives sins and that a person wants to become a follower of Christ. What does the phrase *baptized for* mean? In this case, does it mean "in order to get"? An illustration from daily life might be helpful here. Do you take an aspirin for a headache *to get* a headache or *because* you have a headache? In a passage in Matthew's Gospel, the Greek preposition *eis* is used in a similar manner. "The men of Nineveh will rise up in the judgment with this generation and condemn it, because they repented *at* the preaching of Jonah; and indeed a greater than Jonah is here" (Matt. 12:41; italics added, cf. Luke 11:32). Here *eis* is translated *at*. Jonah's preaching was the cause or reason for the Ninevites' repentance.

This understanding of *eis* does make sense in the case of John's baptizing, and it is in harmony with sound doctrine. The usual or common meaning of *eis*, "in," "into," "toward," does not exhaust the many uses of this preposition, which occurs over sixteen hundred

1. "(f) Translation. . . . Syntax is not translation, though it is the only safe way to reach a correct translation. Exegesis is not syntax, but syntax comes before real exegesis. The importance of syntax is rightly appreciated by Gildersleeve.

"(g) Limits of Syntax. After all is done, instances remain where syntax cannot say the last word, where theological bias will inevitably determine how one interprets the Greek idiom. Take ὕδατι in Ac. 1:5, for instance. In itself the word can be either locative or instrumental with βαπτίζω. So in Ac. 2:38 εἰς does not of itself express design (see Mt. 10:41), but it may be so used. *When the grammarian has finished, the theologian steps in, and sometimes before the grammarian is through.*" Robertson, A. T. A *Grammar of the Greek New Testament in the Light of Historical Research* (New York: Hodder & Stoughton, 1919), 389 (my italics).

See also the discussion by Daniel B. Wallace in, Daniel B. Wallace, *Greek Grammar Beyond the Basics: An Exegetical Syntax of the New Testament With Scripture, Subject, and Greek Word Indexes* (Grand Rapids: Zondervan, 1996), 369–71. I agree with this point of view.

times in the New Testament. That the baptism of John is significant and descriptive but does not effect a change in the one baptized can be discerned elsewhere in two ways. We begin by taking note of Matthew 3:11, where *"for* repentance" (HCSB) is the same grammatical expression as in Acts 2:38, *"for* the remission of sins." The context in Matthew 3 shows that John rejected the hypocrites (the Pharisees and Sadducees) who had not repented but were coming forward to be baptized. John told them to bring "fruits worthy of repentance" if they desired baptism (Matt. 3:8; cf. Luke 3:8): "Then Jerusalem, all Judea, and all the region around the Jordan went out to him and were baptized by him in the Jordan, confessing their sins. But when he saw many of the Pharisees and Sadducees coming to his baptism, he said to them, 'Brood of vipers! Who warned you to flee from the wrath to come? Therefore bear fruits worthy of repentance'" (Matt. 3:5–8).

In Matthew 3:11, the phrase "baptize you with water unto repentance," should be understood as meaning "in reference to repentance," "on account of repentance," or possibly "because of repentance." That the humble, sincere Jews were repentant is evident by the fact that Matthew informs us they were "confessing their sins."

Although "respecting" or "in reference to" are not the usual translations of *eis*, a comparison of several modern translations does demonstrate such a possibility. Below are quotations from the English Standard Version and the New American Standard Bible. I have pointed out the translation of *eis* by marking the words in bold.

"No unbelief made him waver **concerning** the promise of God, but he grew strong in his faith as he gave glory to God" (Rom. 4:20, ESV).

"Yet, **with respect to** the promise of God, he did not waver in unbelief but grew strong in faith, giving glory to God" (Rom. 4:20, NASB).

εἰς δὲ τὴν ἐπαγγελίαν τοῦ θεοῦ οὐ διεκρίθη τῇ ἀπιστίᾳ ἀλλὰ ἐνεδυναμώθη τῇ πίστει, δοὺς δόξαν τῷ θεῷ (Rom. 4:20, SBLGNT).

Adult baptism follows conversion and is a *sign* and seal of repentance. John the Baptist said concerning his baptism, "I indeed baptize you with water unto repentance" (Matt. 3:11). John's baptism was a baptism *unto* (Greek *eis*) *repentance* (*because of* or *as a sign of repentance*) as well as *for the remission of sins*. In Luke 3:3 we read, "He went into all the region around the Jordan, preaching a baptism of repentance *for the remission* of sins." John's baptism didn't grant remission of sins any more than it granted repentance. His baptism was for repentant Jews who longed for the Messiah; it was not for hypocrites. John's ministry as the forerunner was clearly preparatory (Luke 16:16). Under the New Covenant, Christian baptism continues to be a sign of faith, repentance, and conversion for Christians (Acts 10:43). Consequently, because we are not baptized *to get repentance*, we wouldn't get baptized *to get saved* (*remission of sins*).

Furthermore, other passages such as Mark 1:4, Luke 3:3, Acts 13:24, and Acts 19:4 also reveal that repentance was demonstrated by accepting baptism. "Baptism of repentance" involves a descriptive genitive modifying the word *baptism*. It tells us what baptism is all about. So we ask, Of what is baptism a sign? Answer: repentance. Therefore, we can be sure that *eis*, followed by the word *repentance* or the phrase *for the remission of sins,* is descriptive, describing *what is referred to* by this sacrament/ordinance; it shows *the reason for* baptism. John's baptism did not remit sins in and of itself any more than it gave repentance. It is not a question of what his baptism did, but what it represented!

The difference between John's baptism and the baptism into Jesus' name is that those baptized into Jesus receive the Holy Spirit. This was foretold by John the Baptist himself when he said, "I indeed baptize you with water unto repentance, but He who is coming after me is mightier than I, whose sandals I am not worthy to carry. He will baptize you with the Holy Spirit and fire" (Matt. 3:11; cf. John 1:33; Acts 11:15–17).

This difference between the two baptisms becomes clear as we read the following in Acts:

> He said to them, "Did you receive the Holy Spirit when you believed?" So they said to him, "We have not so much as heard whether there is a Holy Spirit." And he said to them, "Into what

then were you baptized?" So they said, "Into John's baptism." Then Paul said, "John indeed baptized with a baptism of repentance, saying to the people that they should believe on Him who would come after him, that is, on Christ Jesus." When they heard this, they were baptized in the name of the Lord Jesus. And when Paul had laid hands on them, the Holy Spirit came upon them, and they spoke with tongues and prophesied. Now the men were about twelve in all. (Acts 19:2–7)

It is important to keep in mind that Christian baptism is a sign of repentance, washing, remission of sins, justification, cleansing—all of these. This is why sacraments or ordinances are called "signs." The visible water applied to our bodies symbolizes the washing away (or "bath," Titus 3:5) of the filth of sin that inhabits our nature. Whereas some of Peter's listeners accepted the message gladly, others turned away, as every evangelist since Peter has experienced.

Let us consider baptism from another angle. Is our sinful nature the source of spiritually good acts? Here is where many people "kick against the goads." The New Testament teaches us that faith, repentance, and conversion are all gifts from God (Acts 11:18; 14:27). When Peter confessed that Christ was the Son of God, Jesus told him that he was blessed because His Father in Heaven had revealed it to him (Matt. 16:16, 17). God opens hearts and grants faith, repentance, and new life,[2] but men often desire the praise that belongs to God alone. Baptism demonstrates death to such feelings when we are baptized into Christ, confessing with all humility, "He saved me." The old sinful nature is counted as dead and buried with Christ in the waters (Rom. 6). Rising from the water symbolizes our union with Him in His resurrection, in new life—victorious, Christian, Spirit-filled, new life.

---

2. "When they heard these things they became silent; and they glorified God, saying, Then God has also granted to the Gentiles repentance to life" (Acts 11:18).

"Now a certain woman named Lydia heard us. She was a seller of purple from the city of Thyatira, who worshiped God. The Lord opened her heart to heed the things spoken by Paul" (Acts 16:14).

"In humility correcting those who are in opposition, if God perhaps will grant them repentance, so that they may know the truth" (2 Tim. 2:25).

"For to you it has been granted on behalf of Christ, not only to believe in Him, but also to suffer for His sake" (Phil. 1:29).

This is New Testament baptism!

What was the result of Peter's Spirit-filled preaching? The newly born church experienced rapid growth. God blessed Peter's bold preaching and "the Lord added to the church daily those who were being saved" (Acts 2:47).[3] In summary, we note gospel preaching, the Holy Spirit touching hearts, repentance, faith and conversion, followed by water baptism and the new disciples assembling with others having the same convictions. These are the necessary elements to establish a sound, Scriptural ecclesia, a church. As we progress, what else might we discover in the book of Acts?

Examples of Baptism in Acts of the Apostles

Here is a list of verses where baptism occurs in the book of Acts. Mention is also made of faith, contrition, conversion, and going *into* the water. Some of these are easy to understand. Others are ambiguous and need to be interpreted in the light of clearer passages. If people will not follow this procedure, they will never make any sense of the Scriptures. We won't examine all of them, but they are provided for those who wish to study them: Acts 1:5, 22; 2:38, 41; 8:12, 16, 36, 38; 9:18; 10:37, 47; 11:16; 13:24; 16:15, 33; 18:8, 25; 19:3ff.; 22:16.

Acts 8:12, 13

"But when they believed Philip as he preached the things concerning the kingdom of God and the name of Jesus Christ, both men and women were baptized. Then Simon himself also believed; and when he was baptized he continued with Philip, and was amazed, seeing the miracles and signs which were done."

This passage is easy enough: when they had believed, they were baptized. The next one is strikingly similar to the baptism Jesus experienced at the hands of John in the Jordan River.

---

3. Perhaps your Bible does not have the words "to the church" in Acts 2:47. Princeton scholar Bruce M. Metzger comments that the alternate Greek phrase ἐπὶ τὸ αὐτό is a technical term and means the same thing as "to the church." Bruce M. Metzger, *A Textual Commentary on the Greek New Testament* (New York: United Bible Societies, 1971), 304–05. See also footnote 22 in Metzger's text.

Acts 8:38, 39

"So he commanded the chariot to stand still. And both Philip and the eunuch went down into the water, and he baptized him. Now when they came up out of the water, the Spirit of the Lord caught Philip away, so that the eunuch saw him no more; and he went on his way rejoicing."

An important question here is, What preceded the baptism? The answer is found in verse 35: "Then Philip opened his mouth, and beginning at this Scripture, preached Jesus to him." The Ethiopian had heard the gospel truth about the Lord Jesus Christ.

Acts 10:47, 48

"'Can anyone forbid water, that these should not be baptized who *have received* the Holy Spirit just as we have?' And he commanded them to be baptized in the name of the Lord. Then they asked him to stay a few days" (italics added).

In this case, the Holy Spirit was given *before* baptism, along with the speaking in tongues, which occurred at Pentecost; in this instance the Spirit fell upon Gentile believers. The Roman centurion Cornelius was already a "devout man," a God-fearer, a believer in the God of Israel. He and those of his house heard Peter preach, and their hearts were purified by faith. They also received the Holy Spirit. The next passage in Acts 10 gives a Scriptural commentary on this event. Tempted evangelicals should ask themselves, What purified their hearts: the waters of baptism or their faith?

Acts 15:7–9

"And when there had been much dispute, Peter rose up and said to them: "Men and brethren, you know that a good while ago God chose among us, that by my mouth the Gentiles should hear the word of the gospel and believe. So God, who knows the heart, acknowledged them by giving them the Holy Spirit, just as He did to us, and made no distinction between us and them, purifying their hearts by faith."

Acts 16:31–33

"So they said, 'Believe on the Lord Jesus Christ, and you will be saved, you and your household.' Then they spoke the word of the Lord to him and to all who were in his house. And he took them the same hour of the night and washed their stripes. And immediately he and all his family were baptized."

Many denominations believe that the baptism of a household means that every single member of the jailor's household was baptized, even the jailer's infant children if he had any. The reasoning behind this is twofold: First, that the Philippian jailer as head of the family would bring his family into the New Covenant, just as Abraham's entire household was circumcised as a sign of their belonging to the Covenant (Gen. 17:10–27). Secondly, the church is the New Israel under a New Covenant as promised to Old Israel in Jeremiah (31:31–34). We cannot deviate from our general theme in an attempt to solve an intramural debate between evangelicals, because this problem has been thoroughly examined in books and debates devoted to baptism. It is best to say that *to surmise* is not a proof of anything.

Acts 3:19; 4:4

"Repent therefore and be converted, that your sins may be blotted out, so that times of refreshing may come from the presence of the Lord."

"However, many of those who heard the word believed; and the number of the men came to be about five thousand."

There is no mention here of baptism, but in light of all we have studied, one can be sure these believers had been baptized as evidenced in Act 2 before being added to the church. This is not an argument from silence because of the statements about baptism made in 2:38 and 41. Again, context is important.

We have almost completed our examination of the ordinance of baptism, yet there remain a few passages that require more explanation. It is important to look at these because they seem to support the idea that water effects what, as we have learned elsewhere, comes through faith and repentance. We will look at these passages in chapter 6.

Baptism in the Early Church—Part 3

DOES BAPTISM ACCOMPLISH something *in and of itself*? Many theologians think so, and they will cite the following Biblical texts to support their doctrine. But do these passages really support such an idea?

Five Difficult Passages

John 3:3–8, *"Born of water and the Spirit"*

> Jesus answered and said to him, "Most assuredly, I say to you, unless one is born again, he cannot see the kingdom of God." Nicodemus said to Him, "How can a man be born when he is old? Can he enter a second time into his mother's womb and be born?" Jesus answered, "Most assuredly, I say to you, unless one is born of water and the Spirit, he cannot enter the kingdom of God. That which is born of the flesh is flesh, and that which is born of the Spirit is spirit. Do not marvel that I said to you, "You must be born again." The wind blows where it wishes, and you hear the sound of it, but cannot tell where it comes from and where it goes. So is everyone who is born of the Spirit."

Some people bend over backward to press this passage into a philosophy or doctrine they hold dear. How can we avoid introducing our own preconceived notions or prejudices into the Bible? First, we must carefully read our Lord's words and then ask ourselves what He emphasized in His conversation with Nicodemus, a Jewish rabbi. Jesus told him, "You must be born again." In Greek, the word *again* can mean either "from above" or "again." Possibly it means both in this passage. To discover how people are "born again," we turn to the wider context in John's Gospel. At John 1:12, the apostle John wrote, "But as many as received Him, to them He gave the right ["power," KJV] to become children of God, to those who believe in His name." Men have no power to grant this new birth. People are not born from the will of man, because we can produce only the first, or natural, birth. The new birth is due to the will of God (v. 13) and involves a person who receives the Messiah (v. 12). In John 3, Jesus emphasizes the Spirit, the agency of regeneration. During Jesus' conversation with Nicodemus, our Lord mentioned *born of the Spirit* two times. He said, "That which is born of the flesh is flesh, and that which is born of the Spirit is spirit." Again He said, "So is every one that is born of the Spirit." This refers to the invisible new nature begotten by God and to that person becoming a new creature or creation (2 Cor. 5:17). In his first letter, John wrote, "Whoever believes that Jesus is the Christ is born [Greek "has been born"] of God, and everyone who loves Him who begot also loves him who is begotten of Him" (1 John 5:1); this clearly shows that the work of the Spirit precedes faith.

Several other passages may help people avoid placing their entire confidence in religious rites. Basic Christian teaching, Scriptural teaching, tells us that "the blood of Jesus Christ His Son cleanses us from all sin" (1 John 1:7; Heb. 9:13, 14). Water is a natural sign of cleansing, but it is the blood shed on Calvary's cross that washes sin away. Furthermore, wind or spirit (*pneuma* carries both meanings) along with water are well-known allusions to the Old Testament teaching on the rebirth of God's people, which probably served as the background for Jesus' dialogue with Nicodemus. Consider Isaiah 44:3–5 and Ezekiel 37:9–14, for example. Was Jesus reminding Nicodemus of what was predicted in the Old Testament?

Isaiah 44:3—"I will pour water on him who is thirsty, and floods on the dry ground; I will pour My Spirit on your descendants, and My blessing on your offspring."

Ezekiel 37:9, 14—"Prophesy to the breath, prophesy, son of man, and say to the breath [wind] . . . 'Thus says the Lord GOD: "Come from the four winds, O breath, and breathe on these slain, that they may live." . . . I will put My Spirit in you, and you shall live, and I will place you in your own land. Then you shall know that I, the LORD, have spoken it and performed it,' says the LORD."

Nicodemus, being a teacher in Israel, would know these things. Would he recognize that the appointed time for the fulfillment of the Old Testament prophecies, types, and shadows had arrived? In His usual manner Jesus led Nicodemus to think about it. But would he *receive* it? The water and the Spirit surely refer to the same event,[1] the Messiah's advent. The Kingdom was at hand; Jesus, the Baptizer in the Holy Spirit, was present; people were being born from above! This was that which was spoken of by John the Baptist.

We have already seen gospel preaching taking place each time a New Testament person was convicted of sin and sought baptism. Through the Holy Spirit, God the Father brings a person to repentance and faith in Jesus Christ. This is how our Lord explains it: "No one can come to Me unless the Father who sent Me draws him; and I will raise him up at the last day" (John 6:44). A person cannot produce his own birth; this is self-evident. Isaiah 44:3 and Ezekiel 37:9, 14 speak of God's "heavenly work" as His sending us the wind and the rain, producing new beginnings, new life, new births—all allusions to and fitting symbols of the Holy Spirit at work. In John 3:3–8, Holy Scripture indicates this by uniting the water and the wind (spirit), a reference to the Holy Spirit's marvelous work upon us.

---

1. "Because a preposition tends to be repeated before each noun in a series of nouns joined by καί, sometimes the non-use of a second or third preposition in New Testament Greek may be significant, indicating that the writer regarded the terms in one list as belonging together in concept or reality. The phrase ἐξ ὕδατος καὶ πνεύματος in John 3:5 is a possible example: 'water and Spirit' together form a single means of regeneration." David Alan Black, *It's Still Greek to Me, An Easy-to-Understand Guide to Intermediate Greek* (Grand Rapids: Baker Books, 1998), 87.

As the rain brings new life in arid soil, the Holy Spirit is *poured out* (ἐκχέω) on mankind in the last days (cf. Acts 2:2, 16–18, 33). In John 4, Jesus speaks of the Holy Spirit as "living water" (v. 10) and as a "fountain of water" (v. 14). In John 7 Jesus proclaims that the Holy Spirit is like "rivers of living water" (v. 38): "On the last day, that great day of the feast, Jesus stood and cried out, saying, 'If anyone thirsts, let him come to Me and drink. He who believes in Me, as the Scripture has said, out of his heart will flow rivers of living water.' But this He spoke concerning the Spirit, whom those believing in Him would receive; for the Holy Spirit was not yet given, because Jesus was not yet glorified" (John 7:37–39).

If water baptism produced the new birth, then a man could be the cause of his own new birth, or he could beget others in the waters of baptism, as claimed in the *Apostolic Constitutions.*

Other interpreters teach that *water* in John 3 refers to the first, or natural, birth and *Spirit* refers to the second, or new, birth. Others would tell us that *water* refers to God's Word. Both of these ideas are rather gratuitous, being far removed from a contextual exegesis of John 3:3–7. It involves reading our own ideas into the passage, which is why I don't think these views are correct.

In an effort to remove any lingering doubts, I offer one more Scriptural testimony. The apostle Peter wrote, "Having been born again, not of corruptible seed but incorruptible, through the word of God which lives and abides forever" (1 Pet. 1:23). Here "through the word," *dia logou* in Greek, indicates the instrumentality of God's Word. God the Holy Spirit works through His Word to bring us under conviction of sin and knowledge of the Savior (John 17:3). Many Bible interpreters have quoted 1 Peter 1:23 to prove that the water refers to the Word of God. I reply as follows: The Holy Spirit is the *direct* agent God uses to bring us to the Savior, to regenerate us. The Bible, preaching and teaching, are the *intermediate* means God uses to stir our hearts. I am not asserting there is never any exception, because God does as He wishes. "The wind [Spirit or wind (same Greek word, *pneuma*)] blows where it wishes."

Wouldn't the simplest interpretation be to understand that the waters of baptism are the outward sign of the Spirit's invisible inner working of washing and cleansing us from sin? This harmonizes easily enough with Mark 16:16 if we bear in mind the entire teaching of the New Testament. Baptism is not an automatic mechanism that produces the new birth *in and of itself.* The waters of baptism are the sign of death, burial, resurrection, union with Christ, purification, and new birth. Salvation is always God's gift to believers (Rom. 6:23). According to Romans 1:16, the gospel "is the power of God to salvation for everyone who believes, for the Jew first and also for the Greek." If we keep this in mind, the difficult passages will not be difficult after all. Evangelicals should not be swayed by those who argue that the sacraments give life (*ex opere operato*).

Acts 22:16, *"Wash away your sins"*

"And now, why delay? Get up and be baptized, and wash away your sins by calling on His name" (HCSB).

No apologist for the liturgical churches would neglect to cite Acts 22:16 in support of baptismal regeneration. I did it. I remember going over this passage, struggling to understand it. It seemed so out of line with the gospel passages that describe conversions in the book of Acts. Before taking up this phrase, we must do two things: remember all that has been said and then seek the context. The context is found in the historical event related in Acts 9:

> But the Lord said to him, "Go, for he is a chosen vessel of Mine to bear My name before Gentiles, kings, and the children of Israel. For I will show him how many things he must suffer for My name's sake." And Ananias went his way and entered the house; and laying his hands on him he said, "Brother Saul, the Lord Jesus, who appeared to you on the road as you came, has sent me that you may receive your sight and be filled with the Holy Spirit." Immediately there fell from his eyes something like scales, and he received his sight at once; and he arose and was baptized. So when he had received food, he was strengthened.

> Then Saul spent some days with the disciples at Damascus.
> Immediately he preached the Christ in the synagogues, that He
> is the Son of God. (Acts 9:15–20)

Did Paul (Saul) ever preach salvation by means of baptism?
Consider. Saul met the Lord Jesus before he was baptized. Ananias
referred to Jesus, and he told Saul that he would "be filled with the
Holy Spirit." This was Paul's personal Pentecost. He had the same
experience that the other apostles had had. Having met the Lord of
Glory, having been blinded by the light, having heard from Christ
Himself, Saul obeyed by waiting for Ananias in Damascus (v. 6) to
follow through in baptism. Saul's baptism indicated his decision to
join the Christian believers he had been sent to persecute and put into
prison. Identifying himself with Christ and His people, Paul humbled
himself. He, the Pharisee (*Pharisee,* a word denoting one who is pure,
set apart), admitted his impurity and need of a Savior. He got up, got
baptized, and called upon the Lord Jesus to wash away his sins, as
all Christians have done: "To the church of God which is at Corinth,
to those who are sanctified in Christ Jesus, called to be saints, with
all who in every place call on the name of Jesus Christ our Lord, both
theirs and ours" (1 Cor. 1:2).

So what washed Saul's sins: the blood of Christ or the water baptism? The ancient churches reply "both," but evangelical Christians
believe that the ordinances, including baptism, are visible signs of
invisible spiritual realities. Ask yourself, Would Saul's sins have been
washed away if Saul had not called upon the name of the Lord? The
Scriptures give the answer, "Whoever calls on the name of the LORD
shall be saved" (Rom. 10:13). Did the scales fall from his eyes as a
result of getting baptized or before he was baptized? The scales being
removed from his eyes speaks clearly of his being able to see again, of
his being blessed, of his faith in our Lord, Whom he now saw with the
"eyes of his heart" (Eph. 1:18, HCSB; "understanding," KJV). Ananias
told Saul that he had been sent to him so "that you may receive your
sight and be filled with the Holy Spirit." Then Saul saw both physically and spiritually. Being illumined interiorly, he received the "bath

of illumination," as Justin Martyr called it: the bath that showed *outwardly* what had transpired *inwardly* in his soul. Saul did not refuse to formalize his new faith before witnesses; he knew he had to call on the name of Jesus to be saved. Thus Saul became Paul, the apostle to the Gentiles (Rom. 1:1).

Galatians 3:27, *"For as many of you as have been baptized into Christ have put on Christ"*

Considering the context with a look at the previous verse, we read, "You are all sons of God through faith in Christ Jesus." So which is it? The sacramentalists reply "both." Nevertheless, their answer makes baptism necessary for salvation, and this is the issue we are addressing. Our answer is faith, and faith alone. This answer is not meant to denigrate or belittle baptism in any way, but we are obliged to confess that baptism is not the gospel (1 Cor. 1:17). Salvation is God's gift and truly good news, because no works of any kind guarantee salvation. Instead, works emerge from salvation as a believer is motivated by God's Holy Spirit. A saved Christian is one who is "created in Christ Jesus for good works," says Paul (Eph. 2:10).

In 1 Corinthians 1, Paul addresses the many divisions in the Corinthian church. Things had come to the point where immature Christians were boasting about the person who had baptized them. Many of us can understand this, because we might desire to tell about having sat at the feet of a famous theologian. If we did, what we would mean is that we have been well taught. In any case, this example helps us to understand the Corinthians' actions. But the problem was that their bond of fellowship, enjoyed through the gospel, was being weakened by their partisanship. Had they not all accepted the same Christ and been baptized in the same Spirit? Had they not all experienced the same water baptism as a sign of this? This state of affairs in their church drove Paul to explain his mission more clearly to them; he was inspired to point them to what was most important:

> Now I say this, that each of you says, "I am of Paul," or "I am of Apollos," or "I am of Cephas," or "I am of Christ." Is Christ

divided? Was Paul crucified for you? Or were you baptized in the name of Paul?

I thank God that I baptized none of you except Crispus and Gaius, lest anyone should say that I had baptized in my own name. Yes, I also baptized the household of Stephanas. Besides, I do not know whether I baptized any other. For Christ did not send me to baptize, but to preach the gospel, not with wisdom of words, lest the cross of Christ should be made of no effect. (1 Cor. 1:12–17)

This paragraph puzzled me for some time: In light of the Great Commission, how could Paul say that he hadn't been sent to baptize? Perhaps Paul engaged in hyperbole to show the Corinthians their mistake. They were exaggerating in their boasts about who had baptized them, and Paul needed to stress the point that baptism is not the gospel. What is impossible through a ceremonial rite is possible through the preaching of the cross. The blood of Christ washes away sins, and the outward washing is a sign of the interior washing that took place when the Holy Spirit came to dwell in us. Baptism is the badge of the Christian.

Ronald Fung writes,

The baptism in view in Gal. 3:27 is almost certainly water baptism; this being the case, its juxtaposition with faith, especially the fact that union with Christ is ascribed both to faith (v. 26) and to baptism (v. 27), raises the question of the exact relationship between the two. An extreme, mechanistic view of baptism would have us believe that it was, "for Paul and his readers, universally and unquestionably accepted as a 'mystery' or sacrament which works ex opera operato," that the moment the believer receives baptism, union with Christ "takes place in him without any cooperation, or exercise of will or thought, on his part" [footnote 27, quoting Lake, etc.]. Such a view simply ignores the close connection between faith and baptism in the present instance; the fact that in this chapter faith is mentioned fifteen times and baptism only once would even by itself compel agreement with the dictum that Paul "by no means unconditionally attributes magic influence to baptism, as if receiving it guaranteed salvation" [footnote 28, quoting Bultmann, etc.].

. . . And the apparent equation of faith and baptism in vv. 26f. may be explained as a natural transference of terms whereby the symbol (baptism) is said to effect that which it symbolizes or as a form of metonymy whereby what is strictly true of faith is predicated of baptism.[2]

Dr. Fung's conclusions find strong support in what Paul wrote toward the end of his letter to the Corinthians. He told them that their reception of his message was salvation for them:

Moreover, brethren, I declare to you the gospel which I preached to you, which also you received and in which you stand, by which also you are saved, if you hold fast that word which I preached to you—unless you believed in vain. For I delivered to you first of all that which I also received: that Christ died for our sins according to the Scriptures, and that He was buried, and that He rose again the third day according to the Scriptures. (1 Cor. 15:1–4)

The point of these baptismal passages is this: The gospel saves the believer who has been baptized into the Body by (or better, *in*) the Holy Spirit, Whom Christ has poured out (1 Cor. 12:13; Acts 2). In 1 Corinthians 12, the apostle Paul writes, "For by one Spirit we were all baptized into one body—whether Jews or Greeks, whether slaves or free—and have all been made to drink into one Spirit" (v. 13).

The various Bible translations of 1 Corinthians 12:13 are divided into two groups regarding this little word *by*. Some translate the Greek preposition ἐν (*en*) *in*; and others, like the KJV, read *by*. It is difficult to tell whether the locative dative (location, sphere) or the instrumental dative is to be understood by the preposition ἐν (*en*) in this verse. My opinion is that the presence of the Greek preposition ἐν reinforces the idea that the simplest reading of the text indicates it is the dative of location or sphere that is meant here; instrumentality

---

2. Ronald Y. K. Fung, *The Epistle to the Galatians*, gen. ed., Gordon D. Fee, The International Commentary on the New Testament (Grand Rapids: Eerdmans, 1988), 173–74.

being secondary but admittedly possible.[3] Christ is the baptizer: He pours out the Holy Spirit; He baptizes people in the Holy Spirit, so the baptism takes place in the medium or sphere of the Holy Spirit, or *by means of* the Holy Spirit. The Holy Spirit *filling* the room with the apostles in it at Pentecost is an example. God places us into the one Body of Christ through the Holy Spirit. That probability is on our side is shown by a statistical table of usage in the New Testament. Usage charts[4] show that in the KJV (AV) the Greek preposition ἐν (*en*) is translated *in* 1,874 times, *by* 141 times, and *with* 134 times.

John baptized *in* (*en*) (or, *with*) water, and Christ baptizes *in* (*en*) (or, *with*) the Holy Spirit (Matt. 3:11; Mark 1:8; John 1:31); in Luke 3:16 the Greek preposition ἐν is absent. In these verses, most translations translate *en hudati* (*in water* or *with water*) as instrumental dative, indicating that John's baptism was performed *with* water. The Greek preposition *en* seems to me to reinforce the idea that John's baptism took place *in* water. Likewise, Christ our God baptizes *in* the Holy Spirit. All in all, it is clear that something happens to us; we *receive* a spiritual baptism whose origin is heavenly, not earthly. God becomes our Father through regeneration. This is demonstrated by the fact that grammatically *baptized* is passive in mood, meaning we receive the baptism (1 Cor. 12:13).

All Christians of Paul's time shared the same two experiences. Salvation and baptism were events that took place close together in time, but they were not the same experience; they were two experiences. One is salvation by "grace . . . through faith," which is a gift, the other

---

3. Although I have striven to avoid a certain level of technicality in this book, it is sometimes unavoidable, especially when considering various possibilities in the translation of certain passages of the Greek New Testament. Concerning 1 Corinthians 12:13 and the matter of the preposition ἐν (in, by, with, etc.), Daniel B. Wallace, writing about Mark 1:8 and referring to these choices, says, "In the five-case system, it is possible to see ὕδατι as both the means and the sphere in which John carried out his baptism. [Thus, his baptism would have been done both by means of water and in the sphere of water.] The same principle applies to Christ's baptism ἐν πνεύματι, which addresses some of the theological issues in 1 Cor. 12:13." Daniel B. Wallace, *Greek Grammar Beyond the Basics: An Exegetical Syntax Of The New Testament With Scripture, Subject, and Greek Word Indexes* (Grand Rapids: Zondervan, 1996), 32.

On page 374, he admits that sphere is possible, although he sees means in Mark 1:8. In my opinion, the Greek construction is similar to that in 1 Corinthians 12:13 and thus sphere is possible without eliminating means. I am pleased to note that in the HSCB, note f on Mark 1:8 reads, "Or in."

4. For example, *Strong's Concordance*, which is available in BibleWorks for Windows.

is baptism (dipping) *in* or *with* water, signifying outwardly the spiritual cleansing they had experienced. Baptism was the common experience of the Galatian Christians, whether rich or slave, male or female. They knew what it meant. Paul had to bring them back, however, to the basic truth they were ignoring. They were listening to deceivers who sought to take away their freedom by making circumcision a requirement. Paul reminded them that baptism was a pledge (*sacramentum* in Latin) because of their oral confession of faith given on the occasion of their baptism (Rom. 10:9, 10, 13); later, by association of ideas, baptism would come to be esteemed an *efficacious* sacrament.

Titus 3:5–7, *"He saved us, through the washing of regeneration and renewing of the Holy Spirit"*

Eastern Orthodox, Roman Catholics, and many others believe that Titus 3 has baptism in view. Commentators attest that the word *washing* (*loutron*) alludes to the "bath" of regeneration, that is, baptism. Although this may be true as an inference, baptism being the sign of salvation, we should not view the visible ordinance as the act that washes away sin. If we were to do so, we would be moving the fulcrum to a point where the tension or balance in the Scriptural teaching about salvation would be upset. An in-depth examination of Titus 3:5–7 already exists, and those interested in extensive discussion are invited to examine it. I refer to Dr. George W. Knight's study in *The New International Greek Testament Commentary.*[5]

In line with my goals, I want to emphasize a few ideas evident in Titus.

> Not by works of righteousness which we have done, but according to His mercy He saved us, through the washing of regeneration and renewing of the Holy Spirit, whom He poured out on us abundantly through Jesus Christ our Savior, that having been justified by His grace we should become heirs according to the hope of eternal life. (Titus 3:5–7)

---

5. George W. Knight III, *Commentary on Titus,* The New International Greek Testament Commentary: The Pastoral Epistles, ed. I. Howard Marshall and W. Ward Gasque (Grand Rapids: Eerdmans, 1992), 335–52.

The first point the apostle makes is *not by works of righteousness*. Paul placed these words at the head of his statement to emphasize a point: salvation is not of works. If baptism were a work that saved souls by a washing away of sins, would it not be a righteous work? Speaking infallibly, God tells us through His servant Paul that we are saved only through faith in Christ. The multitude asked Jesus how they could accomplish godly works, or righteous works. Jesus explained to them, "This is the work of God, *that you believe* in Him whom He sent" (John 6:28, 29; italics added). How do we become just people, righteous people? Paul's answer in Titus is that we are "justified by His grace." Who or what saves? The verse says *God* saves us. How does He accomplish this salvation? Paul says, "Through the washing of regeneration and renewing of the Holy Spirit." And what is the source or origin of regeneration (another word for *rebirth* or *born again*)? Again, Paul says, "Whom He [God the Father] poured out [ἐκχέω: to pour out, shed, spill] on us." Notice that the *pouring out* of the Holy Spirit is "through Jesus Christ our Savior." The Holy Spirit is again spoken of as being poured out like water (cf. Acts 2:33). This baptism in the Holy Spirit cleanses, washes, justifies, and saves (1 Cor. 12:13). All the Persons of the Trinity are involved in the work of salvation (1 Pet. 1:2). There is no new birth without Christ as the object of faith: "And I, if I am lifted up from the earth, will draw all peoples to Myself" (John 12:32). The passage in Titus 3:3–7 says no more than this. If it has anything to do with water baptism, it is because water baptism is the sign of what the Holy Spirit has done in us and for us.

What is impossible through a ceremonial rite is possible through the power of the preaching of the cross. I would ask those who believe that evangelical Christians are wrong, If baptism washes sins away, how could Paul have said, "For in Christ Jesus I have begotten you *through the gospel*" (1 Cor. 4:15; italics added)?

Next in line for our consideration is the only verse that actually says "baptism saves us."

1 Peter 3:21, *"Baptism doth also now save us" (KJV)*

Let us compare the King James Version with the Holman Christian Standard Bible.

"The like figure whereunto even baptism doth also now save us (not the putting away of the filth of the flesh, but the answer of a good conscience toward God,) by the resurrection of Jesus Christ" (KJV).

"Baptism, which corresponds to this, now saves you (not the removal of the filth of the flesh, but the pledge of a good conscience toward God) through the resurrection of Jesus Christ" (HCSB).

We come to what is one of the two strongest Scriptural statements that ancient churches will bring up (cf. Acts 22:16) to support the idea that baptism removes sin. It will necessitate a careful reading on our part. This verse actually helps us to understand how easily the transition came about. The cleansing *signified* by baptism would be thought of later as *produced* by baptism itself. We have seen elsewhere that the new birth is from above, from God, Who adopts us as His children. How could an informed evangelical conceive of a concept that contradicts the plain teaching of the New Testament?

As in Acts 22:16 (cf. Acts 21, the discussion of ritual purification), references to baptism are qualified by their immediate or more remote context. Our studies have shown us that there can be no salvation without faith, without a calling upon the Lord Jesus. According to Peter, baptism is also "a request" (KJV, NKJV, "the answer") or a "pledge of a good conscience" (HCSB). For the Greek word ἐπερώτημα, Arndt-Gingrich's *Greek-English Lexicon* and *Louw-Nida* suggest such definitions as "question," "request," "appeal," and "pledge" instead of "answer."[6]

---

6. Ἐπερώτημα in Walter Bauer, *A Greek-English Lexicon of the New Testament and Other Early Christian Literature,* trans. William F. Arndt and F. Wilbur Gingrich (Chicago: University of Chicago, 1957), 285. Also, *Louw-Nida Lexicon,* 33.162: "ἐπερώτημα, τος n: (derivative of ἐπερωτάω 'to ask for,' 33.161) that which is asked for - 'request, appeal.' βάπτισμα . . . ἀλλὰ συνειδήσεως ἀγαθῆς ἐπερώτημα εἰς θεόν 'but baptism . . . is a request to God for a good conscience' 1 Pe 3.21. It is also possible to interpret ἐπερώτημα in 1 Pe 3.21 as meaning 'pledge' or 'promise,' in which case it may be classified under 33.288 [the content of what is promised]. Accordingly, the phrase συνειδήσεως ἀγαθῆς ἐπερώτημα εἰς θεόν may be rendered as 'a promise made to God from a good conscience.'" J. P. Louw and Eugene Albert Nida, *Greek-English Lexicon of the New Testament: Based on Semantic Domains* (Swindon, Wiltshire: United Bible Societies, 1999). Accessed in BibleWorks for Windows, Version 7. (My brackets to provide the contents of 33.288.)

We need to widen the context in 1 Peter to avoid wrong interpretations that usually arise from a reading of only one or two verses. What is the apostle Peter talking about just before he gets to the section on baptism?

> But even if you should suffer for righteousness' sake, *you are* blessed. "And do not be afraid of their threats, nor be troubled." But sanctify the Lord God in your hearts, and always be ready to give a defense to everyone who asks you a reason for the hope that is in you, with meekness and fear; having a good conscience, that when they defame you as evildoers, those who revile your good conduct in Christ may be ashamed. For *it is* better, if it is the will of God, to suffer for doing good than for doing evil. For Christ also suffered once for sins, the just for the unjust, that He might bring us to God, being put to death in the flesh but made alive by the Spirit, by whom also He went and preached to the spirits in prison, who formerly were disobedient, when once the Divine longsuffering waited in the days of Noah, while the ark was being prepared, in which a few, that is, eight souls, were saved through water. There is also an antitype which now saves us—baptism (not the removal of the filth of the flesh, but the answer of a good conscience toward God), through the resurrection of Jesus Christ, who has gone into heaven and is at the right hand of God, angels and authorities and powers having been made subject to Him. (1 Pet. 3:14–22)

Peter's letter to Christians who were suffering some form of criticism or persecution by non-Christians was meant to encourage them to persevere. The world did not understand what had changed their relatives or former friends; so they, being puzzled, spoke evil of the Christians and belittled their new lifestyle. Peter holds up Christ as a model: He, the innocent One, suffered in their behalf. Noah and his family are named as examples of faithful people who persevered. "Noah walked with God," says Genesis 6:9. Such conduct is an example to Christians. Noah and his family's deliverance through the waters of the deluge becomes an example (figure) for all believers. The Greek is very clear: they were not saved by water except in the sense it buoyed or supported the ark while those outside perished in the water. The Greek says they were saved *through water*; compare all the modern translations. Noah and his family passed through the flood, the Israelites passed through the Red Sea, and Christians pass through the waters of baptism (the antitype) because Christ gave the example and the command. We are dealing with images, types, and figures here. Peter explains that baptism is not a putting away (ἀπόθεσις, "putting off") of the filth of the flesh, but is a request, a pledge, or appeal made to God for a good, clean conscience. We could say that baptism is the promise or pledge that we have received a good conscience because of our obedience to faith.

Peter explains that he was not referring to a cleansing (whether physical or spiritual) of the sinful nature. He corrects such false impressions by emphasizing that baptism is a pledge or a request made (or received) for a good conscience. This pledge is a public confession before a church or before a missionary sent by the church (Rom. 10:9–13).

Christ's victory over death and His resurrection to the right hand of God have made this possible. His resurrection guarantees our future, giving us reason for hope. Peter emphasized this by beginning his letter with a beautiful doxology in praise of the resurrection of our Lord: "Blessed be the God and Father of our Lord Jesus Christ, who according to His abundant mercy has begotten us again to a living hope through the resurrection of Jesus Christ from the dead" (1 Pet. 1:3).

The waters of the flood were a type (figure) of baptism, the antitype, a symbol of our salvation. Could it be that Peter remembered a reference from the Apocrypha? Although a Jewish Christian from Palestine, Peter would have been familiar with the apocryphal Book of Wisdom. The Apocrypha was part of the Septuagint Old Testament, a translation of the Hebrew Bible into Greek. The Septuagint was the common version used in the early church. The Apocrypha was even printed in the older editions of the King James Version, where we find this passage from Wisdom:

> Again, one preparing to sail and about to voyage over raging waves calls upon a piece of wood more fragile than the ship that carries him. For it was desire for gain that planned that vessel, and wisdom was the artisan who built it; but it is your providence, O Father, that steers its course, because you have given it a path in the sea, and a safe way through the waves, showing that you can save from every danger, so that even a person who lacks skill may put to sea. It is your will that works of your wisdom should not be without effect; therefore people trust their lives even to the smallest piece of wood, and passing through the billows on a raft they come safely to land. For even in the beginning, when arrogant giants were perishing, the hope of the world took refuge on a raft, and guided by your hand left to the world the seed of a new generation. For blessed is the wood by which righteousness comes (Wisdom 14:3–7, NRSV).

God gave instructions to Noah and his family on how to avoid destruction at the judgment of the wicked. By faith, Noah built an ark (Heb. 11:7). Each member of Noah's family had to listen to what he told them about God's plan to destroy the earth and the urgency of building an ark to survive. Putting their faith in God's warning in spite of the world's mockery, they obeyed God and began to build. The waters came and covered the earth. But Noah and his family rode it out, the waters carrying them to safety. Notice the emphasis upon the wood in the quotation above. To the first-century Christians familiar with the Apocryphal books, Peter's reference to the flood would not be surprising. I mention this only because the Septuagint was part of the culture of the early church. This passage in the Book of Wisdom is not referenced in the New Testament, but could have been in Peter's mind or memory. G. R. Beasley-Murray has referred to it, and he drew it to my attention.[7]

Are we saved by grace through faith? Is not salvation always because God gives us His grace instead of punishing us for our sins? We have been, we are, and we will always be saved through the death and resurrection of our Lord, Whose blood atoned for our sins: "And

---

7. G. R. Beasley-Murray, *Baptism in the New Testament* (Grand Rapids: Eerdmans, 1973), 259–60. Cf. J. Ramsey Michaels, *1 Peter,* Word Biblical Commentary (Waco, TX: Nelson Reference, 1988), 49:213.

from Jesus Christ, the faithful witness, the firstborn from the dead, and the ruler over the kings of the earth. To Him who loved us and washed us from our sins in His own blood" (Rev. 1:5).

Extremes in Sacramental Teaching

Before leaving this very moving topic, we should take note of the extremes to which some early Christians went in their sacramental teaching. In *The Shepherd of Hermas* (ca. AD 145), Hermas explains baptism: "For, he continued, before a man bears the name of the Son of God he is dead; but when he receives the seal he lays aside his deadness, and obtains life. The seal, then, is the water: they descend into the water dead, and they arise alive. And to them, accordingly, was this seal preached, and they made use of it that they might enter into the kingdom of God."[8]

In his series on early church writings titled *Patrology*, patristic scholar Johannes Quasten points out several problems with the *Shepherd of Hermas*; particularly, he mentions the writer's errors concerning Christology.[9] Later, Quasten points out Hermas's erroneous views on baptism: "Thus Hermas is so thoroughly convinced that baptism is absolutely necessary for salvation that he teaches that the Apostles and teachers descended into limbo after death (*descensus ad inferos*) to baptize the righteous departed of pre-Christian times."[10]

Many errors sprang up early in the church's history, just as Jesus had predicted in the parable of the wheat and the tares. That this could happen so early is startling, and to many it is incredible. For many years I ignored what I have written here. Finally, I had to face the facts: No matter how old or ancient an idea may be, it can be erroneous. But thanks be to God, we have been forewarned!

I hope that this study of baptism (chapters 4–6) has alerted the reader to the issues and to the Scriptures' clear teaching about the gospel and the place of baptism in a Christian's life. The evils of

8. Hermas, "The Shepherd of Hermas," *Fathers of the Second Century*, vol. 2 of Ante-Nicene Fathers, 49.

9. Johannes Quasten, *The Beginnings of Patristic Literature*, 4 vols. (Westminster, MD: Christian Classics, Inc., 1983), 1:99.

10. Ibid., 101.

wrong thinking eventually become evident in their fruits: baptism eventually came to be imposed by force. The absence of a true conversion was the result, and it meant that generally a deep love and commitment to Christ as Savior diminished in the church of Jesus Christ. Should we be surprised when we note the many evils that were practiced in His name? Did not our Lord ask, "I tell you that He will avenge them speedily. Nevertheless, when the Son of Man comes, will He really find faith on the earth?" (Luke 18:8). And did He not also say in Matthew, "The love of many will grow cold" (Matt. 24:12). History demonstrates that the sowing of false doctrines brought an abundant harvest of evil in the church and in the world. A mechanistic view of baptism led to two things: baptism where there is no faith and the belief that water baptism accomplishes the work that belongs only to the Holy Spirit.

In chapter 7 we will turn our attention to the second sacrament, the Lord's Supper, also called the Eucharist.

The Eucharist in the Early Church

The sanctuary is magnificent. Light streams through icons in stained-glass windows. The marble iconostasis (icon screen) separates the altar area from the sanctuary (the nave), where worshipers are gathered to celebrate the Divine Liturgy. The domed cupola overhead is crowned with an awesome mosaic icon of Christ Pantocrator, the "Almighty," seated in judgment.

The congregation stands as a priest, facing the altar, intones, "Blessed is the Kingdom of the Father, and of the Son, and of the Holy Spirit, now and ever, and unto the ages of ages." Crossing themselves and singing out "Amen," the worshipers bow and touch the floor with the fingers of their right hands. The service continues as the priest or a deacon chants the various petitions, and the readers (cantors) or choir responds with the continuous refrain, "Lord, have mercy." The glittering vestments, costly gold chalices, brass ornaments, lighted candles and oil lamps—all contribute to the beauty of the liturgy and draw the attention of the worshipers.

Contrasts

According to the ancient churches, during the worship service the bread and the wine will become the Holy Eucharist, that is, Communion in the body and blood of the Savior for the faithful who have prepared themselves by fasting and confessing their sins. The Holy Communion of bread and wine is received from a spoon dipped in the chalice and given in the mouth to each communicant. This is the high point of worship in the Catholic and Orthodox churches. Whether celebrated in Greek, Arabic, English, or in Slavonic, it is the same service, the Divine Liturgy of Saint John Chrysostom.

How different is this service—which emperors, kings, presidents, senators, and other dignitaries have attended for centuries—from the simple celebration of the Lord's Supper by a small, hated, and persecuted minority that oftentimes met in a home or on the outskirts of a town or village and in remote mountain valleys. The simple fraction, or breaking of bread, reminds Christians of the price paid for our redemption, Jesus Christ's body broken, His blood poured out, our sins atoned and forgiven (Heb. 9:22–26), a church built through the water and the blood that gushed from Emmanuel's pierced side. The Lord of Glory crucified between two felons; apostles and disciples in fear, scattered, apparently abandoned, left to wonder about their future.

What a contrast with the scene of Henry IV, the excommunicated and deposed emperor of the Holy Roman German Empire, kneeling in the snow for three days outside Pope Gregory VII's window during the winter of 1076–77, begging for forgiveness! What a contrast with a pope today being received and applauded at the United Nations in New York or leading an ecumenical meeting of the world's religions in Assisi or Jerusalem to pray for world peace!

Apostolic Fathers

You are invited to journey back in time as we peer into the obscure tunnel of church history. Our Lord told His disciples that the gates of Hell would not prevail against His church; consequently, it seems logical that the apostolic fathers would transmit only what they had learned from the apostles or their successors. The question is, Were they faithful witnesses to Christian truths? What these early records relate is important, yet several questions remain. One is, How do we account for the differences in thought between these writers and the New Testament Scriptures? These and other questions will now occupy us. What did early Christian writers at the beginning of the second century write about the Lord's Supper, also called the Eucharist?

Ignatius, Bishop of Antioch

Our first early "witness" is known as Saint Ignatius. Our examination of early Christian documents will hopefully shine some light on Christianity at the turn of the first century. Ignatius was the second bishop of Antioch. During his journey in chains to Rome, where he would die a martyr (ca. AD 107), Ignatius wrote letters of encouragement to seven churches. Did he promote any new ideas in his letters? The ancient churches say no, but evangelicals believe that he did introduce some novel opinions. What did Ignatius teach about the Lord's Supper? Several pertinent thoughts can be found in his letters to various churches: To Romans he wrote, "I have no delight in corruptible food, nor in the pleasures of this life. I desire the bread of God, the heavenly bread, the bread of life, which is the flesh of Jesus Christ, the Son of God, who became afterwards of the seed of David and Abraham; and I desire the drink of God, namely His blood, which is incorruptible love and eternal life."[1] To the people of Smyrna he wrote,

> But consider those who are of a different opinion with respect to the grace of Christ which has come unto us, how opposed they are to the will of God. . . . They abstain from the Eucharist and from prayer, because they confess not the Eucharist to be the flesh of our Saviour Jesus Christ, which suffered for our sins, and which the Father, of His goodness, raised up again. Those, therefore, who speak against this gift of God, incur death in the midst of their disputes.[2]

These passages surprised me when I first read them. I asked myself which faith they resembled more, the Catholic or my Baptist

---

1. Ignatius of Antioch, "The Epistle of Ignatius to the Romans," 7, in *The Apostolic Fathers with Justin Martyr and Irenaeus*, The Ante-Nicene Fathers, 1:77.

2 Ignatius of Antioch, "The Epistle of Ignatius to the Smyrnæans," 6–7, in *The Apostolic Fathers with Justin Martyr and Irenaeus*, The Ante-Nicene Fathers, 1:88–89.

faith. Grudgingly, I had to admit it all sounded very Roman Catholic. More mature reflection[3] leads me to make the following comments.

The first quotation from the "Letter to the Romans" is not really so far removed from what Christ taught in John 6 and during the Last Supper. Jesus' flesh is the bread of God, heavenly manna. Jesus Christ is God's provision for our salvation. His spilled blood is proof of God's love for us. He Himself said, "Greater love has no one than this, than to lay down one's life for his friends" (John 15:13). His flesh and blood are our food and drink, according to His own words.

The quotation from the "Letter to the Smyrnaeans" leads me to wonder if Ignatius might have been overemphasizing his point in an effort to combat the Gnostics, who did not celebrate the Lord's Supper because they denied the reality of Christ's passion on the cross. Did Ignatius really believe the bread and the wine were transformed to become the very flesh and blood of the Savior? Or was he saying that Christ was a real man with real flesh and blood, Who, as spiritual food and drink, is our nourishment for eternal life? The types and shadows found in the Old Testament (the Passover lamb, the manna, the water from the rock that Moses struck, etc.) all point to Christ. Being Jewish converts, the majority of the new believers were familiar with the Old Testament. As faithful Jews celebrated the Passover, which foreshadowed Christ's death on the cross, so faithful Christians celebrated the Lord's Supper to commemorate (Greek *anamnesis*,[4] "to bring to remembrance") their redemption by means of Messiah's blood. They would have been familiar with Paul's words to the Ephesians: "In Him we have redemption through His blood, the forgiveness of sins, according to the riches of His grace" (Eph. 1:7). Elsewhere, the apostle wrote, "In the same manner He also took the cup after supper, saying, 'This cup is the new covenant in My blood. This do, as often as you drink it, in remembrance of Me'" (1 Cor. 11:25).

Like the Jews of old, God calls us out of Egypt (this world, Rev. 11:8) and sets us free from bondage to the Devil. The bread and wine would

---

3. About twenty years later.

4. "Remembrance," *anamnesis* in Greek, means "a calling to mind."

have absolutely no meaning if Christ had not given His flesh for mankind and poured out His blood for the forgiveness of sins. This is the reality they were reliving[5] through their commemoration of His sacrificial death on the cross. This is clear enough from what the apostle Paul wrote to the Corinthians: "For as often as you eat this bread and drink this cup, you proclaim the Lord's death till He comes. Therefore whoever eats this bread or drinks this cup of the Lord in an unworthy manner will be guilty of the body and blood of the Lord. But let a man examine himself, and so let him eat of the bread and drink of the cup" (1 Cor. 11:26–28).

After the giving of thanks (Greek *eucharistia*), the apostle indicates that the elements are still bread and wine (referring to the contents of the cup). No transformation or "transubstantiation" into flesh and blood has taken place, yet they are fitting symbols of the Lamb of God offered for us (Eph. 5:2; Heb. 10:14). The elements in the Communion service are called the "body" (or "flesh") and "blood" of Christ because this is the reality to which they direct our thoughts (John 6:51, 55). Gazing on the emblems, we see the body and blood of our Lord given for us in atonement for our sins. It was easy for people of that time and culture to call the signs by the name of the object signified; for example, the "Rock was Christ" (1 Cor. 10:4).[6] Christ points out a spiritual reality by pointing to a physical object: "I am the true vine" (John 15:1). Again, "Likewise He also took the cup after supper, saying, 'This cup is the new covenant in My blood, which is shed for you'" (Luke 22:20). Is it too difficult to believe that the words "this cup is the new covenant" mean this cup *stands for* the New Covenant in His blood (1 Cor. 11:25)? First Corinthians 10:16 and 17 seem self-explanatory and may be help-

---

5. See the preceding note.

6. ἡ πέτρα δὲ ἦν ὁ Χριστός; literally, "The Rock was the Christ." In this case, the definite article preceding "Christ" indicates a particular person is intended. Centuries ago, John Calvin commented on this passage: "For, while the sacraments agree in many things, there is also, in this metonymy, a certain community in all respects between them. As, therefore, the apostle says that the rock from which spiritual water flowed forth to the Israelites was Christ (1 Cor. 10:4), and was thus a visible symbol under which, that spiritual drink was truly perceived, though not by the eye, so the body of Christ is now called bread, inasmuch as it is a symbol under which our Lord offers us the true eating of his body." John Calvin, *Institutes of the Christian Religion*, trans. H. Beveridge (Oak Harbor, WA: Logos Research Systems, Inc., 1997), 4:21.

ful here: "The cup of blessing which we bless, is it not the communion of the blood of Christ? The bread which we break, is it not the communion of the body of Christ? For we, though many, are one bread and one body; for we all partake of that one bread."

At this point, several questions may help evangelicals who are tempted by the ancient churches. Are we "bread"? What is the cup of blessing? What is the apostle teaching us? Is it not the unity and harmony of the Body of Christ because of the cross and our baptism? Is this not what we celebrate each time we take part (Greek *koinonia*) in the Lord's Supper?

To the Christians in Ephesus, Ignatius of Antioch wrote, "Take heed, then, often to come together to give thanks (*Eucharistia*) to God, and show forth His praise."[7] How important it is to remember each Lord's Day that Christ came and fulfilled the things prophesied concerning Him in the Old Testament; He died, was buried, and rose again, and now sits at the right hand of God the Father.[8] "For Christ is the end of the law for righteousness to everyone who believes" (Rom. 10:4). How blessed we are every time we remember our Lord's death for us in the celebration of the Lord's Supper!

Again, Ignatius referred Christians to this celebration when he admonished them to maintain the unity of the faith: "Take ye heed, then, to have but one Eucharist. For there is one flesh of our Lord Jesus Christ, and one cup to show forth the unity of His blood; one altar; as there is one bishop, along with the presbytery and deacons, my fellow-servants: that so, whatsoever ye do, ye may do it according to the will of God."[9]

Nothing in Ignatius's writings on the Eucharist goes against a Scriptural understanding of the Lord's Supper, as I have

---

7. Ignatius of Antioch, "The Epistle of Ignatius to the Ephesians," 13, in *The Apostolic Fathers with Justin Martyr and Irenaeus*, The Ante-Nicene Fathers, 1:55.

8. "Then He said to them, 'O foolish ones, and slow of heart to believe in all that the prophets have spoken! Ought not the Christ to have suffered these things and to enter into His glory?' And beginning at Moses and all the Prophets, He expounded to them in all the Scriptures the things concerning Himself" (Luke 24:25–27).

9. Ignatius of Antioch, "The Epistle of Ignatius to the Philadelphians," 4, in *The Apostolic Fathers with Justin Martyr and Irenaeus*, The Ante-Nicene Fathers, 1:81.

demonstrated. The reading and interpretation of these passages clearly depend upon one's presuppositions. His language is flowery, full of images, and truthfully, could be a step in the direction of sacramentalism. If he meant to be taken literally, he has taken a step in that direction and gone beyond apostolic teaching. It is his culture and context that will be determinative. For example, if by "altar" he is referring to Hebrews 13:10, "We have an altar from which those who serve the tabernacle have no right to eat," no issue is at stake. The writer of the "Letter to the Hebrews" indicates that the place of Christ's death (the altar) is the cross where He suffered outside Jerusalem's walls. "Therefore Jesus also, that He might sanctify the people with His own blood, suffered outside the gate. Therefore let us go forth to Him, outside the camp, bearing His reproach" (Heb. 13:12, 13).

According to the Old Testament types and shadows, Christ is not only our high priest, but He is also the victim, the Passover lamb offered once for all. That this is so is clear from 1 Corinthians 5:7, where Paul wrote, "Therefore purge out the old leaven, that you may be a new lump, since you truly are unleavened. For indeed Christ, our Passover, was sacrificed for us." He is the propitiation for sin (1 John 2:2; 4:10). In the New Testament period, Christians considered the Lord's Table to be a time for thanksgiving and offering up of spiritual praises to God because it was a meal that recalled His sacrifice on the cross. They were admonished in Hebrews 13:15, "Therefore by Him let us continually offer the sacrifice of praise to God, that is, the fruit of our lips, giving thanks to His name."

Justin the Philosopher

Justin Martyr was born in the city of Flavia Neapolis (formerly Sichem) in Palestine to Greek immigrant parents around AD 100–110 and was martyred around AD 165. He was called the "Philosopher" because of his studies, Platonism being his favorite philosophy. His goal was to teach Christianity, and his strategy was to set up a school in Rome to teach it as one would any philosophy. Justin is important because he provides us not only a description of baptism and the

Eucharist as practiced during his lifetime, but also an interpretation of these ordinances. He writes,

> And this food is called among us Εὐχαριστία [the Eucharist], of which no one is allowed to partake but the man who believes that the things which we teach are true, and who has been washed with the washing that is for the remission of sins, and unto regeneration [i.e., has received baptism], and who is so living as Christ has enjoined. For not as common bread and common drink do we receive these; but in like manner as Jesus Christ our Saviour, having been made flesh by the Word of God, had both flesh and blood for our salvation, so likewise have we been taught that the food which is blessed by the prayer of His word, and from which our blood and flesh by transmutation are nourished, is the flesh and blood of that Jesus who was made flesh.[10]

It is tempting to ask whether Justin reproduced what Christians held universally or whether he was innovating, introducing new ideas along mystical and philosophical lines.

Clearly Justin appears to have moved away from the simplicity of the Biblical doctrine. Was he calling the types by the names of what is typified? In other words, Christ's flesh and blood in Heaven are typified by the emblems of bread and wine on the table at the Lord's Supper. As a former Platonist, this would come naturally to Justin the Philosopher. J. N. D. Kelly, discussing the Latin Church writer Tertullian, explains, "According to ancient modes of thought a mysterious relationship existed between the thing symbolized and its symbol, figure or type; the symbol in some sense *was* the thing symbolized."[11]

In any case, Justin prepared the ground for what in time would become known as the Roman Catholic teaching of *transubstantiation*. In the West, a scholastic understanding of how the bread would seem to be bread in its appearance and taste—although it had been transformed (or trans-substance-tized; i.e., the substance had changed)

---

10. Justin Martyr, "The First Apology of Justin," 66, in *The Apostolic Fathers with Justin Martyr and Irenaeus*, The Ante-Nicene Fathers, 1:185.

11. Kelly, *Early Christian Doctrines*, 212.

into the body and blood of Christ at the consecration during the Mass—would be given later by Thomas Aquinas (1225–1274). Aquinas employed Aristotelian philosophy to help inquirers understand Christian doctrine.

Without going into great detail, it suffices to say that the Eastern Orthodox Church teaches essentially the same doctrine as the Roman Catholic Church, although Orthodox theologians generally maintain that their church does not wish to go into detail as to how the change takes place.[12] Concerning the Eucharist, Catholic scholar Johannes Quasten tells us that Cyril of Jerusalem (ca. 350) "makes a more definite advance on his predecessors. He expresses himself more clearly regarding the Real Presence than all the earlier writers."[13] Quasten cites Cyril, who in his catechism for baptismal candidates, explains what takes place during the Divine Liturgy (Mass): "That what seems bread is not bread, though bread by taste, but the Body of Christ; and that what seems wine is not wine, though the taste will have it so, but the Blood of Christ."[14] Quasten also informs us that "according to Cyril this Real Presence is brought about by a changing of the substances of the elements (μεταβάλλεσθαι) and thus he is the first theologian to interpret this transformation in the sense of a transubstantiation."[15] If Quasten's assessment of Cyril's "more definite advance" is worth anything, this would be evidence that there was doctrinal development throughout the early period of Christianity. Regarding my use of "development" here, I wish to mention one more observation about Justin Martyr's teaching on the Eucharist, as noted by Kelly. He says, "Altogether it would seem that, while his language is not fully explicit, Justin is feeling his way to the conception of the eucharist as

---

12. Michael Pomazansky, *Orthodox Dogmatic Theology,* trans. and ed. Hieromonk Seraphim Rose, 2nd ed. (Platina, CA: St. Herman of Alaska Brotherhood, 1997), 280n5.

13 Johannes Quasten, *Patrology,* 4 vols. (Allen, TX: Christian Classics, 1993), 3:375.

14. Cyril, "On the Mysteries," *Mystagogical Catecheses,* 22.4.9; cited in Quasten, *Patrology,* 3:375. I have read several Orthodox writers who speak of the "Mystical Supper." I have also questioned several Orthodox priests in different jurisdictions, and I received the same answer to the question whether the Orthodox church believes in transubstantiation. I sum it up this way: the bread and the wine remain bread and wine, but when an Orthodox believer takes Communion, he receives the body and the blood of Christ.

15. Ibid., 3:375.

the offering of the Saviour's passion."[16] From that time onward, the Lord's Supper would come to be regarded as a sacrifice the community offers to the Lord.

Augustine of North Africa, an Important Early Latin Father

Augustine of North Africa was an important early Latin church father. He is highly esteemed by the Roman Catholic Church and many Reformed Protestants. What were his views on the Eucharist? In his lectures on John 6, Augustine comments on Jesus' words, "the work of God." Augustine explains that true drinking and eating are matters of the heart, meaning, faith in him who is the heavenly Manna, the Bread of Life.[17]

> 12. "Jesus answered and said unto them, This is the work of God, that ye believe on Him whom He has sent." This is then to eat the meat, not that which perisheth, but that which endureth unto eternal life. . . . And because He invited them to faith, they, on the other hand, were still asking for signs by which they might believe.

> 14. "And Jesus said unto them, I am the Bread of Life: he that cometh to me shall never hunger; and he that believeth on me shall never thirst." "He that cometh to me;" this is the same thing as "He that believeth on me;" and "shall never hunger" is to be understood to mean the same thing as "shall never thirst." For by both is signified that eternal sufficiency in which there is no want. You desire bread from heaven; you have it before you, and yet you do not eat. "But I said unto you, that ye also have seen me, and ye believed not."

> 17. Let us drink within, let us see within.

In Tractate XXVI on John 6:41–59, Augustine expands on his exposition of the Bread of Life. In reference to the heavenly manna, he

---

16. Kelly, *Early Christian Doctrines*, 197.

17. Augustine of Hippo, "Lectures or Tractates on the Gospel According to St. John," 12, 14, 17, in *St. Augustin: Homilies on the Gospel of John, Homilies on the First Epistle of John, Soliloquies*, ed. Philip Schaff, trans. John Gibb and James Innes, vol. 7, A Select Library of the Nicene and Post-Nicene Fathers of the Christian Church, First Series (New York: Christian Literature Company, 1888), 164–65, 167.

gives a spiritual interpretation to eating and drinking.

> 1. . . . Wherefore, the Lord, about to give the Holy Spirit, said that Himself was the bread that came down from heaven, exhorting us to believe on Him. For to believe on Him is to eat the living bread. He that believes eats; he is sated invisibly, because invisibly is he born again. A babe within, a new man within. Where he is made new, there he is satisfied with food.

> 3. If he is drawn, saith some one, he comes unwillingly. If he comes unwillingly, then he believes not; but if he believes not, neither does he come. For we do not run to Christ on foot, but by believing; . . .

> 18. In a word, He now explains how that which He speaks of comes to pass, and what it is to eat His body and to drink His blood. "He that eateth my flesh, and drinketh my blood, dwelleth in me, and I in him." This it is, therefore, for a man to eat that meat and to drink that drink, to dwell in Christ, and to have Christ dwelling in him. Consequently, he that dwelleth not in Christ, and in whom Christ dwelleth not, doubtless neither eateth His flesh [spiritually] nor drinketh His blood [although he may press the sacrament of the body and blood of Christ carnally and visibly with his teeth], but rather doth he eat and drink the sacrament of so great a thing to his own judgment, because he, being unclean, has presumed to come to the sacraments of Christ, which no man taketh worthily except he that is pure: of such it is said, "Blessed are the pure in heart, for they shall see God."[18]

Other statements of Augustine indicate that he may have held to a sacramental and literal interpretation of Christ's words. Yet he was in fact saying no more than Christ Himself said at the Lord's Supper. So I would ask, is the sign indicative of the reality? Does Augustine call the sign by the name of what is signified? Notice that he still called it bread and wine, as did the apostle Paul (1 Cor. 11:26–28). Here are selections from other of Augustine's writings.

---

18. Augustine of Hippo, "Lectures or Tractates on the Gospel According to St. John," 1, 3, 18, in *St. Augustin: Homilies on the Gospel of John, Homilies on the First Epistle of John, Soliloquies,* A Select Library of the Nicene and Post-Nicene Fathers of the Christian Church, First Series, 7:168–69, 173.

. . . That Bread which you see on the altar, having been sanctified by the word of God is the Body of Christ. That chalice, or rather, what is in that chalice, having been sanctified by the word of God, is the Blood of Christ. Through that bread and wine the Lord Christ willed to commend His Body and Blood, which He poured out for us unto the forgiveness of sins.[19]

The Lord Jesus wanted those whose eyes were held lest they should recognize Him, to recognize Him in the breaking of the bread [Luke 24:16, 30–35]. The faithful know what I am saying. They know Christ in the breaking of the bread. For not all bread, but only that which receives the blessing of Christ, becomes Christ's body.[20]

Patristic scholar J. N. D. Kelly opines that "one could multiply texts like these which show Augustine taking for granted the traditional identification of the elements with the sacred body and blood. There can be no doubt that he shared the realism held by almost all his contemporaries and predecessors."[21]

Figuratively or Literally

Many Bible readers interpret John 6 as evidence that the literal flesh of Christ is eaten in the Eucharist. It is tempting to think that it is too difficult to determine just what early writers really taught. For instance, in *Against Heresies* Irenaeus speaks of the body and the blood of Christ in the Eucharist, but he also speaks of these celebrations as figures of the true things which are in Heaven.[22] Several early writers such as Tertullian and Hippolytus called the emblems antitypes or figures.[23] Four hundred years later, John Damascene (ca. 650), a great Eastern church father and authority, drew up a confession of faith in which he stated without any ambiguity:

19. William A. Jurgens, trans., "Sermon 227," *The Faith of the Early Fathers* (Collegeville, MN: The Liturgical Press, 1979), 3:30.

20. Ibid., "Sermon, 234.2," 3:30–31.

21. Kelly, *Early Christian Doctrines*, 446–47.

22. Irenaeus of Lyons, "Irenæus Against Heresies," 4.18.6–19.1, in *The Apostolic Fathers with Justin Martyr and Irenaeus*, The Ante-Nicene Fathers, 1:486–487.

23. Henry Chadwick, *The Early Church*, The Penguin History of the Church, rev. ed. (New York: Penguin Books, 1993), 1:266.

Further, bread and wine are employed: for God knoweth man's infirmity: for in general man turns away discontentedly from what is not well-worn by custom: and so with His usual indulgence He performs His supernatural works through familiar objects: and just as, in the case of baptism, since it is man's custom to wash himself with water and anoint himself with oil, He connected the grace of the Spirit with the oil and the water and made it the water of regeneration, in like manner since it is man's custom to eat and to drink water and wine, He connected His divinity with these and made them His body and blood in order that we may rise to what is supernatural through what is familiar and natural. . . .

The bread and the wine are not merely figures of the body and blood of Christ (God forbid!) but the deified body of the Lord itself: for the Lord has said, "This is My body," not, this is a figure of My body: and "My blood," not, a figure of My blood. And on a previous occasion He had said to the Jews, Except ye eat the flesh of the Son of Man and drink His blood, ye have no life in you. For My flesh is meat indeed and My blood is drink indeed. And again, He that eateth Me, shall live.[24]

Now, having examined the teaching of several early church fathers, we must squarely face the issues. If the second or third generation of Christians did believe that during the Lord's Supper the emblems of bread and wine become the actual body and blood of Christ, it would be another example of the apostles' timely warnings about antichrists and an apostasy already at work in the first century (2 Pet. 2:1, 2 "false teachers"; 1 John 2:18). In situations like this, what should the evangelical Christian think while reading early church history along with the church fathers? The answer is in fact rather simple: a Christian must always remain faithful to the Word of God. If one lets go of God's Word, he becomes dependent upon man's word.

---

24. John Damascene, "An Exact Exposition of the Orthodox Faith," 4.13, in *St. Hilary of Poitiers, John of Damascus*, ed. Philip Schaff and Henry Wace, trans. S. D. F. Salmond, vol. 9b, A Select Library of the Nicene and Post-Nicene Fathers of the Christian Church, Second Series (New York: Christian Literature Company, 1899), 83.

He no longer follows the Way, the Truth, and the Life, because he is relying on the uninspired opinions of men. A glance at science and health books over a period of fifty years demonstrates how opinions change from one generation to the next. Just as people grow old and die and are replaced by their progeny, so various scientific opinions come and go like fads. In contrast, the apostle Peter says the Word of God endures forever, and he quotes Scripture to substantiate it: "Having been born again, not of corruptible seed but incorruptible, through the word of God which lives and abides forever, because 'All flesh is as grass, and all the glory of man as the flower of the grass. The grass withers, and its flower falls away, but the word of the LORD endures forever'" (1 Pet. 1:23–25).

Our body's senses are God-given gifts that equip us to live in a physical world. Of course, anyone can be deceived by his senses, but that is not the point here. If an institution asks its members to believe something that goes against their experience of sight, touch, smell, taste, and hearing, there is probably good reason to doubt. Although the Eastern Orthodox Church does not formally teach transubstantiation, members are bound to accept whatever their church teaches on the Eucharist. In the case of transubstantiation, Roman Catholics are required to take their church's word for something that goes against normal life experience. After the priest says a few words over the bread and the wine, the church tells them the bread is no longer bread and the wine is no longer wine, but has become the body and the blood of Jesus Christ. Transubstantiation (i.e., eating flesh and blood) shocks many people because it sounds disgusting, akin to cannibalism. But a person could believe what contradicts the physical senses if his faith were based only upon an a priori: taking the church's word for what is simply a nonsensical doctrine. If one showed a picture of a loved one to a neighbor and said, "This is my daughter," would the neighbor understand the picture to be anything more than a picture of the daughter?

Imagine you needed to withdraw money from your bank account, and the teller took out a ten dollar bill, said a few words over it, then lifted it over his head, gazed at it reverently, dropped his arms, and then put the ten dollar bill into your hands, telling you that it is now a one hundred dollar bill. It looks the same as before, but would you meekly accept something that goes against your better judgment because of a famous bank's name? Are not these ancient churches doing the same thing when they ask people to accept the doctrine of transubstantiation?

So far our studies of baptism and the Eucharist have not exhausted all there is to say; clearly, the subject of sacramentalism will require more analysis. Recognizing that this is a vast field for investigation and scholarly debate, and acknowledging the limitations of this book, the next chapter will give a brief account of the world to which Jesus Christ was sent by His Father. History records Christendom's bloody expansion, followed by a bloody resistance to change during the sixteenth and seventeenth centuries. Do not forget the many clerical abuses throughout those centuries and, sadly, more recently. Such a study will help the reader understand better the foundations for the Catholic and the Orthodox churches' practices that they believe to be apostolic.

PART 2

CHAPTER 8

Liturgical Developments and the Sacralization of the Clergy

What is the church, and how is it different from God's covenant people of the Old Testament? A summary of the Old and the New Testament systems will help us better see God's plan and purpose for His church. Such a sketch reveals that God formed a nation from twelve tribes descended from Abraham, Isaac, and Jacob.

Israel, God's Old Covenant People

Worship in Israel was originally organized around a portable tabernacle and a hieratic leadership led by two strong personalities, the prophet and mediator Moses and his brother Aaron, the first high priest. A covenant (agreement, treaty, promise) existed between God and His Chosen People. The work of the priesthood involved receiving offerings and sacrificing animals the people brought daily, first to the tabernacle in the wilderness and later to King Solomon's magnificent temple. The priests also taught the people the nation's religious laws contained in the book of the Law. These laws governed their worship and moral conduct; the civil laws detailed their duties toward one another and to the strangers dwelling in their midst (see Exodus 19:5–8). Bible students acknowledge that the nation was well organized and sufficiently structured. Still, one question may yet linger: Why did God desire a nation based on race and heredity? Wasn't this rather narrow, ignoring the rest of mankind?

An examination of the messianic promises found in Genesis will help us better understand God's purpose. In Genesis 3 we find that God made a gracious promise to Adam and Eve; this promise is also called the Proto-Gospel. God promised He wouldn't permit Satan to be victorious over His creation because He would send a Savior Who would redeem His people from sin and death. In God's plan, this Savior would bring about a restoration of all of creation so that every created thing would bring glory to God as He originally purposed (Gen. 3:15; see Matt. 19:28, 29; Acts 3:19–26; Rom. 8:18–25; Eph. 1:3–14; Rev. 21:5). In the Proto-Gospel God promised that the Seed (posterity) of the woman would crush the serpent's head. This promise demonstrates that God did not abandon His creation but that He would be actively involved in the lives of those He has created in His image. Sometime later, Abram, one of Noah's descendants, received a promise. The line of blessing was to pass through Noah and his son Shem to Abram (Abraham). The account is given in Genesis 12:2 and 3; the Lord spoke to Abram, saying, "I will make you a great nation; I will bless you and make your name great; and you shall be a blessing. I will bless those who bless you, and I will curse him who curses you; and in you all the families of the earth shall be blessed."

The Abrahamic Covenant takes its name from *Abraham,* which means "father of a multitude." The whole world—that is, all nations, tribes, and tongues, without exception—would be blessed through Abraham's seed (cf. Gen. 18:18; 22:18). This should give pause to all who are anti-Semitic. We learn that God's plan was not restricted to only one nation. He desires to bless all peoples, races, and tribes. Abraham's line would eventually bring forth the Promised Seed of the woman, Who would bruise the serpent's head. In a word, this is God's eternal plan to remedy Adam and Eve's transgression. Their fall from innocence brought them and their children into bondage to Satan, which ends in spiritual and physical death (Gen. 2:17). Sin, which is disobedience, separated them from God, the all-holy One. Their children inherited their parents' fallen, corrupt, and dying nature. What else could they transmit but what they were themselves? In spite of the apparent hopelessness of it all, light would break forth in the midst of darkness according to the Creator's eternal purpose. A Savior would be sent to liberate them, "for God so loved the world that He gave His only begotten Son, that whoever believes in him should not perish but have everlasting life." This is the gospel, or good news about Jesus Christ, the Liberator, the power of God unto salvation to all who believe (Rom. 1:16; cf. John 8:34–36).

After God freed Abraham's descendants from slavery in Egypt, He confirmed His covenant with them at Mount Sinai. He made a contract or covenant with them and ratified it by the sprinkling of animal blood on the altar and then on the people who agreed to keep the covenant (Exod. 24:3–8). By this covenant, the Israelites were set apart (sanctified) to be God's special possession out of all the nations of the earth. God told them through Moses, "Now therefore, if you will indeed obey My voice and keep My covenant, then you shall be a special treasure to Me above all people; for all the earth is Mine. And you shall be to Me a kingdom of priests and a holy nation.' These are the words which you shall speak to the children of Israel" (Exod. 19:5, 6).

Around fifteen hundred years later, the apostle Paul reminded believers in Christ of the gracious covenant made with Abraham when he wrote, "And the Scripture, foreseeing that God would justify the Gentiles by faith, preached the gospel to Abraham beforehand, saying, 'In you all the nations shall be blessed'" (Gal. 3:8). Acts 15 relates how the Jewish council of apostles and elders met in Jerusalem to discuss a situation that had arisen. Gentiles were converting to the Christian faith! What was the church to do with them? Should they be obliged to accept circumcision? Must they keep the law? How could they mix with Jewish believers who in the past had no personal relationships with Gentiles? These questions needed answers. Standing, James took the floor and related that the Old Testament prophets had foretold that God would take people from among the nations (Gentiles) to constitute "a people for His name" (Acts 15:13–18). The Seed of Abraham had come. He was a descendant of the royal line of David, but He was more than that. He was also the Son of God (Luke 1:27–35).

God preserved one nation to bring forth the Messiah. He gave them a law, priests, and prophets, a king, and a land. In the course of time God sent His own Son, born of a woman under the law, and those who received Him by faith received the promised blessing (Gal. 4:4, 5). In Galatians 3:14, Paul wrote, "That the blessing of Abraham might come upon the Gentiles in Christ Jesus, that we might receive the promise of the Spirit through faith." The blessing would no longer be linked to a particular blood line, the Jewish people; the blessing would go out to all peoples, to every nation and tribe.

To summarize: God chose and preserved the Jewish people to bring forth the Messiah. All the Old Testament prophecies served to pinpoint His identity at His appearance. Israel had a God-given covenant, circumcision as the sign of that covenant, a law, a priesthood, a king, armies, cities, national boundaries, and a language. All of these marked Israel as God's special possession. What about God's chosen people from the New Testament period until now? What distinguishes Christians from their neighbors? Are there notable differences or similarities between us and Israel? It is time to look at the New Testament church and God's plan to bless believers in Christ.

The New Testament Church

Introduction

How do you see the church? More importantly, how does God see the church? Perhaps a reminder would be appropriate: God's ways are not our ways, and His thoughts are not our thoughts (Isa. 55:8, 9). We should never ignore the fact that culture, history, politics, and influential people had a lot to do with the church's move into basilicas and the development of lengthy liturgies. Some Christians believe they should meet only in a living room, while others think that a large and beautiful Gothic cathedral is more worthy as a sanctuary for

God. They want to house God; they tell us He is present in the bread (hosts) in their tabernacles. Other successful churches consider those who attend. Striving to satisfy perceived needs, they have ministries for those with handicaps, singles, couples, and the elderly. These churches build gymnasiums, dining halls, and classrooms. They set aside space in their auditoriums for an orchestra or a beautiful organ, all to God's glory of course. I am sure everyone will agree that these are the externals and that a group of Christians does not have to have all of these things even though much of this may be justifiable. Perhaps you have noticed how noisy some churches are; everyone is joyfully greeting friends, talking with them or with their families. Yet other church sanctuaries are quiet, reserved, dimly lit by light streaming in from beautiful stained-glass windows; there is a hush, a respectful silence. A person can take a seat, pray quietly, and prepare his heart for the service. Some churches will not display even a cross on their building, whereas others use incense, bells, icons, or statues. In some churches the priest or minister is robed in beautiful vestments, but a number of others consider such things nonsense and entirely out of line with God's will for ministers. Be that as it may, it actually has nothing to do with the New Testament's description of the church.

Since we are considering the ancient churches, specifically, the Roman Catholic and the Eastern Orthodox Churches, we need to focus on certain questions such as, What happened to the simplicity of the early Christians? What led Christians to worship in a style that is more reminiscent of Israel with its temple, priesthood, sacrifices, and ranks of priests serving altars? How did the simplicity of the gospel become a powerful ecclesiastical system? Why have liturgical services been celebrated in a dead language for centuries? (This is certainly not a dead issue in either the Orthodox or the Catholic church today.) And how did a persecuted church become a persecuting church?

People generally consider the gradual evolution of the church in history to be a normal and legitimate development. This is especially true since John Henry Newman wrote his book *An Essay on the Development of Christian Doctrine* before he entered the Roman Catholic

Church. He argued that growth and development include necessary changes but that the church remains the same. Christ's church developed just as an oak tree from the acorn or a baby from an embryo, yet there is no change in nature. Natural growth is simply normal for any living organism. For our part, proceeding century by century, it is easy to note the various changes introduced into the church, but if we focus on details during a particular period, we often lose sight of the overall view. Roman Catholic and Orthodox believers reproach Protestants for ignoring much of church history because of their desire to restore the New Testament church model. They accuse Protestants of being "fundamentalists" and "sectarian," people lacking confidence in Christ's promise to preserve His church. These ancient churches also charge them with not taking seriously the church fathers and their teachings.

After reading Newman's book and being convinced by his arguments, I made the same charge against Protestants. I no longer stand by that conviction. I suggest it would be helpful to take a step back and look at how the church existed in the first century, and then look at the church as it developed across the centuries. While doing so, we need to keep in mind what the New Testament teaches about the gospel, grace, and salvation, comparing that teaching with what the ancient-liturgical churches teach. It is a simple matter of comparing *A* with *Z* in the alphabet. There are many steps (letters) to get to the end of the alphabet. When a word is spelled, *Z* is definitely not *A*, even though they are both letters of the alphabet. *A* is a vowel, while *Z* is a consonant, and one does not replace the other. We know they are different. This method of looking at things has helped me to come back to personal freedom in the gospel. My in-depth and personal study of Paul's letter to the Galatians and my reading the entire New Testament again and again brought God's clear teachings to mind. I noted the passages opposed to Orthodox and Roman Catholic teachings. The remainder of this book deals with these.

Changes in Church Government

Church government is one clear example of change due to

development. How should a person view changes in church government, or other changes people call natural development, an unfolding of what existed in germ. Our Lord Jesus has given us an important principle to help us identify deviations from His teaching. In Matthew's Gospel Christ said,

> Beware of false prophets, who come to you in sheep's clothing, but inwardly they are ravenous wolves. You will know them by their fruits. Do men gather grapes from thornbushes or figs from thistles? Even so, every good tree bears good fruit, but a bad tree bears bad fruit. A good tree cannot bear bad fruit, nor can a bad tree bear good fruit. Every tree that does not bear good fruit is cut down and thrown into the fire. Therefore by their fruits you will know them. (Matt. 7:15–20)

In a nutshell, the principle He gave us involves what the fruits are and the consequences of adopting certain changes. Our Lord's teachings are the absolute truth, the standard, because their source is the omniscient Deity. His apostles, indwelled and filled with the Holy Spirit, set up churches and established overseers (elders) over them. Our Lord gave the churches deacons to minister to their material needs. This pattern for church government is found in the New Testament. Why would anyone think he needs to improve on it? Why did the ancient churches abandon the apostolic model? When the tabernacle was to be constructed in the wilderness, God told Moses, "Be careful to make everything *according to the model* of them you have been shown on the mountain" (Exod. 25:40, HCSB, italics added). Can we say God's pattern has been respected? What do historians tell us about the changes that took place in church government?

Early in the twentieth century Philip Schaff wrote a history of the church that is still in print. Concerning church government during the first and second centuries, Schaff quoted Dean Stanley,

> It is certain that they [church offices] arose gradually out of the preexisting institutions either of the Jewish synagogue, or of the Roman empire, or of the Greek municipalities, or under

the pressure of local emergencies. It is certain that throughout the first century, and for the first years of the second, that is, through the later chapters of the Acts, the Apostolic Epistles, and the writings of Clement and Hermas, Bishop and Presbyter were convertible terms, and that the body of men so-called were the rulers—so far as any permanent rulers existed—of the early church. It is certain that, as the necessities of the time demanded, first at Jerusalem, then in Asia Minor, the elevation of one Presbyter above the rest by the almost universal law, which even in republics engenders a monarchial element, the word 'Bishop' gradually changed its meaning, and by the middle of the second century became restricted to the chief Presbyter of the locality. It is certain that in no instance were the apostles called 'Bishops' in any other sense than they were equally called 'Presbyters' and 'Deacons.' It is certain that in no instance before the beginning of the third century the title or function of the Pagan or Jewish priesthood is applied to the Christian pastors.[1]

The Roman Catholic priest Thomas Bokenkotter explains, "These elders or bishops governed the churches collectively at first. But gradually one man took over the power and concentrated the various ministries in his hands. He was now called 'bishop' to distinguish him from the presbyters, who were his subordinates." By 150 or 160 this system of authority was established practically everywhere.[2] Bokenkotter's statement is a little fuller than what is quoted here, but the quotation here is the essential part.

Another important source is J. B. Lightfoot's study from the 1800s. He wrote,

> With the opening of a second century a new phraseology begins. In the epistles of Ignatius the terms [bishops and presbyters] are used in their more modern sense. . . . The bishop is always singled out by this writer, as the chief officer of the Church.

---

1. Dean Stanley, *Christian Institutions: Essays on Ecclesiastical Subjects* (London: John Murray, 1881), 187, 188, quoted in Philip Schaff, *History of the Christian Church* (New York, 1910; Grand Rapids: Eerdmans, 1975), 1:487–88. See note 2 in chapter 10.

2. Thomas Bokenkotter, *A Concise History of the Catholic Church*, rev. ed. (New York: Doubleday, 2004), 33.

> But in the fourth century, when the fathers of the Church began
> to examine the apostolic records, with a more critical eye, they at
> once detected the fact. No one states it more clearly than Jerome.
> "Among the ancients," he says, "bishops and presbyters are the
> same, for the one is a term of dignity, the other of age."[3]

Lightfoot's excellent study explains how and why the apostles adopted a simple, practical system of government, one with which they were familiar: "Over every Jewish synagogue, whether at home or abroad, a council of 'elders' presided. It was not unnatural therefore that, when the Christian synagogue took its place by the side of the Jewish, a similar organization should be adopted with such modifications as circumstances required; and thus the name [presbyter] familiar under the old dispensation was retained under the new."[4]

Bishop Lightfoot buttresses his study by noting the New Testament passages that demonstrate that the Christian assemblies had only two offices: elders and deacons. In support of this he listed Acts 20:17, 28; 1 Peter 5:1, 2; 1 Timothy 3:1–7, 8–13; and Titus 1:5–7. Lightfoot also showed that this simple church structure was still in existence at the end of the first century. He also provided several references from Clement of Rome as evidence.[5]

We need only compare his first quotation, Acts 20:17, "From Miletus he sent to Ephesus, and called for the elders of the church," with Acts 20:28, "Therefore take heed to yourselves and to all the flock, among which the Holy Spirit has made you overseers." Clearly the elders were the overseers in the church. It is time to examine how developments in the early church transformed the ecclesia from a body of priestly saints with appointed officers into a body divided: rulers and the ruled, that is, clergy and laity.

William McNeill describes the immense changes that took place when the church became an established religion: "During and after

---

3. J. B. Lightfoot, *St. Paul's Epistle to the Philippians* (New York, 1903; Lynn, MA: Hendrickson, 1981), 98.
4. Ibid., 96.
5. Ibid. See pages 97–98, quoting First Clement 42 and 44. Compare page 230 for comments on the substantial identity of the two terms "bishop" and "presbyter" still being recognized in the fourth and fifth centuries.

the time of Constantine the Christian Church underwent rapid change. First of all, worldly advantages were heaped upon the clergy. Constantine assigned state funds for the erection of church buildings, exempted the clergy from ordinary taxes, and allowed them free use of the imperial post service when traveling on ecclesiastical business."[6]

Sacerdotalism and the Sacralization of the Clergy

The pattern set forth for the church in the New Testament is deducted from the following passages:

"But you are a chosen race, a royal priesthood, a holy nation, a people for His possession, so that you may proclaim the praises of the One who called you out of darkness into His marvelous light" (1 Pet. 2:9, HCSB).

"And do not be drunk with wine, in which is dissipation; but be filled with the Spirit, speaking to one another in psalms and hymns and spiritual songs, singing and making melody in your heart to the Lord, giving thanks always for all things to God the Father in the name of our Lord Jesus Christ" (Eph. 5:18–20).

"And let us consider one another in order to stir up love and good works, not forsaking the assembling of ourselves together, as is the manner of some, but exhorting one another, and so much the more as you see the Day approaching" (Heb. 10:24, 25).

"Therefore by Him let us continually offer the sacrifice of praise to God, that is, the fruit of our lips, giving thanks to His name" (Heb. 13:15).

The entire congregation is called to participate in the worship of God in spirit and in truth. Members are to exhort one another and to sing praises to God because the "fruit of [their] lips" is the sacrifice that pleases the Lord. Of course, the elders take the lead, rule, preach, and exhort the brethren as their shepherds and servants, and the deacons carry out their assigned duties to care for the physical needs of the people and the church edifice. But what ever happened to this simplicity? A single paragraph can summarize what took place over several centuries.

---

6. McNeill, *History of Western Civilization*, 191–92.

As time went on (and it did not require the passage of many decades), the president or leader among the elders began to receive more responsibilities and consequently more honor from his fellow elders who, acknowledging his leadership and supporting his ministry, gave up their positions of co-elders and eventually became his inferiors, receiving direction from him. Again, as time passed, those appointed to take the lead, to baptize new ones, and to serve the Lord's Supper were those who offered the emblems to God. As the liturgy was lengthened, the eucharistic prayers recited during the Eucharist by the bishop (*episkopos*) or by an elder (presbyter) in his absence were and are still known as the *anaphora* during which a remembrance (*anamnesis*) is made of salvation history, followed by the offering (*anaphora*) composed of the holy gifts, the leavened bread to be consecrated (the *prosphora*), and then the calling down of the Holy Spirit to complete the change (the *epiclesis*). These are the terms one encounters when reading literature that describes the Christian *synaxis,* or meeting, in liturgical churches. The Lord's Supper became enshrouded more and more in mystery and sacredness. It became the "awesome sacrifice" of the Mass.

'Clericalization'

Church historians and scholars have documented this evolution. They detail the "clericalization" and the sacralization that took place, leading to a division of the Body of Christ into clergy and laity. The following paragraphs trace this progression. Henry Chadwick notes the changes that occurred during the second century:

> [T]he ministry achieved its universal threefold shape of bishop, presbyter, and deacon. . . .

> The way in which the second-century Church solved the questions of authority, however, produced its own problems. Emphasis on the local bishop as the fundamental principle of unity (Ignatius) and on the sacredness of the 'tradition' (Irenaeus) was necessary enough for survival, but had its byproduct in a measure of clericalization of the Church. The part of the

people in the sacraments began to become less important than the acts of the priest in the mystery; and the priest became rather more remote, especially after the fourth century, when the Greeks started to veil the altar from the congregation's view.[7]

Bokenkotter says that "the clergy at first were not sharply differentiated from the laity in their lifestyle: The clergy married, raised families, and earned their livelihood at some trade or profession. But as the practice grew of paying them for their clerical work, they withdrew more and more from secular pursuits, until by the fourth century such withdrawal was deemed obligatory." And,

> An important factor in this change was the increasing stress laid on the cultic and ritualistic aspects of the ministry. At first the Christian presbyter or elder avoided any resemblance to the pagan or Jewish priests and, in fact, even deliberately refused to be called a priest. He saw His primary function as the ministry of the Word. The ritualistic features of His sacramental ministry were kept in a low key. Even as late as the fifth century, John Chrysostom still stressed preaching as the main task of the Christian minister. But the image of the Christian presbyter gradually took on a sacral character.[8]

Lightfoot tells us, "The progress of the *sacerdotal* view of the ministry is one of the most striking and important phenomena in the

---

7. Chadwick, *The Early Church*, 1:286.
8. Bokenkotter, 53. Along the same lines,

Still, from the apostolic age onwards, there was an increasing tendency to widen the distance between clergy and laity. It was felt necessary to guard against the growing dangers of heresy and schism by emphasizing the dignity of the standing officers and leaders of the Church. As numbers and wealth increased, there was both more occasion and more opportunity for the ministry to abandon secular callings, and to give themselves wholly to their sacred vocation. Jewish ideas upon the subject of the priesthood unduly colored the thinking of some minds. As the heathen world had also its sacrificing priesthood, converts from within its borders not unnaturally were inclined to seek in Christianity for a counterpart to their old system of altars and officiating priests. From these several causes, there resulted a positive growth of priestly ideas and customs. As early as the closing part of the second century, there was a noticeable drift towards sacerdotalism, or the high-church theory of Christ's kingdom on earth. Henry C. Sheldon, *The History of the Christian Church* (Cambridge: University Press, 1894), 1:241–42.

history of the Church." He adds, "It has been pointed out already that the sacerdotal functions and privileges, which alone are mentioned in the apostolic writings, pertain to all believers alike and do not refer solely or specially to the ministerial office."[9] Lightfoot also explains what he means by *sacerdotalism*: "In speaking of sacerdotalism, I assume the term to have essentially the same force as when applied to the Jewish priesthood."[10] Could anything be clearer than this? Again, "For, though no distinct traces of sacerdotalism are visible in the ages immediately after the Apostles, yet having once taken root in the Church it shot up rapidly into maturity. Towards the close of the second century we discern the first germs appearing above the surface: yet, shortly after the middle of the third, the plant has all but attained its full growth."[11]

Lightfoot also explains how the term *clergy* came into use. It seems to be derived from the Greek word for a lot; lots were cast to choose a successor to the traitor Judas (Acts 1:17–26). The Greek word is *kleros,* which, when transliterated into English letters, gave us *clerus: clergy.* Lightfoot tells us that the "earliest instance of 'clerus', meaning clergy, seems to occur in Tertullian, who belongs to the next generation."[12]

I trust that this review has served to somewhat lift the veil over the most obscure centuries of the Christian faith. Understanding how clericalization developed in the church, logically the next step would be to trace how the sacralization of the clergy evolved.

Sacralization

In *A Concise History of the Catholic Church*, Bokenkotter provides an excellent explanation of this process:

> This sacralization of the clergy was brought about by various developments—theological, liturgical, and legal. *The Old Testament priesthood,* for instance, *was seen as the type and model* for

---

9. Lightfoot, 244–45.
10. Ibid., 245 n1.
11. Ibid., 246.
12. Ibid., 248.

the New Testament priesthood. The more elaborate liturgy of the post-Constantinian era, *with its features borrowed from paganism*, enhanced the image of the minister as a sacred personage. The ministry of the Word diminished in importance when infant baptism became the rule rather than the exception, for infants could not be preached to. Imperial legislation established the clergy as an independent corporation with its own rights and immunities.

In line with these developments, there was a big shift in the very idea of the sacred. Before Constantine the whole church was considered the realm of the sacred as opposed to the profane world outside; after Constantine and the breakdown of the separation between church and world, the polarity between sacred and profane was transformed into one between sacred clergy and profane laity.[13]

In his next paragraph, Bokenkotter observes how celibacy increased the distance between clergy and laity in the West. Now that the general outline is in place, we turn our attention to the further development of a sacrificial and hierarchal system within the church.

A Priesthood Must Offer Sacrifices

As time passed and Christianity was legalized and supported by the empire, eventually government officials began to attend the *synaxis* (gathering, or worship service). Christians no longer had to hide; they were favored with gifts and public support. They could have large public meetings in temples abandoned by the pagans. Church services were crowded as everywhere disaffected pagans beheld Christianity victorious. As people flowed into the church, the church became more worldly, and the liturgies became longer, more mysterious, more awe-inspiring. According to Chadwick, "As the congregations swelled in size during the fourth century, so the liturgy tended to be extended. Sometimes these enlargements could

13. Bokenkotter, 54 (my italics). See also, Alexander Schmemann, *The Eucharist, Sacrament of the Kingdom*, trans. Paul Kachur (Crestwood, NY: St. Vladimir's Seminary, 1988), 89. Schmemann writes, "The deficiency in contemporary church psychology lies in regarding the whole life of the Church in terms of the interrelation of clergy and laity. We have equated the Church with the clergy, and the 'laity' with the world."

go to enormous lengths, as in the Eucharistic formulas provided in the eighth book of the *Apostolic Constitutions.* . . . Greek clergy began to wear ornate clothes, and the ritual acquired high dramatic splendour."[14]

In the book *Orthodox Worship*, Orthodox author Benjamin Wilson, writing under the heading "The Conversion of Constantine," says,

> Although he was not baptized until just prior to His death in A.D. 337, Constantine embraced Christianity, made it legal, and for all practical purposes made it the religion of the state. With the edict of Milan in 313 A.D., he granted free religious worship and recognition by the state. As a result, the persecution of the Church finally ended, as did the need for secrecy. This caused the first of the major changes in the form of the Liturgy.
>
> . . . With the acceptance brought about by Constantine, all this changed. Now it became possible to publicly erect churches dedicated to the worship of God, and to do so with state support. Christian worship became a public affair, and these changes out of necessity resulted in an elaboration of the ceremonial aspect of worship. Christian worship was now being seen by non-believers; thus it not only had to be understandable to them, but the necessary sense of reverence and thanksgiving had to be conveyed.
>
> These enhancements in act and ceremony manifested themselves in a variety of ways. The Church had always worshiped in homes, but during times of toleration, it began taking over secular buildings, and converting them for Christian worship. The new public places of worship were larger, and there was amplification of the service over what had been celebrated in earlier times. Clerical vestments began to appear. The use of chanting and hymnody, *having their basis in Jewish worship*, became more highly developed in this more public worship and proclamation. There was a heightened sense of drama, with entrances, processions and censing, also built upon Old Testament worship. Icons, as a means of remembering Christ, His saints and

---

14. Chadwick, *The Early Church*, 266.

martyrs, spread in their use. These changes occurred in response to the cultural change which the Church was experiencing with the end of persecution and its open acceptance within society.

Perhaps nothing better illustrates this process than the development of clerical vestments. The most striking aspect of the development of vestments is that they came out of everyday culture. In the early church, in fact, there was a marked attitude that there should be no liturgical vestments; that the celebration of worship and of the Eucharist should take place in everyday dress. . . .

Dix[15] goes on to point out that to this "accidental" distinction which developed between lay and clerical clothing added "symbolic enrichment" to add Christian meaning to things that had utilitarian origins; and that included the use of lights and censing during the Eucharist as well. *Again we see elements of Old Testament worship being retained and in fact taking on new meaning in the worship of the New Covenant.*[16]

Casimir Kucharek, a liturgical expert and priest from the Eastern Catholic Church, informs us that "by the middle of that century [sixth century], however, the splendor of the procession had become excessive. . . . Also, the lavish procession attracted all the attention, while the offering itself seemed incidental. The magnitude of the procession at Hagia Sophia, as early as in the days of Justinian, may be inferred

---

15. Gregory Dix (1901–1952), an English monk and priest of an Anglican Benedictine community, was a specialist on the liturgy.

16. Benjamin Wilson, "The Conversion of Constantine" in Benjamin D. Williams and Harold B. Anstall, *Orthodox Worship, A Living Continuity With the Synagogue, the Temple and the Early Church* (Minneapolis: Light and Life, 1990), 45–47 (my italics). Page 52 contains an account of how the church became a worldly ruler:

The Church became a source of authority and often exerted itself as the authority in the world. This historical situation directly involved the Church in politics—in the world—and the Western Church, in part out of necessity and in part out of choice, elected to assert itself in this arena. The result was clericalism, what Fr. Schmemann describes as the "hierarchical subordination of the state to the church." Out of this came the religious-political struggles which raged in the Dark Ages, through the period of Charlemagne into the Middle Ages, and ultimately culminated in the Reformation. All this from the Church opting to operate as an entity in "the world."

How different this is from the tone of the New Testament description where we find in passages such as James 4:4, "Know ye not that the friendship with the world is enmity with God?"

from His decree of A.D. 535, ordering that the clergy of Hagia Sophia and the three churches annexed to it number no more than four hundred and twenty-five."[17]

A quotation from John Henry Newman reveals how many "Christian" practices were adopted from the pagan cultic world:

> The use of temples, and these dedicated to particular saints, and ornamented on occasions with branches of trees; incense, lamps, and candles; votive offerings on recovery from illness; holy water; asylums; holydays and seasons, use of calendars, processions, blessings on the fields; sacerdotal vestments, the tonsure, the ring in marriage, turning to the East, images at a later date, perhaps the ecclesiastical chant, and the Kyrie Eleison, are all of pagan origin, and sanctified by their adoption into the Church.[18]

Of course, we know that some of these items were also used in the Old Testament worship rendered to Yahweh. The point is that Christianity is different. It is not a national religion; it is not based upon a certain language group or a cultural community. The Christian faith involves a new and a spiritual relationship with God, and it demands personal conversion and a commitment to our Lord. Yet very early, as the pagan religious people acknowledged Christianity's superiority and began entering the church in droves, the church adopted the customs and usages of the pagans. The leadership believed that this facilitated the pagans' acceptance of Christianity.

I was raised in the Roman Catholic Church before Vatican II brought changes to the celebration of the Mass. I remember the awe I experienced as a child when I heard the prayers in Latin, viewed the candles and the stained-glass windows, and heard the chimes or bells rung as the priest said the words of consecration to change the bread and wine into the body and blood of Christ. Later, after the recitation of the "Our Father" prayer and the breaking of the bread, we

---

17. Casimir Kucharek, *The Byzantine-Slav Liturgy of St. John Chrysostom: Its Origin and Evolution* (Combermere, Ontario: Alleluia, 1971), 493.

18. John Henry Newman, *An Essay on the Development of Christian Doctrine* (1878; Notre Dame, IN: Univ. of Notre Dame, 1989), 373.

knelt and recited as the host was elevated, "Lamb of God who takes away the sins of the world" (*Agnus Dei, qui tollis pecata mundi*; I still remember the words). I also remember later on the "awesome mysteries," as they are called in the Orthodox church. When attending the Divine Liturgy, we bowed and touched the floor, crossing ourselves at the invocation of the Holy Spirit, as the priest said, "Making the change." Chadwick wrote about this: "John Chrysostom . . . speaks of the Lord's Table as a place of 'terror and shuddering'. . . . Before the end of the fourth century in the East it began to be thought necessary to screen off the holy Table by curtains."[19] "Hippolytus accordingly enjoins on the faithful intense reverence for the eucharist. It should be received early before any other food, and the greatest care should be taken to see that nothing was dropped or spilt."[20]

Although ancient, a custom or practice (icon screen, etc.) must be rejected if it is wrong. The evidence just presented should be sufficient to convince any open-minded person that the early church underwent many transformations that led to a return to the Old Covenant system of worship. The early church leaders quickly forgot that Christ established a New Covenant based upon the bloody offering of Himself *once for all time*. The Scriptures tell us, "So Christ was offered once to bear the sins of many. To those who eagerly wait for Him He will appear a second time, apart from sin, for salvation" (Heb. 9:28). This offering can never be repeated or re-offered. Why? Because it was and is an infinite sacrifice made by God Himself, sufficient to atone for all the sins of His people; it remains perfect forever, needing no repetition. It would be disrespectful and erroneous to even think we need to present or offer it again on another altar. Christians recognize only the cross of Calvary, where the Lamb of God was sacrificed to take away the sins of the world. We need no other altar! The Lord's Supper is our remembrance of that finished sacrifice: "Do this in remembrance of Me" (Luke 22:19).

Why was the primitive church so easily influenced in spite of leaders who searched the Holy Writings for prophecies to support their

---

19. Chadwick, *The Early Church*, 267.
20. Ibid., 266.

faith in the face of Jewish and pagan attacks on their beliefs? We do not know for sure. Perhaps the many priests that converted to Christianity exerted undue influence (Acts 6:7)? Did their training and habits influence the worship format of the church? Why did the simple Christian synagogue service come to look more and more like the temple services? Was this a sincere effort to strengthen or heighten piety? Did their search of the Scriptures, so imprinted on their minds, lead them to unwittingly copy the Old Testament style of worship, which they thought prefigured so clearly the final sacrifice, Christ our Lord?

Apparently, a transformation did take place in spite of warnings such as these:

"But evil men and impostors will grow worse and worse, deceiving and being deceived" (2 Tim. 3:13).

"For the time will come when they will not endure sound doctrine, but according to their own desires, because they have itching ears, they will heap up for themselves teachers, and they will turn their ears away from the truth, and be turned aside to fables" (2 Tim. 4:3, 4,).

"For there are many insubordinate, both idle talkers and deceivers, especially those of the circumcision, whose mouths must be stopped, who subvert whole households, teaching things which they ought not, for the sake of dishonest gain. One of them, a prophet of their own, said, 'Cretans are always liars, evil beasts, lazy gluttons.' This testimony is true. Therefore rebuke them sharply, that they may be sound in the faith, not giving heed to Jewish fables and commandments of men who turn from the truth" (Titus 1:10–14).

Our study leads us to conclude that this is what happened. The A became Z, and Z is not A. This is why I invite every evangelical convert to Roman Catholicism or to the Eastern Orthodox Church to return to the simplicity of worship offered in "Spirit and in truth," and to "walk by faith and not by sight" (John 4:24; 2 Cor. 5:7).

I trust these explanations are sufficient. They are important to this study because they help us to see how the church got from A to Z. The changes were so great that the churches we call A, the simple first-century New Testament gatherings of members of the Body of

Christ, quickly evolved through all the steps from A to Z, that is, the Roman Catholic and Eastern Orthodox Churches (not excluding the non-Chalcedonian, the Armenian churches, and other such-like churches), that is, all the ancient liturgical churches. These two entities are very different in essence, although they both have the Holy Scriptures and believe in Jesus Christ. The liturgical churches lost the simplicity and clarity of the gospel because of such practices as the invocation of saints and angels and trust in relics, icons, and asceticism (fasting and abstinence, even from sexual relations). These churches teach their members that these practices are necessary to mortify the flesh, to become holy, to achieve divinization. Mary, the angels, and the saints grant healings, as well as salvation from floods, volcanic lava flows, droughts, and victory over foreign armies. Memorials and Liturgies (Masses) are paid for in order to help their dead loved ones, to alleviate their sufferings. Z is definitely not A!

CHAPTER 9

Further Dilution
of Biblical Christianity

BIBLICAL WORSHIP in Western civilization has been diluted and degraded over the centuries. We have already observed how Christianity underwent a transformation during a relatively short period of time. As theologian Paul Jewett wrote, "It must not be forgotten, however, that the earliest ages of Christian history are marked not only by rapid expansion, but also by rapid change."[1] What led the early church to believe that Christians ought to pray to Mary, to saints and angels; that their images should be kissed and incensed; that bows and prostrations should be made in front of them?

The transformation of the church began to snowball when the church became a state-supported entity and when pagan temples and their appendages, customs, and usages were christianized.

From Paganism to Patron Saints, Icons, and Statues

W. H. C. Frend, in his highly readable book *The Rise of Christianity,* describes some of the changes the church underwent in the fourth and fifth centuries:

> A century after its triumph during the reign of Constantius II the Church had become the most powerful single factor in the lives of the peoples of the [Roman] empire. *The Virgin and the*

---

1. Paul K. Jewett, *Infant Baptism and the Covenant of Grace* (Grand Rapids: Eerdmans, 1978), 19.

saints had replaced the gods as patrons of cities. The bishops were equated in precedence and often in salary with a provincial governor. . . . The century had seen fundamental shifts in the structure of society to the church's advantage.

She [the *Theotokos*] was Ever-Virgin "queen of heaven," mediator between the spiritual and the material worlds, protector of cities, and guardian over the welfare of the empire. . . . Whereas in the fourth century [in Palestine] churches would be dedicated usually to Christ, in the sixth the Virgin and the military saints, reputed heroes of the Great Persecution, now held pride of place.[2]

The ancient worship of the Madonna and child was widespread in the East. Many evangelicals who enter either the Catholic church or the Orthodox church are obliged to dismiss any possible connection between that Eastern cult and what occurred in the Christian church, but have they done so too easily? At the very least, we should concede that the minds of the empire's inhabitants were fertile enough ground, already prepared for the developments that led to the veneration of saints. Take for example, Ephesus. *Easton's Bible Dictionary* says,

Diana, so called by the Romans; called Artemis by the Greeks, the "great" goddess worshipped among heathen nations under various modifications. Her most noted temple was that at Ephesus. It was built outside the city walls, and was one of the seven wonders of the ancient world. "First and last it was the work of 220 years; built of shining marble; 342 feet long by 164 feet broad; supported by a forest of columns, each 56 feet high; a sacred museum of masterpieces of sculpture and painting. At the centre, hidden by curtains, within a gorgeous shrine, stood the very ancient image of the goddess, on wood or ebony reputed to have fallen from the sky. Behind the shrine was a treasury, where, as in 'the safest bank in Asia,' nations and kings stored their most precious things. The temple as St. Paul saw

---

2. Frend, *The Rise of Christianity,* 773, 836.
    Also, see page 755, where Frend discusses the early gnostic writings and the origin of the title *Theotokos,* "God-bearer" and relates how Mary became the patron and protector of cities.

it subsisted till A.D. 262, when it was ruined by the Goths" Ac 19:23–41, Moule on Ephesians: Introd.[3]

The bishops that met in council in Ephesus gave Mary the title "Mother of God" or *Theotokos,* the "God-bearer."

The Life and Epistles of St. Paul describes another pagan practice in Ephesus:

> One of the idolatrous customs of the ancient world was the use of portable images or shrines, which were little models of the more celebrated objects of devotion. They were carried in processions, on journeys and military expeditions, and sometimes set up as household gods in private dwellings.... From the expressions used by St. Luke, it is evident that an extensive and lucrative trade grew up at Ephesus, from the manufacture and sale of these shrines. Few of those who came to Ephesus would willingly go away without a memorial of the goddess, and a model of her temple.[4]

This is all very familiar to Catholics who have visited shrines like those in Lourdes and Fatima, or Orthodox who have also visited monasteries and holy places where one is able to buy statues or icons, prayer ropes or rosaries, holy water, or oils and incense to take home for an icon corner or other areas set apart for daily prayers and worship.

Historian William McNeill notes the following about Europe several centuries later:

> Despite the efforts of individual popes, of monks and of Irish missionaries, the Church of Western Europe underwent a profound intellectual and moral decay during the sixth and seventh centuries. Among the Franks and other German peoples many pagan ideas and practices survived; and the educated population almost wholly disappeared. Under such circumstances many superstitious practices penetrated Christian rituals, and pagan deities not infrequently reappeared as Christian saints.[5]

---

3. Entry #1030, *Easton's Bible Dictionary* in BibleWorks 7.

4. W. J. Conybeare and J. S. Howson, *The Life and Epistles of St. Paul* (1856; Grand Rapids: Eerdmans, 1974), 424.

5. McNeill, *History of Western Civilization, a Handbook,* 215.

James C. Russell has also documented some of the changes that occurred in the church. Having made a sociological study of the progress of Christianity in Europe during the Middle Ages, he arrived at similar conclusions. Although the references provided here are from studies of Western Europe, the same principles apply to the Eastern Roman Empire, where the Orthodox church developed. The reason is that these common sociological transformations and events occur unless there is a conscious and tireless effort to resist them. The desire to assimilate the pagan populations and to facilitate their evangelization led the church to adopt similar methods in both the East and the West. Russell quotes Gregory Dix, a well-known specialist on the liturgy: "The barbarians followed their chiefs submissively into the fold of the church, . . . [b]ut that did not in fact make them responsible Christians. Their mass-movements into christianity or from Arianism to orthodoxy did not betoken any sort of change of heart."[6] Then Russell informs us that "the general missionary policy of Gregory, and later Boniface, may be summarized as 'that which cannot be supplanted by preaching or coercion, may be accommodated.'"[7]

Such accretions transformed true Christianity into a "fusion religion." We should be asking ourselves, What was the driving force or motivation behind such innovations? Apparently a "success matters" philosophy was at work. The return to certain Judaic practices and the blending of Christianity with the pagan religious customs and practices produced a composite religion with which anyone could easily identify. The same philosophical sword, pragmatism, continues to strike at the heart of the church today. The only possible conclusion is this: Christendom *did not* remain steadfast in the apostles' doctrine (Acts 2:42). This principle is clearly manifest in the Orthodox and Roman Catholic dogmatic teaching about "relative worship"[8] of Mary,

---

6. Gregory Dix, *The Shape of the Liturgy* (1945; New York: Seabury Press, 1982), 595–96; cited in, James C. Russell, *The Germanization of Early Medieval Christianity* (New York: Oxford, 1996), 199.

7. James C. Russell, *The Germanization of Early Medieval Christianity,* 187. The reference is to Pope Gregory the Great (AD 590–604).

8. In relation to the worship of God, this is considered a lesser form of worship; therefore, it is "relative" worship.

the saints, and angels. I certainly have no desire to offend anybody's sensibilities, but necessity constrains me to speak the truth in love (Eph. 4:14, 15). My sincere desire is to help those attracted to any ancient church because he thinks the weight of antiquity is in favor of the church's history and authority.

Prayers Addressed to Mary, Saints, and Angels

Evangelicals who are considering becoming Catholic or Orthodox must face a number of questions: Is prayer to saints a form of worship, which belongs to God alone? Is there any Biblical command to address prayers to saints or, at the very least, an example in the New Testament that would lead us to think such prayers are permissible? How can we be sure any given person is really in Heaven? Is it not true that God alone knows the heart of man and that He alone can judge a person to be worthy of Heaven (Rev. 2:23)? Finally, is prayer to saints in Heaven any different from asking a friend to pray for us?

Mary

First, we consider the one called the "Virgin Mary" because she is esteemed to be the first and highest of all the saints and angels. Her statues and icons are famous in every country. I remember kneeling as a child before a statue of Mary standing on a globe, with a crown on her head and a serpent crushed under her feet. I was taught that this statue depicted the fulfillment of Genesis 3:15, which meant that a woman would crush the serpent. On December 12, Mexicans, Hispanics, and North Americans celebrate the Virgin of Guadalupe, whom Pope John Paul II proclaimed "Patroness of the Americas." We often hear the famous hymn "Ave Maria" interpreted by well-known singers, and Eastern Orthodox Christians have a special service called the Akathist that poetically proclaims the virtues of the *Theotokos*.

The historian Jaroslav Pelikan wrote a book on Mary that can enlighten us concerning the development of these doctrines. He presents evidence on the sources for the ancient churches' doctrines on Mary. Prospective converts to those churches should note it: "Although it [the Protoevangel of James] was an apocryphal Gospel,— one that did not achieve official status as part of the canon of the New Testament—it nevertheless 'has dominated the development of the Marian legend, providing much of the basic material for Mary's biography.'"[9]

Pelikan goes on to enumerate ideas familiar to Orthodox believers, but prospective converts to Orthodoxy need to realize that the origins of many Orthodox beliefs about Mary are found in the apocryphal writings, and gnostic ones at that!

As to the rosary in the Latin church, Pelikan mentions its similarity to the prayer habits of other religions: "Following a devotional practice that appeared also outside Christianity, for example in Hinduism, Buddhism, and Islam, the rosary was a string of beads to be used as a mnemonic device for the recitation of prayers."[10]

Prayer addressed to anyone other than God involves the veneration or worship of creatures. The ancient churches admit that only God is worshiped as God and Creator. They tell us that this kind of worship is described by the Latin word *latria*, which is derived from the Greek word *latreuo*. They explain further that the saints and their images and relics receive veneration of a lesser form of worship called *dulia*, from the Greek noun *douleia*, meaning "slavery" or "bondage," and the Greek verb *douleuo*, meaning, "to serve" or "to worship gods."[11] They say that Christ's mother, Mary, is worthy of a higher veneration called *hyperdulia*, because she has been elevated to a position higher than other saints due to her being the "Mother of God." They tell us further that this *worship* should be understood as veneration or reverence. The subtleties that separate the God Who seems so distant and the always tender Mary, "our Mother," are lost on many. Addressing these distinctions of *latria* and *dulia*, which could be a

---

9. Pelikan, "The Daughter of Zion and the Fulfillment of Prophecy," *Mary Through the Centuries: Her Place in the History of Culture*, 47. This is an excellent book with beautiful plates. It is also a good example of the development of doctrine, especially of the history of Mary, in the church through the ages..

10. Ibid., 98.

11. Joseph Thayer, *Thayer's Greek-English Lexicon* (Peabody, MA: Hendrickson Publishers, 1996).

form of Mariolatry, Pelikan mentions the Protestant reaction and the need for such educated distinctions, even if they are problematic for the uneducated. Note what he says about Mary's position in Heaven, which justifies her receiving *hyperdulia*: "This distinction was intended to stand as a barrier against 'Mariolatry'—albeit a barrier that may sometimes have been all but invisible to the piety of ordinary believers, whether Western or Eastern, in their prayers to her and to her icon."[12]

Pelikan sums up Mary's position in Catholicism, saying, "It was perceived as an appropriate honor and an authentic expression of her position in the divine order when Mary was acclaimed as second in dignity only to God himself, who had taken up habitation in her."

Pelikan adds, "Because she was the one who held first place among the entire celestial host, whether human or angelic, she, next to God himself, should receive the praises of the whole world. There was, in short, 'nothing equal to Mary and nothing but God greater than Mary.'"[13]

Prospective converts need to take the time to carefully review all the various arguments, taking note that there is neither a command in the New Testament nor any clear example indicating that prayers to anyone other than God are permissible. After reviewing a number of arguments given in the book *Fundamentals of Catholic Dogma*, I found nothing substantial to support these practices. Doctrines such as praying to Mary and saints and angels, the immaculate conception of Mary, and the veneration of images are based more on church authority than on any Scriptural authority, in spite of attempts to document these doctrines in the Scriptures. The ancient churches' reasoning is based upon deductive and/or wishful thinking, upon nothing more than allusions and allegories. They seek to justify practices that entered the church from outside her. The Marian doctrines satisfy a human desire for a sweet mother image—someone who always hears our prayers

---

12. Ibid., 102. See his pages 100–02 for a discussion of *latria* and *dulia*. He also informs us that Augustine of Hippo was among the first to make these distinctions in his City of God.

13. Ibid., 134. See also pages 201–05 for the 1950 papal proclamation and Protestant reaction.

and brings them to her Son, Jesus. The pious person believes that his requests of Mary will not fail to secure the desired answer. The loftiness of a male God Who is the judge is attenuated by the image of a tender mother who cares for her children. Mary (or the *Theotokos*) has as many names as the cities and towns where she is supposed to have appeared through the centuries and where she is supposed to have accomplished miracles and healings and protected cities and countries. Admittedly, I have here in these pages presented my conclusions before examining the evidence, but I have done so in the interest of economy, because entire books are devoted to this one subject. It is time, however, for us to review a few of the arguments Catholic theologian Ludwig Ott has developed.

Saints and Angels

Ott, quoting the Council of Trent in *Fundamentals of Catholic Dogma*, argues, "It is good and profitable to appeal to them [saints] for help." Then Ott admits, "Holy Writ does not explicitly refer to the veneration and invocation of saints. . . . Our right to venerate the saints can be deduced from the veneration offered to the angels as attested by Holy Writ. . . . Since the saints also are immediately joined to God (1 Cor. 13, 12; 1 John 3, 2), it follows that they too are worthy of veneration."[14]

What does "immediately joined to God" mean? Does Ott imagine they are part of God, members of Christ's Body, or what? I can't imagine. If anyone will take the time to examine Ott's book, he may note that Ott's arguments are based upon deductions, several references to the apocryphal (deuterocanonical) Old Testament books, and wishful thinking. Ott also says, "According to Tob. 12, 12; Apoc. 5, 8; and 8, 3, the angels and the saints lay the prayers of the holy at the feet of God." This may be a touching scene, but it does not occur in these passages. Rather, it appears that the saints offer prayers to God, which is in harmony with Holy Writ. The angel offers the incense accompanied by the saints' prayers. It is remarkable that Revelation 8:3 in the Catholic

---

14. Ott, *Fundamentals of Catholic Dogma*, 318.

edition of the Bible reads, "Another angel came and stood at the altar, holding a gold censer. He was given a great quantity of incense to offer, along with the prayers of all the holy ones, on the gold altar that was before the throne" (New American Bible, New English Translation).

In other words, the incense offered is accompanied by the prayers of God's faithful servants.[15] We must not forget that Revelation is an apocalyptic book filled with images. The passage concerns a heavenly vision given to John. It can be interpreted as speaking of the saints in Heaven, of the saints still alive on earth, or of those who were martyred. In any case, what the Old Testament high priest did is pictured by the angel in the heavenly temple, in line with the teaching that angels are ministers to the saints. The incense symbolizes the rising of prayers to God. This was a well-known part of worship in Israel. Psalm 141:2 says, "Let my prayer be set before You as incense, the lifting up of my hands as the evening sacrifice." According to Revelation 5:8, just like incense rising up to our God, our prayers reach up to Him, and He is pleased. Liturgical churches once again seek support from the Scriptures with a naked literalism *when it suits them*. This reminds us of what they have done with the bread and the wine, emblems of our Lord's body and blood.

Ott becomes an excellent witness to the development of "Christian" worship when he admits that "the veneration of images (by kissing, bowing down before them, burning of candles, incensing) chiefly developed in the Greek Church from the fifth to the seventh centuries. The Iconoclasts of the eighth and the ninth centuries saw in the veneration of images a relapse into paganism."[16]

Ott informs us as well that the invocation of saints was first attested by Hippolytus of Rome [d. AD 235].[17] About Hippolytus, William Jurgens says, "He exhibits a thorough knowledge of Greek philosophy and his theological attitudes betray a dependence upon

---

15. In Revelation 8:3 and 4, the "prayers" are dative in Greek and explained as a dative of association or accompaniment. See Wallace, *Greek Grammar Beyond the Basics*, 159–60.

16. Ibid., 320–21.

17. Ott, *Fundamentals of Catholic Dogma*, 319.

Alexandrian thought."[18] By distancing himself from apostolic practice, Hippolytus became a speculative innovator in theology.

Before concluding this section, it would be well to point out how
such practices get started and to say a little more concerning Catholic
and Orthodox reasoning on these matters.

I beg the reader's patience due to what may appear to be a change
of subject by bringing up the doctrine of the immaculate conception of Mary. This teaching provides a better insight into the type of
reasoning that led to changes in practices and beliefs in the ancient
churches. In Ott's book we read, "Reason bases the dogma on the
Scholastic axiom which is already found in the writings of Eadmer;
Potuit, decuit, ergo fecit (God could do it, He ought to do it, therefore
He did it). This, it is true, gives no certainty, but still, it rationally
establishes for the dogma a high degree of probability."[19]

True, Orthodox theologians tell us they reject scholastic reasoning,
and most of them do not accept this Roman dogma. Still, this method
of reasoning is typical, and it caused the church to sully the pure
waters of truth. The argumentation we have been examining together
demonstrates how simple church services in which Christians met to
celebrate the Lord's Supper, to read the Scriptures, and to pray and
sing hymns were transformed into temple worship, with processions,
ranks of clergy, icons or statues adorning the temple, and people
bowing and lighting candles before their favorite saints and addressing prayers to them. These numerous changes transformed the church
from a community of brothers and sisters where spiritual worship
was offered to a temple where dignitaries and nobles were received in
grand procession. The emphasis was on the visual, the experiential,
and the external. All of this was due to rationalism, pragmatism, and
influences that can be traced to philosophy and worldliness.

Catholic and Orthodox theologians and apologists explain that
it is all right to ask the saints in Heaven to pray for us, because all
Christians (whether alive or dead) are members of the one mystical

---

18. Jurgens, *The Faith of the Early Fathers*, 1:162.
19. Ott, *Fundamentals of Catholic Dogma*, 202.

Body of Christ. They will point out that the saints are very much alive in Christ (Mark 12:26, 27). Moreover, Christ is a mediator in a special sense, but all Christians are mediators or intercessors for one another in a lesser sense.

Although someone may object to the word *mediators* because he thinks of their prayers for others as intercessory prayer, the real issue is this: Is not Jesus Christ an all-sufficient mediator? Again, are we permitted to pray to anyone other than God? Is there any support for this practice in the New Testament? The answer is no! One Orthodox author (a priest) says that the Orthodox don't pray to the saints. Yet in practice this is not true, as observation proves. True Christians pray to God alone because He is our Father, our God, and because He is able to answer our prayers. In the Gospels, our Lord Himself taught us to pray to the Father, Who meets all our needs (Luke 11:1–4).

The God-Man, Jesus Christ, is our ever-present intercessor and mediator as God's perfect man and man's perfect God. A true evangelical would never need to pray to saints for two simple reasons: (1) because he knows God is able to meet his every need and (2) because God commands believers to worship Him alone (Exod. 20:1–6).

In the next chapter we will consider Biblical worship vs. diluted worship.

CHAPTER 10

Biblical Worship vs. Diluted Worship

C HRISTIANS SERVE AND WORSHIP God the Creator because of Who He is: worthy, holy, life-giver. Worship is due to Him alone. In the Holy Scriptures He tells us that He is a jealous God and does not share His glory with another (Exod. 20:5; Isa. 42:8; 48:11).

The Nature of Worship

If the reader will take the time to look up Exodus 20:5; 23:24; Deuteronomy 5:9; Judges 2:19; and 2 Kings 17:35, he will note the repetition of the words *bow down* and *serve*. To bow down before idols is to serve them and the false gods they represent. The lexicological meaning of *serve* in Hebrew (*abad*) and in Greek (*douleuo*) can also refer to bondage or slavery, and it means that one belongs to the god one worships. A feature of the Hebrew Bible is parallelism, repeating the same idea using different words or expressions to emphasize an idea. So the words *bow, worship,* and *serve* may appear together in the same sentence. *Latria* (from *latreuo*) is quite often translated *serve* in the Bible because worship is service to the true God or to a false god.

In the Greek Septuagint, Exodus 23:24 is a good example because both *proskyneo* and *latreuo* are present: "You shall not bow down [*proskyneo*; Latin Vulgate: *adorabis*] to their gods, nor serve [*latreuo*] them, nor do according to their works; but you shall utterly overthrow them and completely break down their sacred pillars." Who would deny that bowing down before these gods is worship and that serving them also implies worship! The prospective convert to the ancient churches should observe the manner in which icons are treated in the Orthodox and Roman churches, where both statues and icons are found.

A Matter of Words

The Catholic and Orthodox argument that prostration before a saint's image is permissible and covered by *dulia* in Latin (*douleia* in Greek) is without Scriptural support. Their apologists will reply that the Greek word *proskyneo* does not indicate a degree of worship as high as *latria*. Clearly, Exodus 23:24 offers no support to their arguments when *proskyneo* has to do with statues or images. Is not their reasoning based only on wishful thinking? Rather than allow presumption or fantasy to run wild, should we not accept God's supreme laws and the Scriptural context as definitive?

Another example is found in 2 Chronicles 7:19: "But if you turn away and forsake My statutes and My commandments which I have set before you, and go and serve other gods, and worship them." Both verbs *latreuo*, "to serve," and *proskyneo*, "to bow," are present here in the Greek Bible. But you should be aware that where the Greek Bible has the verb *proskyneo*, the Hebrew Bible has *shachach*, "worship." We conclude, therefore, that *proskyneo* is a correct translation of the Hebrew word for worship.

In the King James Version, 1 Kings 9:6 reads "if you . . . serve [*abad*] other gods, and worship [*shachach*] them," whereas in Judges 2:19 the translators rendered the exact same Hebrew words as "serve them, and to bow down unto them." Why should anyone insist that bowing down is only "relative worship," not real worship? Is it because they prefer to accept man's word rather than God's on the matter?

The Work of Man's Hands

Deuteronomy 4:28, "And there you will serve gods, the work of men's hands, wood and stone, which neither see nor hear nor eat nor smell," should be a warning to all of God's people. The Orthodox and Roman Catholic theologians who promote the veneration of Mary, saints, and angels through icons or statues cannot escape the clear teaching of Holy Scripture. To bow the knee before, or to fall prostrate before them, amounts to the worship of "the work of men's hands." Also, there is one more point to add. To even bring the hand to the mouth *to kiss* is esteemed idolatry in the Old Testament (see 1 Kings 19:18; Job 31:24–28; Hos. 13:2; Ps. 2:12 [*Kiss the Son* means "worship God's Son"]). The only one who represents God for us is Jesus Christ in Whom we know God the Father; Christ alone is the *icon* (image) of God. Colossians 1:15 tells us that our Savior "is the image [Greek *eikon*, "icon"] of the invisible God, the firstborn over all creation." No wonder Philippians 2:10 and 11 tell us "that at the name of Jesus every knee should bow, of those in heaven, and of those on earth, and of those under the earth, and that every tongue should confess that Jesus Christ is Lord, to the glory of God the Father."

It is evident that it is wrong for a church to set itself above God's Word and to insist on a difference between *latria* and *dulia,* because God's Word alone, not a church hierarchy that may be disobedient to God's Word, determines our conduct. Remember Exodus 23:24: "You shall not bow down to their gods, nor serve them, nor do according to their works; but you shall utterly overthrow them and completely break down their sacred pillars."

The Difference with Israel's Kings

The people of Israel were commanded to not bow down to the false gods and to not serve (worship) them, but they were never told to refuse to bow before their king, who represented God's invisible reign over Israel. Two Bible translations show this. Upon the occasion of Solomon's succession to the throne in Israel, King David told the people:

"Now bless the LORD your God. And all the congregation blessed the LORD God of their fathers, and bowed down their heads, and worshipped [*shachach*] the LORD, and the king" (1 Chron. 29:20, KJV).

"Then David said to the whole assembly, 'Praise the LORD your God.' So the whole assembly praised the LORD God of their ancestors. They bowed down and paid homage to the LORD and the king" (HCSB).

This is nothing more than an example of an oriental king receiving homage (a reverential regard). Someone told me the passage means that the people paid homage (worship) to the Lord and that King David worshiped God along with his people. I don't believe this interpretation will stand from either the Hebrew or the Greek text. As God's representative on earth, David received homage, whereas Yahweh received worship. How do we know this is correct? Well, the simplest way would be to consult the context of the passage before us:

> And they made sacrifices to the LORD and offered burnt offerings to the LORD on the next day: a thousand bulls, a thousand rams, a thousand lambs, with their drink offerings, and sacrifices in abundance for all Israel. So they ate and drank before the LORD with great gladness on that day. And they made Solomon the son of David king the second time, and anointed him before the LORD to be the leader, and Zadok to be priest. Then Solomon sat on the throne of the LORD as king instead of David his father, and prospered; and all Israel obeyed him. All the leaders and the mighty men, and also all the sons of King David, submitted themselves to King Solomon. (1 Chron. 29:21–24)

To whom did the people offer their sacrifices and burnt offerings? Certainly not to King David. Notice also that Solomon sat on the "throne of the LORD" as God's representative on earth. Therefore, they did not worship David as God but prostrated themselves before him because he was their king, God's representative. This is quite different from prostrating oneself before icons or statues made of wood and paint, precious metals, stone, or marble: "I am the LORD, that is My name; and My glory I will not give to another, nor My praise to carved images" (Isa. 42:8).

"Saints" do not sit upon God's throne, ruling in His place on earth. Norman Cantor has described the importance of theocratic and monarchial rule through human history up to the Middle Ages:

> Again, medieval men worked within the system of divine mon-
> archy mainly because they had no clear consciousness and
> scarcely even an awareness of any other system. Theocratic
> (divinely ordained) monarchy was not only the orthodox politi-
> cal form, but, as far as they knew, it was the best-functioning
> form. The king represented God; he represented the divine forces
> in this world; he was the image of God on Earth. His subjects
> obeyed him not only because that was the useful, virtuous
> course of action or because his soldiers enforced his wishes,
> but because they believed that was what God wanted them to
> do. This was an essential fact of western history from 3200 B.C.
> down to the eighteenth century.[1]

Before entering the Promised Land, Joshua warned the Israelites
about worshiping other gods. Such worship involves service; remember, the Hebrew word for *service* is *abad*. Here and in other places,
the Greek version of the Hebrew Old Testament translated *abad* by
latreuo, "to work," "to serve." Joshua told God's people that they
must choose whom they would serve, but he and his house would
serve the Lord. It is evident in Joshua 24 that the word *serve* stands
for worship.

> "Now therefore, fear the LORD, serve Him in sincerity and in
> truth, and put away the gods which your fathers served on the
> other side of the River and in Egypt. Serve the LORD! And if it
> seems evil to you to serve the LORD, choose for yourselves this
> day whom you will serve, whether the gods which your fathers
> served that were on the other side of the River, or the gods of
> the Amorites, in whose land you dwell. But as for me and my
> house, we will serve the LORD." So the people answered and
> said: "Far be it from us that we should forsake the LORD to serve
> other gods." (Josh. 24:14–16)

Turning to the New Testament, we note in the Gospels the
same Semitic manner of expression. Here is the account of Satan's

---

1. Cantor, *Medieval History, the Life and Death of a Civilization*, 6.

temptation of Jesus when he invited Him to bow before him:

> And the devil said to Him, "All this authority I will give You, and their glory; for this has been delivered to me, and I give it to whomever I wish. Therefore, if You will worship [*proskyneo*: "worship, "bow," reverence"] before me, all will be Yours." And Jesus answered and said to him, "Get behind Me, Satan! For it is written, 'You shall worship [*proskyneo*] the LORD your God, and Him only you shall serve [*latreuo*: "serve," "worship"].'" (Luke 4:6–8)

The reader can check sources online or in a seminary library to get a better grasp of our subject or consult a concordance such as George Wigram's *The Englishman's Hebrew and Chaldee Concordance to the Old Testament*. In Wigram, note the various listings for worship where the contexts have the words *bow down, serve,* and *worship*.[2]

On Whose Authority?

The whole matter boils down to one of authority. Will we follow what God's Word teaches, or the opinions or teachings of others? The same principles we just studied are found in the New Testament but more strongly advanced (Acts 10:25, 26; Rev. 19:10; 22:8, 9). The last book of the Bible informs us that we are not allowed to bow down before angels. What happened when the apostle John fell at the feet of an angel? Revelation 19:10 says, "And I fell at his feet to worship him. But he said to me, 'See that you do not do that! I am your fellow servant, and of your brethren who have the testimony of Jesus. Worship God! For the testimony of Jesus is the spirit of prophecy.'"

As we are now well aware, the Greek word for *worship* is *proskyneo*. According to the *Shorter Lexicon of the Greek New Testament*, it means "to fall down and worship, do obeisance to, prostrate oneself before, do reverence to."[3] If the apostle John was forbidden to prostrate him-

---

2. George Wigram's *The Englishman's Hebrew and Chaldee Concordance to the Old Testament* (Grand Rapids: Zondervan, 1972), 1249. Zondervan has reprinted *The Englishman's Greek Concordance to the New Testament* as well.

3. F. Wilbur Gingrich, *Shorter Lexicon of the Greek New Testament* (Chicago: University of Chicago Press, 1965), 186–87.

self before an angel, no matter how one may seek to dilute the word *worship,* why do Roman Catholics and Orthodox worshipers disobey this clear warning? Again a question comes to mind: would the apostle John really *worship* an angel? Undoubtedly, John thought he was honoring only a powerful and eminent emissary of God, as was customary in oriental cultures. Still he was warned not to do it. Would this not indicate that relative worship *(dulia)* is forbidden? Christians recognize only one God, one Lord, one Savior. This fact was a source of persecution for the early Christians who obstinately refused to place a pinch of incense upon an altar to honor Caesar. They refused to accept him as "lord and savior" as the Romans demanded. Maybe the Eastern customs of bowing at the feet of someone were no longer to be practiced by Christians because the King, the only Potentate, had come, and His name is Lord Jesus (1 Cor. 12:3; Phil. 2:10, 11; 1 Tim. 6:15; Titus 2:11–13)! Perhaps it was permissible as a recognition of authority, but not if it could be considered a form of *worship.*

Christians have direct access to God Almighty, omnipotence being one of God's attributes (Rev. 19:6). Therefore, why would anyone imagine it would be advantageous to pray to or venerate someone less powerful? The fact that God is also immanent (near to—as opposed to "transcendent," far away, majestic, in "light unapproachable" [1 Tim. 6:16]) plays a role here. No creature can be said to be immanent, because immanence belongs to God alone. God is near to us in Word, Spirit, and covenant. If God is with us and in us, would He be pleased if we turned away from Him to pray to someone else? Would this not show a lack of faith on the part of a child of God toward his Heavenly Father? The apostle Peter encourages the downcast, "Therefore humble yourselves under the mighty hand of God, that He may exalt you in due time, casting all your care upon Him, for He cares for you" (1 Pet. 5:6, 7). A true Christian would never deliberately ignore Peter's inspired words. Christ says that if the blind lead the blind, they will both fall into a ditch (Matt. 15:14).

Another issue is communication with the dead. To believe that Mary, angels, and saints are going to favor us with appearances or visions is to open the door to all kinds of deception and exaggeration. Remember, the Devil turns himself into an angel of light (2 Cor. 11:14). This must be considered before making a decision to join an ancient church.

Veneration of the 'Ever-Virgin Mary'

Here are a few questions concerning true worship. Where does one find a description of *true worship* in the New Testament? Where does one find any description of *relative worship* in the New Testament? What would undoubtedly distinguish the two? To better understand what is meant by these questions, I present a typical scene in an Orthodox church. It is August 15, the feast of the Dormition of Mary (Greek, *kimisis*). The fourteen-day fast is now over; the church is almost full. The icon of the *Theotokos* (Mary) lying on her deathbed is displayed on an icon stand. *Dormition* means "sleep." The Orthodox people believe that when the "Most Pure Mother of God" died, her body was taken up by the angels into Heaven to be with her Son. (It seems that many customs pertaining to the veneration of Mary imitate important events in the life of Jesus!)

The priest and the deacon circle the icon as the priest censes it and the choir or chanters sing the appropriate hymn. When they are done, the deacon takes the flask with the oil and the priest takes a brush to dip into the oil as the people line up to venerate the icon and, afterward, to be blessed with the holy oil.

An observer watches from the back of the sanctuary as the people file up to "worship" the icon of the Dormition. As a worshiper approaches the icon, he makes the sign of the cross, drops to his knees, and makes a full prostration, touching the ground with his forehead. Then he gets to his feet and repeats the same actions. When he arrives at the icon, he makes the sign of the cross on himself, and for the third time he drops to the ground on his knees and, bending over, touches the ground with his forehead. He gets up and kisses the icon of the image of Mary on the bier at her shoulders and feet. He may even rest his forehead on the icon as he whispers a brief prayer to

Mary, such as, "Most Holy Theotokos, save us!" All the while the choir sings the troparion:

> In giving birth, you preserved your virginity!
> In falling asleep you did not forsake the world, O Theotokos!
> You were translated to life, O Mother of Life,
> and by your prayers you deliver our souls from death!

When the Orthodox Christian has finished his prostrations, he passes before the priest and the deacon, and the priest anoints his forehead with holy oil. The worshiper receives a piece of holy bread, which has a nice fragrance, and then he leaves the church to go home. Now that the fast is over, the people can celebrate the feast with oil, milk, butter, meat, and wine.

The visitor wonders in his heart, why do they worship Mary? He has witnessed the prostrations, her icon censed and kissed, and prayers and praises being addressed to her. He wonders what these Orthodox people would or could do more for God Almighty Himself that would be any different, any better. He leaves perplexed. No wonder Protestants think that Roman Catholics and the Eastern Orthodox worship Mary!

This prayer to the *Theotokos* will serve as an example:

> I sing of thy grace, O sovereign Lady, and I pray thee to grace my mind. Teach me to step aright in the way of Christ's commandments. Strengthen me to keep awake in song, and drive away the sleep of despondency. O Bride of God, by thy prayers release me, bound with the bonds of sin. Guard me by night and by day, and deliver me from foes that defeat me. O bearer of God the Life-giver, enliven me who am deadened by passions. O bearer of the unwaning Light, enlighten my blinded soul. O marvelous palace of the Master, make me to be a house of the Divine Spirit. O bearer of the Healer, heal the perennial passions of my soul. Guide me to the path of repentance, for I am tossed in the storm of life. Deliver me from eternal fire, and from evil worms, and from Tartarus. Let me not be exposed to the rejoicing of demons, guilty as I am of many sins. Renew me, grown old from senseless sins, O most immaculate one. Present

me untouched by all torments, and pray for me to the Master of all. Vouchsafe me to find the joys of heaven with all the saints. O most holy Virgin, hearken unto the voice of thine unprofitable servant. Grant me torrents of tears, O most pure one, to cleanse my soul from impurity. I offer the groans of my heart to thee unceasingly, strive for me, O Sovereign Lady. Accept my service of supplication and offer it to compassionate God. O thou who art above the angels, raise me above this world's confusion. O Light-bearing heavenly tabernacle, direct the grace of the Spirit in me. I raise my hands and lips in thy praise, defiled as they are by impurity, O all-immaculate one. Deliver me from soul-corrupting evils, and fervently intercede with Christ, to Whom is due honour and worship, now and ever, and unto the ages of ages. Amen.[4]

Along the same lines is Kontakion 13, from the Akathist (to be chanted standing) praises to the *Theotokos*:

O all-praised Mother who didst bear the Word holiest of all the saints, accept now our offering, and deliver us from all misfortune, and rescue from the torment to come those that cry to thee: Alleluia![5]

The evangelical reader must judge for himself whether these prayers are in harmony with God's commandments and declarations that He alone is our God and Savior and that He does not share His glory with another (see Isaiah 44—46). In the Roman Catholic Church, Mary is considered the "neck" of the Body of Christ. Indeed, this is the nexus of the problem. No one other than Christ can occupy a position between us and God. It is a dogmatic article of faith that Christ the incarnate Word stands at the point where union is made between God and man. Jesus Christ—the Logos, God incarnate, the God-Man—is the only mediator for mankind. Orthodox theologian Alexis Kniazeff tells us that the doctrine of the universal mediation of Mary began to

---

4. Laurence Campbell, trans., *Prayer Book*, 4th ed. (Jordanville, NY: Holy Trinity Monastery, 2003), 21–23.
   5. Ibid., 311.

appear with Andrew of Crete, who died in AD 740.[6]

Worship in the Roman Catholic Church declined to the point that even Marian expert René Laurentin admits that the fifteenth century was a mediocre century. The people were no longer able to understand the Latin language used in the liturgy, so they sought comfort in their private devotions.[7] No wonder Bokenkotter says,

> It was at the Mass that the separation of clergy from people was made dramatically evident. While the Mass had retained its basic meal structure, even in the early centuries it began to move away from its original character as an action of the whole community. This tendency was intensified during the early Middle Ages. The people were gradually excluded from all participation, and the Mass became exclusively the priest's business, with the people reduced to the role of spectators. In the Medieval Mass the priest no longer wore his ordinary street clothes as he once did, but glided into the sanctuary draped in a heavily embroidered chasuble and began to whisper the prayers in a language no longer understood by the people. . . . Nor were they allowed to take the wafer in their hands, standing as they once did; now they had to kneel and receive it on the tongue, while the chalice was withheld from them.[8]

I myself often observed this before the Second Vatican Council encouraged using national languages in the Mass. In Europe, I observed people wandering around the church during Mass and kneeling before the statues of their favorite saints at side altars, lighting candles, or praying the rosary, seemingly unaware of the Mass being celebrated.

Prayer Ropes and Rosaries

Most Protestants know that Catholics repeat the "Hail Mary" prayer on each bead of a rosary as they meditate on the mysteries

---

6. Alexis Kniazeff, *La Mère de Dieu dans l'Eglise orthodoxe* (Paris: Cerf, 1990), 184. Kniazeff is an Orthodox theologian and professor at the Saint Serge Institute of Orthodox Theology.

7. René Laurentin, *Court traité sur la Vierge Marie*, 5th rev. ed. (Paris: P. Lethielleux, 1967), 80.

8. Bokenkotter, *A Concise History of the Catholic Church*, 145–46.

and events that took place during the Lord's life. Catholics also say an "Our Father" (the Lord's Prayer) as they begin a set of ten beads (called a decade) and then conclude with a "Glory Be." I will not go into any more detail than this, because the purpose of this section is to explain the prayer rope used by Orthodox Christians, especially monastics. The same principles apply to the rosary. These practices developed some time after the apostles died. It is right to question whether these devices follow Scriptural principles for Christian meditation and worship. When a person becomes a monastic in the Orthodox church, that person receives a prayer rope at the time of tonsure. Prayer ropes may have ten, fifty, one hundred, or more knots, usually made of black wool. The idea is to fulfill the apostle Paul's exhortation to pray without ceasing (1 Thess. 5:17).

The Orthodox believer is advised to practice his prayer rule in the morning and in the evening in a customary place in his home or monastery. This means he will pray before the icons, standing with head bowed, repeating the "Jesus Prayer" on each knot of the prayer rope. He will strive to shut out every distraction and thought from his mind, concentrating on the words "Jesus Christ, Son of God, have mercy on me, a sinner." (There is also a shorter form of this.) He says this prayer on each knot. He may even finish the last ten knots saying, "Most Holy *Theotokos,* save me." Or he could say the latter prayer on all the knots. In any case, the prayer rope and a prayer rule are given to a monk or a disciple by his spiritual director, who tells him how many prayer ropes, prostrations, and prayers he is to repeat to accomplish his prayer rule. This teaches the Orthodox Christian to be obedient, to pray, and to develop discipline, which are key factors in the life of these people. It is said that the time comes when the prayer will enter the heart and become automatic, continuous. I heard a Greek bishop tell the story of a young girl he knew who said the prayer during her sleep! When one arrives at this point, it is believed that the person has become united with God because the mind dwells constantly on Him. This union is *theosis,* divinization.

Many people attend services where they don't understand the language used in the liturgy; in this case they may repeat "the prayer" during the services. Those who can't attend services because of illness or who are illiterate say the prayer rope. A prayer rule is imposed by a spiritual father. It leads to undue subjection to men, but more importantly, it is disobedience to our Lord, Who said we are not to pray as do the "heathen." When our Lord gave us the Lord's Prayer (Matt. 6), He prefaced it with these words: "And when you pray, do not use vain repetitions as the heathen do. For they think that they will be heard for their many words. "Therefore do not be like them. For your Father knows the things you have need of before you ask Him" (vv. 7, 8).

Knowing that the Scriptures are God's Word to us, a wise person will listen to and obey them. Peter said in Acts 4:12, "Nor is there salvation in any other, for there is no other name under heaven given among men by which we must be saved." And 1 Peter 5:8, "Be sober, be vigilant; because your adversary the devil walks about like a roaring lion, seeking whom he may devour."

Judge for yourself what is true, traditional, Biblical worship. The evangelical must decide whether the ancient liturgical religions with the traditions we have been examining are following apostolic teaching. True faith is based upon God's Word, where pure worship is offered in spirit and in truth, and where real freedom and joy in the Holy Spirit are enjoyed!

CHAPTER 11

The Church Defined

IN CHAPTERS 4–7 WE LEARNED something about the history of the New Testament church. The Christian church is different from Israel in that she now has no outward, fleshly conditions such as circumcision of the flesh, nationality, language, armies, or national boundaries. The church is truly a spiritual nation, a chosen people who offer spiritual sacrifices, being a holy priesthood in which all the members form a tightly knit body (1 Pet. 2:9; Col. 2:2, 19). All those who have been born of God have received a new nature through the Savior Jesus Christ, God having made them "partakers of the divine nature" (2 Pet. 1:4; 1 John 5:20).

A person's way of life will be based upon one of two clear-cut authorities: the Word of God or the word of men. In fact, this book boils down to one simple idea: who or what directs one's life. Am I my own guide? Is my church my guide? Is my spouse my guide? Is my life inspired by a particular philosophy? Or do I strive to follow the Word of God as the only sensible rule of life? Do I really believe that God's Word is sufficient to lead me into a closer relationship with my Creator and peace with my neighbor? Here are four quotations from the book of praises, Psalms:

"Blessed are You, O Lord! Teach me Your statutes" (Psalm 119:12).

"Your word is a lamp to my feet and a light to my path" (Psalm 119:105).

"The entirety of Your word is truth, and every one of Your righteous judgments endures forever" (Psalm 119:160).

"Great peace have those who love Your law, and nothing causes them to stumble" (Psalm 119:165).

Identifiers: The Church, the Bride of Christ

God's New Testament people are very different from what people generally have in mind. Although often scattered, despised, and persecuted, they are identifiable. One identifying mark is that they all say the same thing. They speak the same language. What is this language? The Hebrew prophet Zephaniah answers, "For then I will restore to the peoples a pure language, that they all may call on the name of the Lord, to serve Him with one accord" (Zeph. 3:9). Many Christians think this passage applies only to Israel in the millennial Kingdom. Others, including me, think the passage is susceptible to the following interpretation: From the least of them to the greatest, God's people know their Lord, and their worship "in Spirit and truth" identifies them as His special possession. As one redeemed people, they have no inequalities in relation to salvation; they are no longer divided by racial or linguistic differences, by social pecking order, or as male or female. All Christians offer the same simple worship to God, through Christ the Lord (Gal. 3:27, 28; Eph. 4:1–6).

The reader will note that I am speaking of worship and am not using this text as an argument to support feminist goals in the church. The writer to the Hebrews describes Christians this way (Heb. 8:10, 11): "For this is the covenant that I will make with the house of Israel after those days, says the Lord: I will put My laws in their mind and write them on their hearts; and I will be their God, and they shall be My people. *None of them shall teach his neighbor, and none his brother, saying, 'Know the Lord,' for all shall know Me, from the least of them to the greatest of them*" (italics added).

This is not the church of the rich and the influential. Those people are usually part of this world, and Satan has no problem with them. But God's chosen ones? Satan seeks to annihilate them, for they are the seed of the woman, Christ's church, "called out" of Satan's world (Gen. 3:15; Rev. 12:17). They are not aligned with the governments, and they will never be received at the UN. You might possibly find them meeting in a rented hall or a small storefront, maybe worshiping in grass huts in Africa, or in someone's apartment in Iran or China. There is a difference between how the world sees and evaluates Christians and the way God sees them. Is not the church the Bride of Christ? Have her members not been washed in the blood of the Lamb? Do they not stand in white robes before God presenting themselves as living sacrifices, constantly resisting the world's overtures (1 John 2:15–17), prepared to die for their Lord (Rev. 7:9, 14–17)?

We need to review several Scriptural thoughts. First of all, the prophetic book of Revelation speaks of things past and things to come. Due to the nature of apocalyptic writing, there are numerous interpretations of this book, yet the general picture we get is quite clear. There will be continual warfare between God's children and the Devil's offspring (Matt. 10:17–25). John the Revelator paints the scene this way: "So the dragon was furious with the woman and left to wage war against the rest of her offspring—those who keep the commandments of God and have the testimony about Jesus" (Rev. 12:17, HCSB).

This picture of the Seed of the woman is a fulfillment of the prophecy found in Genesis 3:15. Although this verse speaks principally of Christ, it also includes all who belong to Christ Jesus, who, being joined to Him, have become part of the seed (Gal. 3:29). Should we imagine, therefore, that God's people will be the great, the high, and the mighty of this world? Or is it more in line with Christ's prediction that as they persecuted Him, they will also persecute His disciples, who will be hated by all nations for His name's sake (Matt. 10:17–25; 24:9; John 15:18–21)?

What a contrast with the glorious roles of the state churches whose pomp and ceremonies dazzle crowds so much that the prophetic description of true Christians is no longer recognizable! The members of the true church are often a scattered few, hiding in the caves and forests of a wilderness. On the other hand, those who have abandoned the Word of God for the word of men are the people in power, the persecutors of the "little flock." Although unpleasant to many, the truth is that the true church is not always a visible organization, but she is composed of all those whose names are written in the Lamb's Book of Life (Phil. 4:3; Rev. 3:5; 13:8; 17:8). God knows them all and sees them as victorious believers who belong to Him. This is why many in the church visible are not God's, while some of those not meeting with us locally are. This is God's choice, not ours. God can call a man on a deserted island and make him a member of Christ's Body, and his Body is His church! God sees the members of Christ's Body as gathered in Heaven as part of that harvest of good wheat, although not yet garnered in the heavenly storehouse (Heb. 12:22, 23). This is the true church, often invisible to mankind but known to God. The various denominations may have both wheat and tares as members, but the task of separating them has been given to the angels who will separate the weeds (tares) from the wheat.

It is possible to reduce the Scriptural teaching to a few short sentences in question form. If Christ's disciples be few, weak, and scattered, are they any less His disciples? He bought them by His blood; are they not precious in His sight? Does He not see them as His flock although weak, suffering, interned in camps, unable to meet with others? Are they not Christ's friends (John 15:15), no matter how the world views them? Will they not bear fruit due to being the branches abiding faithfully in Him? Are they not His elect, known to Him from all eternity (Eph. 1:4)? Does Christ not see them as already with Him in Heaven (Heb. 12:23)? Does the church exist because it has an external, visible organization, or because her members are God's children? Are they not contenders for the apostolic deposit of faith (Jude 3)? So, what role do true faith and practice play? Revelation 2 gives Christ's answer: "I know your works, your labor, your patience, and that you cannot bear those who are evil. And you have tested those who say they are apostles and are not, and have found them liars; and you have persevered and have patience, and have labored for My name's sake and have not become weary" (vv. 2, 3).

Finally, the names of the wicked are not written in the Lamb's Book of Life (Rev. 13:8). Would it not be wise, therefore, for us to examine ourselves to see whether we really belong to the "household of faith" (Gal. 6:10; 2 Cor. 13:5)? The converts to the liturgical churches oblige us to contrast what we have written above with their liturgical churches' doctrines and practices. Who are the ones walking in "spirit and truth," faithful to the doctrine of the Lord and His apostles?

God Does Not Inhabit Material Temples

God dwells in the heavens. He is pure spirit and desires that we worship Him in spirit and in truth. Because He is infinitely superior to us in His essence, we finite creatures cannot comprehend God beyond what He has deigned to reveal to us. The Scriptures and His visible creation demonstrate His majesty, power, holiness, omniscience, justice, love, and unmerited favor (grace). He does not live in temples made by men, and we cannot see Him or touch Him. Although all this is true, God the Father has revealed Himself to us in a very personal way through His Son, Jesus Christ. His Son took flesh so we might know the Father through knowing the Son: "All things have been delivered to Me by My Father, and no one knows who the Son is except the Father, and who the Father is except the Son, and the one to whom the Son wills to reveal Him" (Luke 10:22).

On another occasion, Jesus told His disciples that if they had known Him, they had known His Father too. He said that from then on, they did know Him and had seen Him. Philip said, "Lord, show us the Father, and it is sufficient for us." Jesus responded by asking whether Philip did not know Him even though He had been with the disciples for such a long time. Jesus then stated, "He who has seen Me has seen the Father; so how can you say, 'Show us the Father'?" (John 14:7–9).

Could it be that the majority of evangelicals considering becoming Orthodox or Catholic have lost touch with reality? Were they poorly instructed in the past, or have they never experienced the powerful reality of Christ's saving life? The apostle Paul wrote in the epistle to the Galatians that it is possible to forsake grace as the ruling principle in the Christian life. Consider what the apostle wrote to the Galatians who were looking to the law or were considering circumcision as necessary to be a true Christian: "You have become estranged from Christ, you who attempt to be justified by law; you have fallen from grace" (Gal. 5:4).

Yes, it is true that God manifested His presence in the Jewish temple through the Shekinah light over the ark of the covenant and through a cloud that filled the first temple at its inauguration, but such manifestations were only glimmers of the real tabernacle, or dwelling among us, which was yet to come. In John's Gospel we read, "And the Word became flesh and dwelt among us, and we beheld His glory, the glory as of the only begotten of the Father, full of grace and truth" (1:14). This doctrine is known as the incarnation of the Son of God. The word *dwelt* is pregnant with meaning for Bible students. That presence, that dwelling, called tabernacling, came about when God sent His Son to dwell temporarily among us so that we might come to know Him.

What a beautiful fulfillment of God's desire to dwell among us! He walked with Adam in the Garden; next, Noah walked with God; then God led His people out of Egypt and dwelt in the midst of Israel, His chosen nation. He commanded them to build a tabernacle so they could approach Him in worship. These events foreshadowed Christ's incarnation and dwelling among us, not just a theophany, as often occurred in the Old Testament, but actually living among men, to teach, to heal, to lead, to nourish, to save. Who would want to return to the ways of an earthly temple with screens and closed-off areas such as exist in the Orthodox church? Who prefers shadows to realities, types over antitypes? Christians understand that the prophecies are fulfilled in Christ (see Hebrews 1:1 and 2; Jesus Christ is identified as the antitype of the Seed, tabernacle, temple, sacrifices, kingdom, manna, rock, etc.). "For in Him dwells all the fullness of the Godhead bodily" (Col. 2:9).

Evangelicals who join the Roman Catholic Church or one of the Orthodox churches are actually returning to Old Testament ways of worship, to sacrifices and priesthood! These churches teach that God can be contained in bread and wine and kept within a gilded box or in a vessel in which the consecrated Host is exposed for the adoration of the faithful (i.e., a monstrance). Such thinking constitutes a rejection of the apostle Paul's declaration found in Acts 17:24 and 25. Paul said that God made the world and everything in it and is, therefore, Lord of heaven and earth. Further, He does not dwell in constructed temples. Neither is He "worshiped with men's hands, as though He needed anything, since He gives to all life, breath, and all things."

There is nothing to misunderstand here. I have described Christianity in its pristine, primitive simplicity. Those who build temples and tabernacles wherein God is supposed to dwell have returned to either Old Testament ways or pagan practices. They have rejected God's Word for their own imaginations. This is why they do not practice New Testament Christianity but a hybrid. Although John Henry Newman tried to get around this objection, at least he recorded the objections of several pagans to early Christianity before giving his own justification for these practices. Here is Newman's comment:

> In like manner Celsus objects that Christians did not "endure the sight of temples, altars, and statues;" Porphyry, that "they blame the rites of worship, victims, and frankincense;" the heathen disputant in Minucius asks, "Why have Christians no altars, no temples, no conspicuous images?" and "no sacrifices;" and yet it is plain from Tertullian that Christians had altars of their own, and sacrifices and priests."[1]

Quoting Gregory Thaumaturgus, Newman went on to compare the pagan gods and heroes who, having lost favor with the populace, were replaced with the new Christian saints and martyrs. He wrote,

> Nay, of the so-called gods, so utterly have the sacred places been destroyed, that not even their outline remains, nor the shape of their altars is known to men of this generation, while their materials have been dedicated to the shrines of the Martyrs. For

---

1. Newman, *An Essay on the Development of Christian Doctrine*, 370.

the Lord has introduced His own dead in place of your gods; of the one He hath made a riddance, on the other He hath conferred their honours. For the Pandian festival, the Diasia, and the Dionysia, and your other such, we have the feasts of Peter, of Paul, of Thomas, of Sergius, of Marcellus, of Leontius, of Panteleëmon, of Antony, of Maurice, and of the other Martyrs; and for that old-world procession, and indecency of work and word, are held modest festivities, without intemperance, or revel, or laughter, but with divine hymns, and attendance on holy discourses and prayers, adorned with laudable tears." This was the view of the "Evidences of Christianity" which a Bishop of the fifth century offered for the conversion of unbelievers.[2]

The churchmen believed they were Christianizing such practices, making Christianity more palatable to the pagans who in their idolatrous worship were accustomed to bells, incense, holy water, statues, and prayers addressed to various gods of war, fertility, and good fortune. Yes, pagan holidays were Christianized. The names of pagan deities were exchanged for the names of saints and martyrs who were the new celebrated heroes. Not only did liturgical development occur, but pagan temples were replaced by "Christian" temples, pagan gods by "Christian gods," pagan customs, festivals, and practices were introduced into God's holy place, among the chosen people of God.[3] The transformation of Christianity proceeded apace, and soon uniformity was imposed and objections and protestations were outlawed. The house of God became a house of merchandize: the centers for pilgrimages grew famous; the commerce in icons, statues, and rosaries added to the financial capitalization of Christianity. Anyone who has visited Lourdes, France, a center of Marian devotion, has seen the streets lined with boutiques selling all these items and more.

---

2. Ibid., 375–76.
3. Modifications like these also took place in Israel. Idolatry replaced the pure worship of Yahweh in the very house of God, and the priests were the leaders in it. See Ezekiel 8 and 9.

CHAPTER 12

Should We Reject Sacerdotalism?

ERRIAM-WEBSTER DEFINES *sacerdotalism* as the doctrine "that assumes a necessity for an authorized priesthood as a mediator between men and their divine needs or aspirations." In the sacerdotal system, only priests can commune directly with God. Priests, it is believed, "exercise within the Church a function of the apostles. They are empowered to perform the ministry of the Word, by which men are formed into the People of God. They catch up and draw into the Eucharistic Sacrifice the spiritual sacrifice of the common priesthood of the faithful."[1] This chapter examines practices that are part of sacerdotalism. Evangelicals who are considering the ancient churches must ask themselves, How should I respond to the sacerdotalism in these churches? Please consider the following.

The Eucharist: Sacrificing and Eating Jesus Christ

The ancient churches believe they actually handle God when they take Communion in their hands or mouths. And what is more incredible, they think they sacrifice their God Jesus Christ upon their altars, and then they eat God. Is this an exaggeration? No! Roman Catholics believe they consume the resurrected Christ, body, soul, and divinity. Yes, they truly believe this. They teach that the Divine Liturgy (the

---

1. Walter M. Abbott, ed. *The Documents of Vatican II* (New York: The America Press, 1966), 535.

Mass) is a sacrifice and that the bread and the wine become the body and the blood of Christ, which they take in their hands and consume. You are invited to read the official doctrine of the Catholic Church in the *Catechism of the Catholic Church.*

> The sacrifice of Christ and the sacrifice of the Eucharist are one single sacrifice: "The victim is one and the same: the same now offers through the ministry of priests, who then offered himself on the cross; only the manner of offering is different." "And since in this divine sacrifice which is celebrated in the Mass, the same Christ who offered himself once in a bloody manner on the altar of the cross is contained and is offered in an unbloody manner. . . . This sacrifice is truly propitiatory."[2]

According to the church, the mode of Christ's presence under the Eucharistic species is unique. It raises the Eucharist above all the sacraments as "the perfection of the spiritual life and the end to which all the sacraments tend." The church affirms that the body, blood, soul, and divinity of the Lord Jesus Christ—that is, the whole Christ—"is truly, really, and substantially contained" in what is called "the most blessed sacrament" of the Eucharist. Further, this presence is called "real," although that is not intended to exclude the other types of presence as though they could not be real too, "but because it is presence in the fullest sense: that is to say, it is a substantial presence by which Christ, God and man, makes himself wholly and entirely present."[3] Further, "by the consecration the transubstantiation of the bread and wine into the Body and Blood of Christ is brought about. Under the consecrated species of bread and wine Christ himself, living and glorious, is present in a true, real, and substantial manner: his Body and his Blood, with his soul and his divinity (cf. Council of Trent: DS 1640; 1651)."[4] These statements are clear enough; what other conclusions could be drawn than those already stated?

---

2. *Catechism of the Catholic Church,* #1367.
3. Ibid., #1374.
4. Ibid., #1413.

What are the consequences of such doctrines? If the churches' beliefs regarding the bread and the wine were true, the digestive system would consume the flesh and blood of Christ (God), breaking Him down into chemicals that are afterward evacuated along with other wastes. I truly find this too gross to imagine and extremely distasteful to even mention, but I feel compelled to do so. Please pardon me for saying it. Catholic speakers often state that after one has received Communion, the Eucharist remains about fifteen minutes within the communicant. Is this an attempt to sidestep the obvious?

If these ancient churches really believed the Scriptures (*sola scriptura*), they would never teach people that their church is a temple where sacrifices are offered daily. They would teach their members that Christ was sacrificed once for all time, that His sacrifice was a perfect atonement for sins, and that there is no need to repeat it. The only command the disciples received was to *remember* it. These ancient churches tell us they are celebrating the one sacrifice made on Calvary's cross. Then the Orthodox tell us that during the Divine Liturgy they are united with the heavenly kingdom, where time is no more, and so Christ's one sacrifice is made present to those in attendance. But these are only words and metaphysics, lofty, but not in harmony with the Scriptures, because they teach that Christ is truly sacrificed during the liturgy. Contrary to this, the writer of the letter to the Hebrews told the first-century Christians:

> By that will we have been sanctified through the offering of the body of Jesus Christ once for all [Gr. ἐφάπαξ, *ephapax*]. And every priest stands ministering daily and offering repeatedly the same sacrifices, which can never take away sins. But this Man, after He had offered one sacrifice for sins forever, sat down at the right hand of God, from that time waiting till His enemies are made His footstool. For by one offering He has perfected forever those who are being sanctified. (Heb. 10:10–14)

The Greek word *ephapax* is found five times in the New Testament.[5] It means "once"; that is, "a single time." Why not just listen to God's Word? Here is another pertinent passage about Christ's offering in the epistle to the Hebrews: "Who does not need daily, as those high priests, to offer up sacrifices, first for His own sins and then for the people's, for this He did once for all when He offered up Himself" (7:27). A priesthood being a special class in the church enjoys special powers and privileges. One has a right to wonder if this may be the reason for its having been adopted so quickly, so easily. According to Roman Catholic priest Newman Eberhardt, "The fruits of redemption are to be applied to men through the sacraments. . . . These sacraments are administered by men endowed with Christ's powers."[6]

Theosis, or Deification: Struggling to Become God or 'Gods'

The Orthodox church teaches that divinization is possible only through the church's sacraments, the Divine Liturgy, prayer, and asceticism, the goal being to become a "god," that is, "godlike." Irenaeus, in *Against All Heresies,* is the earliest church father to speak of this. The gist of it can be found in the preface to Book V, where he said, "The Word of God, our Lord Jesus Christ, who did, through His transcendent love, become what we are, that He might bring us to be even what He is Himself."[7]

Jack D. Kinneer is a Presbyterian who attended St. Vladimir's Orthodox Seminary in New York State. Here is his understanding of the doctrine of *theosis*:

> First, in my experience, the Orthodox do not understand justification by faith. Some reject it. Others tolerate it, but no one I met

---

5. Compare the following occurrences of this word in the New Testament, where it always means "once" (Gr. ἐφάπαξ, *ephapax*): Rom. 6:10; 1 Cor. 15:6; Heb. 7:27; 9:12; 10:10.

6. Newman C. Eberhardt, *A Summary of Catholic History,* 2 vols. (St. Louis: Herder, 1961), 1:43–44.

7. Irenaeus of Lyons, "Irenæus Against Heresies," 5, in *The Apostolic Fathers with Justin Martyr and Irenaeus,* The Ante-Nicene Fathers, 1:526.

or read seemed to really understand it. Just as Protestants can make justification the whole (rather than the beginning) of the gospel, so the Orthodox tend to make sanctification (which they call "theosis" or deification) the whole gospel. In my estimation, this is a serious defect. It weakens the Orthodox understanding of the nature of saving faith.[8]

This touches the heart of the theological errors in the Orthodox church. This is why I decided I could no longer remain a member of the Orthodox church. If a church is correct in some of its beliefs but is in error on the doctrine of salvation, it is time to look elsewhere, because salvation is the whole point of Christ's incarnation and the Bible's message. Unfortunately, the Orthodox church has confused *theosis* with sanctification. The result is bondage to burdensome unscriptural practices that diminish the joy one should experience from a true union with Christ.

Kinneer is not quite clear enough in the paragraph quoted above. He says that "the Orthodox tend to make sanctification (which they call 'theosis' or deification) the whole gospel." *Theosis* does involve sanctification, but we have seen that *theosis* is the terminus ad quem, the goal of a Christian's struggle for salvation. *This is what is wrong with Orthodoxy!* Progressive sanctification is what takes place in a Christian's life as he matures in the faith. The Orthodox church teaches that Christians must cooperate *with* God's work *in order to be* saved; this cooperative effort is called *synergy*. For them, salvation is a process requiring man's effort, often called struggle.

The Scriptures teach that salvation is by faith alone and by grace alone, that eternal life is a present experience because of the believer's union in Christ Jesus. The Bible also tells us that we must be holy even as God is holy (1 Pet. 1:15, 16). This is known as the doctrine of sanctification, a growth in grace, a maturing to become more like

---

8. Jack D. Kinneer, "A Calvinist Looks at Orthodoxy," in *New Horizons,* a publication of the Orthodox Presbyterian Church. (http://opc.org/new_horizons/calvinist_on_orthodoxy.html). The church site is http://opc.org.

Christ. It is definitely not a question of Christians becoming God or gods because they are His adopted children (Gal. 4:5), who, although they have a human nature, have received a new kind of life, eternal life. The apostle John wrote, "And this is the testimony: that God has given us eternal life, and this life is in His Son. He who has the Son has life; he who does not have the Son of God does not have life. These things I have written to you who believe in the name of the Son of God, that you may know that you have eternal life, and that you may continue to believe in the name of the Son of God" (1 John 5:11–13).

We do not receive God's nature (essence), but a new nature when God restores our sinful souls to a blessed communion with Him. It is indeed a resurrection from the dead! The Holy Spirit indwells us, taking up residence in our spirits (John 14:16, 17, 23; 1 Cor. 6:19, 20). Our soul is spiritual and proper to us, therefore adequate for the life we shall experience in eternity. We never become a part of God, but "we shall be like Him" when Christ returns to take us up, incorruptible and immortal (1 John 3:2). Until then, the fight against the flesh, the "old nature" or "old man," continues (Eph. 4:22, 24; Col. 3:9).

In an attempt to review briefly the Orthodox church's teaching on man's deification, I am avoiding copious footnoting. First point: Orthodox scholars teach there is a difference between God in His essence, which we will never know, and God in His activities or operations, which we experience. God is super-essence, unknowable. According to Orthodox theology, here is the problem: How can man know God and attain to union with the unknowable, the unattainable? Again, this reminds us of Neoplatonism, although the Orthodox church rejects such a comparison. Yet several Orthodox theologians have admitted a similarity does exist. This Gordian knot was something over which Irenaeus struggled.

Iranaeus sought to answer the problem posed by gnostic syncretists who claimed secret knowledge of these matters. This explains Irenaeus's statement cited above: "The Word of God, our Lord Jesus Christ, who did, through His transcendent love, become what we are, that He might bring us to be even what He is Himself." The gnos-tic teachers obliged Irenaeus to emphasize the reasons for Christ's incarnation. A little later, the famous Athanasius of Alexandria in a small treatise called *On the Incarnation,* wrote, "He, indeed, assumed humanity that we might become God" (section #54). This is the goal of deification as explained by Dumitru Staniloae, an Orthodox theo-logian from Romania, who wrote, "This greatest possible union with God wherein the fullness of God is stamped upon the human being, yet without the human being thereby being dissolved into God—this is the human being's deification."

Staniloae explains how one receives knowledge of God and how deification occurs: "In his descent to us, God communicates to us in modes adapted to our condition something of what he is in fact, lead-ing us to stages which correspond more and more to himself."

Now we need to see what man does to receive these divine activities, also called energies. According to the ancient churches, Christians are united to Christ through baptism. Also in the Eucharist, Christ gives Christians His flesh and blood to maintain spiritual life; in eating Him *He assimilates* the worshiper, not the worshiper Him. At baptism sins are forgiven, and the baptized receive a new nature that restores the image of God in them. As life goes on, Christians fre-quently fall short of God's perfect standard. This is where the struggle occurs. Asceticism is struggle involving prayer, fasting, abstinence, and obedience to a spiritual father, or director of conscience. This is how the Orthodox Christian fights against the passions of the flesh and becomes more receptive to spiritual things. Such a person is, according to the church, climbing the rungs of a spiritual ladder as he becomes more obedient, more Godlike. The idea is to put the flesh to death in order to live more fully the spiritual life. When an Orthodox Christian falls into sinful acts or omissions of doing God's will, the sacrament of penance (confession) serves to restore friendship and union with God.

The Orthodox church's calendar lists the various fast days and feast days. Major feasts are preceded by strict fasting, or abstinence from wine and oil (signs of joy), fish, dairy, and meat products as well as sexual relations. When some fast periods allow fish, oil, and wine but no meat or dairy, increased giving or sharing with the poor is suggested. The idea is to return to the type of eating and living that Adam and Eve enjoyed in the Garden of Eden before sin came into the world. The Orthodox Christian eats simple vegetables without olive oil. It is believed that fasting helps him avoid lethargy during prayers and is a means of combating fleshly desires. If someone can resist certain foods—so the reasoning goes—he can learn to master his body and the animal passions that take his mind off spiritual matters. Later, when the feast or celebration arrives (for example, Easter), Orthodox Christians enjoy a feast of foods such as lamb, wine, oil, and ouzo or vodka (depending on their ethnic origins or the church's affiliation). To prepare for feasts like Pascha (Easter) or Nativity (Christmas), the Orthodox adherent should fast, go to confession, and attend a greater number of liturgical services. Afterward, he can joyfully partake of the Eucharist and celebrate the feast day. This lifestyle has promoted the publication of many cookbooks to help the Orthodox prepare tasty foods and desserts without olive oil and/or milk products and still remain obedient to the fasting rules. A number of Orthodox people are vegetarians, which makes keeping the fasts much easier.

I don't believe this fasting is a sign of true spirituality. It can be nothing more than a sign of strong willpower. Before going to a restaurant or accepting an invitation to a home, the faithful Orthodox Christian checks his liturgical calendar. He prepares his day and his menu according to the calendar. Think of the office parties and the times he has to refuse to eat or drink certain foods. This can mark him as odd, but many Orthodox gladly do it.

Will evangelicals really find joy and liberty in Orthodoxy such as they experienced when they came to know Jesus Christ through God's grace? Each individual will answer according to his own experience. As for me, after a number of years in Orthodoxy, I began to long for the freedom I had once enjoyed in my evangelical faith when knowing Jesus Christ was real freedom (Gal. 5:1). In fact, the Orthodox system is reminiscent of Buddhism and gnosticism with a disdain for the flesh. Evidently, these practices entered into the early church through the influence of the desert fathers, or monastics, and the common people's desire to emulate their practices.

In Orthodoxy, members are taught that it is possible to experience union with God through the practice of the Jesus Prayer and obedience to a spiritual father. Progress toward *theosis* involves three stages: purification, illumination, and *theosis*. Accordingly, no one ever becomes God in essence (that is impossible), but the Orthodox Christian can be united to God through God's energies (divine activities). When the ascetic participates fully in the energies of God, he becomes one with God. This is how miracles are accomplished. An ascetic who constantly practices the Jesus Prayer ("Lord Jesus Christ, Son of God, have mercy on me a sinner" or the shortened form of it) arrives at the point where he is constantly in remembrance of God, never being separated from Him. He may possibly see a marvelous light during his prayers and become aware of things happening in faraway places. He may know about events not humanly possible to know, be able to read men's hearts and counsel them accordingly, and even foretell events. When an ascetic can accomplish these things, it is, says the Orthodox church, because he has been *divinized* or *deified* in this life; this is *theosis*. This goal is set before all Orthodox Christians, but most never achieve it. They will, therefore, have to wait for Heaven to experience it. The deified Christian, says the church, is a *real* Christian, a person who has *truly* experienced Christ and is one with Him. Because he is deified, he is qualified to guide other souls to salvation.

Daniel B. Clendenin is an evangelical scholar who taught in Russia and knows Orthodoxy from firsthand observation. His book *Eastern Orthodox Christianity* is a good summary of Orthodoxy and the attraction it holds for evangelicals who are dissatisfied with the contemporary worship styles in Protestantism. In his chapter "The Deification of Humanity," Clendenin examines Orthodoxy in a respectful manner. He is not as critical as I am, but his purpose in writing is also different from mine. He is an academic and writes as one. Bear in mind, he is not a former member of the Orthodox church and has not experienced that faith as I have. I invite readers who wish to investigate the matter further to consult Clendenin's book and then go on to read either the Orthodox theologian Vladimir Lossky or Metropolitan Hierotheos of Greece.[9]

I have not yet undertaken a thorough rebuttal of the Orthodox church's doctrine of *theosis* because I deemed it important to first introduce the reader to the teaching. Nevertheless, we shall return to the subject later on and again in chapters 13 and 14. We must now turn our attention to other practices that strangers will consider odd for a church that claims apostolicity.

Other Doctrines and Practices

Eucharistic Adoration

Eucharistic adoration is a late practice in the development of doctrine in the Catholic church. It is clearly a new doctrine. Although attempts have been made to trace the adoration of the host (bread) to very early times, they are not convincing. It is clear that popular Eucharistic devotion had grown to the point that in 1264 the pope promulgated the feast of Corpus Christi (Body of Christ). The monastic orders also played a big role in popularizing this worship.

In the Orthodox church, however, there is no Eucharistic hour for people to gather to adore what Roman Catholics call "The Blessed Sacrament." In his encyclical letter *Mysterium Fidei*, Pope Paul VI sought to base this Catholic practice upon ancient tradition by citing Augustine:

> Moreover the Catholic Church has held on to this faith in the presence in the Eucharist of the Body and Blood of Christ, not

---

9. Daniel B. Clendenin, *Eastern Orthodox Christianity, a Western Perspective*, 2d ed. (Grand Rapids: Baker Academic, 2003). See his chapter 6, "The Deification of Humanity," page 117. In-depth treatment can be found in chapter 10, "The Way of Union," in Vladimir Lossky, *The Mystical Theology of the Eastern Church* (Crestwood, NY: St. Vladimir's Seminary, 1976); and in Hierotheos Vlachos, *The Person in the Orthodox Tradition*, trans. Esther Williams (Levadia, Greece: Birth of the Theotokos Monastery, 1999) and *Saint Gregory Palamas as a Hagiorite* (Levadia, Greece: Birth of the Theotokos Monastery, 1997).

only in her teaching but also in her practice, since she has at all times given to this great Sacrament the worship which is known as Latria and which may be given to God alone. As St. Augustine says: "It was in His flesh that Christ walked among us and it is His flesh that He has given us to eat for our salvation. No one, however, eats of this flesh without having first adored it . . . and not only do we not sin in thus adoring it, but we would sin if we did not do so."

The Catholic Church has always offered and still offers the cult of Latria to the Sacrament of the Eucharist, not only during Mass, but also outside of it, reserving Consecrated Hosts with the utmost care, exposing them to solemn veneration, and carrying them processionally to the joy of great crowds of the faithful.[10]

Remember the thorough discussion of the words *latria, worship, dulia,* and *veneration* presented in chapter 10. The reformer John Calvin in his *Institutes of the Christian Religion,* Book IV, mentions that the apostles ate the bread and drank from the cup as Christ commanded them to eat and drink but that He gave no command to adore them.

In the Roman Catholic Church, the host (a wafer of unleavened bread) is placed in a "monstrance" that has a section in glass in the center for the wafer or host to be seen and adored.

It is important for the evangelical to grasp what is taught here. The person who worships the elements of bread or wine thinks he is worshiping Jesus Christ in the bread, which is supposed to *have been transformed into His flesh.* When the priest offers the host to the communicant, the priest says, "The body of Christ." Think of it! If transubstantiation never occurred—and it hasn't because it is not a Biblical teaching—would the worshiper be guilty of worshiping the creation (ordinary bread) rather than the Creator? Writing to the Roman church, Paul said, "They [barbarian nations] exchanged the truth of God for a lie, and worshiped and served something created instead of the Creator, who is blessed forever" (Rom. 1:25, HCSB).

To conclude this discussion of Eucharistic adoration, consider

---

10. Pope Paul VI, Encyclical Letter "Mystery of Faith," September 3, 1965.

what Jesuit priest Luis M. Bermejo says:

> In contrast with this ancient faith the practice of veneration of
> the Sacrament (c. 6 of Trent) is only a creation of the second
> millennium. [ft. 28].
>
> [ft. 28] Ironically, the first recorded instance of any such eucha-
> ristic veneration seems to come from England: Lanfranc,
> archbishop of Canterbury took the Bl. Sacrament in procession
> on Palm Sunday 1089 and this was the beginning of a sweeping
> tide of eucharistic devotions which proliferated exceedingly in
> subsequent centuries. . . . Late Popes (Pius XII, Paul VI) have
> tried to justify this development by having recourse to argu-
> ments of doubtful value, like the attribution of these devotions
> to "the inspiration of divine grace" (encyclical *Mysterium Fidei:*
> AAS 57, 1965, p. 770). There exists a Catholic propensity to easily
> assume that historical evolutions either in doctrinal or in devo-
> tional areas take place always under the guidance of the H.
> Spirit. . . . The same encyclical of Paul VI, in its desire to show
> that the veneration of the Eucharist sinks its roots in the early
> centuries, refers to testimonies of Hippolytus, Origen, Novatian,
> Cyril of Alexandria and Basil (cf ASS 57, 769–770). An impressive
> array of early witnesses, no doubt—until a careful check of all
> five references given shows that none of them has anything to
> do with the veneration of the Sacrament. . . . It is simply futile to
> look for supporting testimonies of the practice of veneration in
> the entire first millennium, for this search will only reveal a com-
> plete void. And this silence of the first millennium accounts for
> the fact that even today this practice is totally unknown among
> the Orthodox.[11]

Acceptance of Islam

Do Christians worship Allah? This is another matter that gives us
pause concerning the Roman Catholic Church. This church concedes
a privileged place to Islam when it declares that Muslims worship
the same God as Christians. In *The Catechism of the Catholic Church*

---

11. Luis M. Bermejo, *Towards Christian Reunion: Vatican I: Obstacles and Opportunities* (Anand,
India: Gujarat Sahitya Prakash, 1984; Lanham, MD: Univ. of America, 1987), 246–47.

under the heading "The Church's relationship with the Muslims," the Catholic church leaves no room for doubt. "The plan of salvation also includes those who acknowledge the Creator, in the first place amongst whom are the Muslims; these profess to hold the faith of Abraham, and together with us they adore the one, merciful God, mankind's judge on the last day."[12]

The Catechism obviously based this teaching on the Second Vatican Council document *Lumen Gentium* (chap. II, para. 16), which dogmatically states the same idea.

Another Vatican Council document also addresses the question of interfaith. What is the Catholic church's position vis-à-vis the non-Christian religions? Concerning Muslims, the Roman church tells us,

> The Church regards with esteem also the Moslems. They adore the one God, living and subsisting in Himself; merciful and all-powerful, the Creator of heaven and earth, who has spoken to men; they take pains to submit wholeheartedly to even His inscrutable decrees, just as Abraham, with whom the faith of Islam takes pleasure in linking itself, submitted to God. Though they do not acknowledge Jesus as God, they revere Him as a prophet. They also honor Mary, His virgin Mother; at times they even call on her with devotion. In addition, they await the day of judgment when God will render their deserts to all those who have been raised up from the dead. Finally, they value the moral life and worship God especially through prayer, almsgiving and fasting.[13]

Who can agree with the statements above except those upon whom necessity is laid because of living in Muslim lands and under their domination? Christians worship the true God, Who is a triunity, one in essence, but three in Persons. Muslims strongly reject the idea that God has a Son Who is one in nature with God the Father.

---

12. *Catechism of the Catholic Church*, #841.

13. Vatican Council II, *Nostra Aetate*, #3. Note: The evangelical reader may want to compare these Catholic statements with Muslim teaching. Islam denies that Christ's death was an atonement for our sins. Muslims do not believe that God could have a Son and they do not accept his deity. See, Charles R. Marsh, *Share Your Faith with a Muslim* (Chicago: Moody, 1975), 41–43, 54; David Gunn, "Understanding Islam, Reaching Muslims," in *Current Culture: A Biblical Understanding and Response*, ed. Alex Bauman (Arlington Heights, IL: Regular Baptist Press, 2015), 113.

In their holy book, the Quran, Sura nine, verses 30 and 31 say, "The Jews say, 'Ezra is the son of Allah'; and the Christians say, 'The Messiah is the son of Allah.' That is their statement from their mouths; they imitate the saying of those who disbelieved [before them]. May Allah destroy them; how are they deluded? . . . There is no deity except Him."

Does not the Roman Catholic doctrine make you uncomfortable? It did me when I was considering returning to the Catholic church in which I had been raised. I refused to accept such an idea. If you believe God has a Son Who died as an atonement for our sins, and if you worship one God in Trinity, you must question the Catholic church's doctrine. But the Catholic church insists she is comfortable with the idea that Muslims are included in God's plan of salvation. Does this mean the church is comfortable with this teaching even if the Muslims reject Jesus Christ as the *Son of God* Who said, "I am the way, the truth and the life"? Prospective converts should question the Roman Catholic Church's position because it is one more example of pragmatism without any basis in either the Holy Scriptures or history.

Another religious idiosyncrasy should strike evangelicals as odd: the Orthodox and Catholic practice of holding religious meetings with religions that deny the deity of Christ and joining them in prayers for peace (Assisi) or unity. New York after 9/11, Washington National Cathedral, and Jerusalem (2014) are just a few examples. Of course, we have read the excuses or reasons for it, but it is strange in light of God's prohibition against such activities:

> Do not be unequally yoked together with unbelievers. For what fellowship has righteousness with lawlessness? And what communion has light with darkness? And what accord has Christ with Belial? Or what part has a believer with an unbeliever? And what agreement has the temple of God with idols? For you are the temple of the living God. As God has said: "I will dwell in them and walk among them. I will be their God, and they shall be My people." (2 Cor. 6:14–18)

We are fast coming to the end of our lament, although there

remain several more items to mention. They are important to every-one because they demonstrate how the ancient churches have moved the markers, the boundaries of an apostolic faith, step by step along the road from A to Z. The central and most important act that takes place in the ancient churches' system is the Mass or Divine Liturgy. Such a sacrificial system demeans the "once for all" (Gr. ἅπαξ, *hapax*; Heb. 9:24–28; 10:10, 14) act of our Savior, Who having died once, ascended into Heaven and there presented His blood to His Father. How many times does Christ have to do that as if His death on Cal-vary's cross were insufficient? If one reads in the New Testament that Christ suffered *once* for sins (1 Pet. 3:18), he should ask, How many times has He suffered? *Once* means "once," thus it must mean that such a sacrifice will never be repeated, whether in a Mass or in a Divine Liturgy.[14] If Jude wrote that the faith was "once for all deliv-ered," how many times was the true faith given to the church (Jude 3)? Yes, I know that these churches teach it is the same sacrifice that is offered, never a different one, but this argument is rationalism and a justification for something that is clearly wrong.

The Communion service (Lord's Supper) is not a sacrifice in the sense of Christ being offered during the worship service; it is a spiritual memorial and a sacrifice of praise in which prayers and thanksgiving are offered to God *in remembrance* of our Lord's death on the cross (Heb. 13:15).

Feasts, Dietary Laws, and Fasting

In earlier chapters, we discovered that church leaders sought to heighten the mystery of the Eucharistic service when they decided to veil the altar area. Fasting and prayer had already been enjoined upon the people who had to prepare themselves for the reception of the Eucharist. Henry Chadwick writes, "Hippolytus accordingly enjoins on the faithful intense reverence for the eucharist. It should

---

14. Hapax is defined as follows: "Pert[aining] to a single occurrence, once; pert[aining] to a single occurrence and decisively unique, once and for all." William Arndt, Frederick W. Danker, and Walter Bauer, *A Greek-English Lexicon of the New Testament and Other Early Christian Literature* (Chicago: University of Chicago Press, 2000), 97. This word occurs fourteen times in the New Testament.

be received early before any other food, and the greatest care should be taken to see that nothing was dropped or spilt."[15]

Similarly, the Orthodox church requires preparation for Communion by keeping the fasts and confessing sins. Partaking of Communion is deemed necessary for the Orthodox Christian to make progress toward salvation. Augustine, in AD 412, writing against the Pelagians concerning the sacraments of baptism and the Eucharist, said,

> The Christians of Carthage have an excellent name for the sacraments, when they say that baptism is nothing else than "salvation," and the sacrament of the body of Christ nothing else than "life." Whence, however, was this derived, but from that primitive, as I suppose, and apostolic tradition, by which the Churches of Christ maintain it to be an inherent principle, that without baptism and partaking of the supper of the Lord it is impossible for any man to attain either to the kingdom of God or to salvation and everlasting life?[16]

Nothing could be clearer than this. A Christian is to be a communicant; the Eucharist is life for him.

Why is fasting so important in the Orthodox church? Here are a few items from a volume I have before me: Fasting bridles the desires of the flesh and it strengthens the will. It is a means of perfection, "a visible sign of our zeal and struggle to acquire the likeness of God and His angels"; fasting "strengthens and toughens the body and cleanses the soul."[17] Other spiritual writers tell us that fasting is a return to the life of Adam and Eve in the Garden, when they did not kill animals to eat their flesh. It reflects a desire for that time when mankind was in communion with God. Tradition, the Scriptures, and canon law are quoted, along with the church fathers to support fasting and its benefits.

---

15. Chadwick, *The Penguin History of the Church*, 1:266.

16. Augustine, *Anti-Pelagian Writings*, "A Treatise on the Merits and the Forgiveness of Sins and on the Baptism of Infants," Book 1, chap.34 [xxiv] in *Nicene and Post-Nicene Fathers*, First Series, 5:28; also, in William A. Jurgens, *The Faith of the Early Fathers*, 3:91.

17. Elder Cleopa, *The Truth of our Faith: Discourses from Holy Scripture on the Tenets of Christian Orthodoxy*, Peter Alban Heers, trans. and ed. (Thessalonica, Greece: Uncut Mountain Press, 2000), 142.

Although one may respect people who wish to become godlike or Christlike, it is necessary to be critical when examining their methodology. If the methods employed to reach "perfection" have more in common with the philosophical and oriental schools of religion than with Biblical practices, we should reject them. Are they contrary to the teaching in the Pauline Epistles? As I read the Scriptures when still an Orthodox Christian, a number of passages struck me concerning fasting. After looking at them quickly, I will offer only a few comments.

"For the kingdom of God is not eating and drinking, but righteousness and peace and joy in the Holy Spirit" (Rom. 14:17).

"But food does not commend us to God; for neither if we eat are we the better, nor if we do not eat are we the worse" (1 Cor. 8:8).

"You observe days and months and seasons and years. I am afraid for you, lest I have labored for you in vain" (Gal. 4:10, 11).

"Forbidding to marry, and commanding to abstain from foods which God created to be received with thanksgiving by those who believe and know the truth" (1 Tim. 4:3).

After an unbiased reading of these passages, how could anyone dispute that Christians are not to be overly concerned with certain foods? Believers know they are no longer under the Jewish ceremonial and dietary laws. (Of course, this doesn't mean we can go and ruin our health.)

Certainly other principles are articulated in Romans 14 and elsewhere, such as that we should not cause our brothers or sisters to stumble because of our overindulgence, and abstinence is preferable to scandal. We are to give thanks for what we have because we are neither gnostics nor Jews, neither Buddhist nor Hindu ascetics struggling for mastery over our bodies. Higher principles govern our walk with the Lord. Simply put, we allow Jesus Christ to live out His life through us (Gal. 2:22). This principle rules our daily conduct. We no longer lie because Christ is not a liar; we no longer steal because Christ is not a thief; and so forth. Monks in the Orthodox church—and I understand also that those under vows in certain Roman Catholic orders—never eat meat. The Christian approach to this subject is very different from the legalistic approach found in the ancient churches.

Deification, Divinization

A single verse in the New Testament has served as the basis for the ancient churches' teaching that Christians must struggle to become partakers or sharers in God's divinity. What, then, should we think about 2 Peter 1:4? Here is the passage in its context:

> Grace and peace be multiplied to you in the knowledge of God and of Jesus our Lord, as His divine power has given to us all things that pertain to life and godliness, *through* the knowledge of Him who called us by glory and virtue, by which have been given to us exceedingly great and precious promises, that through these *you may be partakers of the divine nature*, [Gr. γένησθε θείας κοινωνοὶ φύσεως] having escaped the corruption that is in the world through lust. (2 Pet. 1:2–4, italics added)

This passage in 2 Peter tells us that we become partakers of the divine nature through the "great and precious promises," not through works or personal efforts, as the ancient churches repeatedly tell us. End of discussion!

As already stated, the Orthodox church's teaching on asceticism and the emphasis placed on "struggle" to attain a degree of sanctity *in this life,* that is, to become more like Christ, is closely related to her teaching on salvation. We need to understand the Orthodox mind-set through a better knowledge of Orthodox teachings.

For a Christian, fasting serves the purpose of freeing him from physical cares in order to keep his mind fixed on Christ through prayer.[18] The Orthodox do not reject the Biblical passages on fasting, but they tend to place the emphasis elsewhere. For example, see how they read Paul's statement in 1 Corinthians 13:8–10. According to the Orthodox interpretation of this text, personal knowledge of God is achievable in this life through unceasing prayer and asceticism. When

---

18. Positive references to Jewish and Christian fasting are Matt. 4:2; 6:16–18; 17:21 (KJV); Luke 2:37; Acts 10:30; 13:2, 3; 14:23; 1 Cor. 7:5.

an ascetic sees God as uncreated light, he has attained deification, or divinization, as mentioned in 2 Peter. Ninety-nine percent of Orthodox church members are not going to experience this "blessing." But Orthodox teaching maintains that a person who attains to deification has been cured of his sin, has been healed, and has now attained to the *likeness* of God (Gen. 1:26). This disappoints a lot of people who would like to experience this blessing; who have tried through endless repetition of the Jesus Prayer and through ceaseless fasting, etc., to achieve their goal but have not; and who will never attain to such a degree of perfection and holiness. Another Orthodox description of *theosis* may prove helpful here:

> Man, who was created "in the image and according to the likeness" of God, acts as a mirror (ἔσοπτρον) that resonates or reflects God Himself. The person who reaches perfection becomes god in all things, "without the identification of nature." This, however, becomes possible only when the mirror's (ἔσοπτρον) surface is clean. Whatever is on this surface, not only a black mark or dust, but also valuable gems or pearls, prohibits the proper reflection, or, at best, creates misshapen refractions.

> The monk's goal is his release from every worldly obstacle: his liberation from passions, belongings, and his own will. It is complete kenosis and it is to this end that the three monastic virtues: virginity, poverty, and obedience, are directed. Obedience in particular, which is the chief monastic virtue, aims at perfect kenosis and humility. In fact, no virtue is an end in itself, but is the means for the cultivation of humility; that is, man's complete release from everything that separates him from God and neighbor.[19]

This "emptying" (*kenosis*) has the familiar ring of the ancient mystery religions. It is amazing how such descriptions can sound almost right to an interested party, but something is not quite right. In contrast, the Scriptural method of sanctification is *filling*, not

---

19. Herman A. Middleton, *Precious Vessels of the Holy Spirit: The Lives and Counsels of Contemporary Elders of Greece*, 2d ed. (Thessaloniki, Greece and Ashville, N.C.: Protecting Veil, 2004), 29.

emptying. We are told that we should be filled with the Holy Spirit (Eph. 5:18).

What does "partakers of the divine nature" mean in 2 Peter? A simple, clear explanation was given by John Gill, a Baptist minister of the eighteenth century:

> Exceeding great and precious promises; meaning the promises of the new and everlasting covenant, of which Christ is the Mediator, surety, and messenger; and which are "exceeding great", if we consider the author of them, who is the great God of heaven and earth, and who was under no obligation to make promises of anything to his creatures; and therefore must arise from great grace and favour, of which they are largely expressive, and are like himself; are such as become his greatness and goodness, and are confirmed by his oath, and made good by his power and faithfulness: and they are also great, as to the nature and matter of them; they are better promises than those of the covenant of works; they are not merely temporal ones, nor are they conditional and legal; but as they relate to things spiritual and eternal, to grace here and glory hereafter, so they are absolute, free, and unconditional, and are irreversible and unchangeable; and they answer great ends and purposes, the glory of God, and the everlasting good and happiness of his people; and therefore must be "precious", of more value and worth than thousands of gold and silver, and to be rejoiced at more than at the finding of a great spoil, being every way suited to the cases of God's people, and which never fail. The end of giving them is, that by these you might be partakers of the divine nature; not essentially, or of the essence of God, so as to be deified, *this is impossible, for the nature, perfections, and glory of God, are incommunicable to creatures;* nor, hypostatically and personally, so as the human nature of Christ, in union with the Son of God, is a partaker of the divine nature in him; but by way of resemblance and likeness, the new man or principle of grace, being formed in the heart in regeneration, after the image of God, and bearing a likeness to the image of his Son, and this is styled, Christ formed in the heart, into which image and likeness the saints are more and

more changed, from glory to glory, through the application of the Gospel, and the promises of it, by which they have such sights of Christ as do transform them, and assimilate them to him; and which resemblance will be perfected hereafter, when they shall be entirely like him, and see him as he is.[20]

Beautifully stated, but we must keep in mind that Gill is referring to the new birth by which we become God's children who bear the image of the Heavenly One and who are beginning their progress in sanctification to be conformed to Christ's glory (Rom. 8:29; Col. 1:26–29).

Justification

The principal error found in the Catholic and Orthodox systems is their confusion of salvation with sanctification. This leads to a salvation earned by faith plus works. No wonder they teach that a Christian once saved can be lost if ultimately salvation depends on the believer's works. Their sacramental theology leads to a third error: that a person is inherently just. This is called "intrinsic justification" received in baptism; the sacrament causes the desired end. Baptism becomes instrumental, the means by which the individual receives God's grace.

The Scriptural view is that Christ's justice or righteousness is imputed to everyone who believes in Him. This means that justification is imputed to a believer even though he is not righteous in himself and can never merit justification. It is imputed on the basis of the merits of Jesus Christ, Who alone paid the price for our sins. A person "in Christ" experiences sanctification and growth in the Spirit as he matures in his faith, becoming evermore conformed to the image of his Lord and Savior, Jesus Christ (Col. 1:28).

Comparing the two views, someone has said, "The Protestant trusts Christ to save him; the Catholic [or Orthodox] trusts Christ to help him save himself." Whereas faith plus works leads to justification in sacramental theology (sacerdotalism), according to the

---

20. John Gill, "2 Peter 1:3–4," *John Gill's Exposition on the Entire Bible* from the electronic edition found in E-Sword Bible software, copyright Rick Meyers (my italics).

Reformers' teaching, justification is imputed through faith alone. But it is not a faith that is alone, because works will follow just as surely as an apple tree produces apples (Eph. 2:8–10). Works will never earn Heaven for anyone, but they are proof of a genuine faith (James 2).

Differences between Sacerdotalism and New Testament Churches

The true church is built on the Rock (Matt. 16:18; 1 Cor. 3:11), Jesus Christ Himself. This church ever looks to its Lord for salvation and grace, protection and strength (Rom. 9:33). By God's grace a person who believes in the Christ (Messiah), Jesus, *has passed* from death to life (a "resurrection," John 5:24–30).[21] The members of this church are members of Christ's Body and are secure, because Satan is not able to overcome and defeat the One Who keeps His sheep (John 10). This doctrine is based upon our Lord's promise to Peter and to us, that "the gates of hell shall not prevail against it [αὐτῆς, feminine, i.e., the church]." This church is not a denomination or a sect, but God's elect. The apostle John gives us another witness to this encouraging truth: "For whatever is born of God overcomes the world. And this is the victory that has overcome the world—our faith. Who is he who over-comes the world, but he who believes that Jesus is the Son of God?" (1 John 5:4, 5)

Neither temples nor priests nor sacrifices can any longer satisfy either God or a child of God. The Apex of all prophecies, all prophets, and types has come. The Seed of the woman has come. The Prophet, King, and Priest has come; and He has fulfilled everything on our behalf. Hebrews 10:14 tells us that by one offering He has perfected in perpetuity the ones being sanctified. The purpose of this magnificent epistle revolves around the question, Will we, like the Judaizers, return to the elementary things of the past (Heb. 6:1–3)? The child of God should always answer no! Christ is superior to angels, priests, and sac-rifices. He is the final Word of God incarnate (Heb. 1:1–3; John 1:14, 17)!

---

21. "Has passed" is a verb, perfect, active, indicative, showing that what has happened in the past has continuing results in the present.

Addressing the prospective convert, we ask, Have you found sufficient reason to reject sacerdotalism and everything connected with it? Christianity is not just one among many religions; it is nothing more and nothing less than a living relationship with the Creator of the universe through His Son Jesus Christ, sent from Heaven to show us the way.

The Good News is that Jesus Christ saves us from our sins, granting (gifting) us everlasting life: "For the wages of sin is death, but the gift of God is eternal life in Christ Jesus our Lord" (Rom. 6:23). This chapter could be summarized by these wonderful words in Romans 3:24: "Being justified freely by His grace through the redemption that is in Christ Jesus"!

CHAPTER 13

The Worst of All Errors

IF YOU KNOW AND LOVE JESUS CHRIST, you also know He loved you before you ever loved Him and He has prepared a home for you! Yet are you wondering if you "made a decision for Him" without any real understanding of what the Christian life entails? Maybe you were very young, and you realize now that you had only wanted to please a parent or a friend. Perhaps you were caught up with the crowd in an emotional moment and never gave your decision the serious contemplation it deserved. This chapter may not answer all your personal questions, but hopefully it will address various issues relating to salvation and at the very least, point out where security and hope are found. Could anything be worse than someone being a devout religious person who never heard God's truth concerning salvation? That would be the worst of all errors.

The Gospel: Justification by Faith (Rom. 3:28)

Martin Luther calls justification "the article upon which the church stands or falls."[1] This article of faith was considered so important that men were willing to risk their lives while the Western church became embroiled in spiritual and physical warfare for several centuries. Thousands of lives were lost on both sides until political leaders decided that enough was enough. It behooves us,

---

1. Cited by R. C. Sproul in, "Introduction," Francis Turretin, *Justification*, ed. James T. Dennison Jr. (Phillipsburg, N.J.: P&R, Introduction copyright, R. C. Sproul, 2004), vii.

therefore, to not dismiss lightly these issues as of no consequence in these days of "live and let live." Times have changed, and many Protestants, Catholics, and evangelicals believe that the time has come for healing the divisions and making common cause together against the evils of our day.

The Roman Catholic Church has been engaged in a number of ecumenical meetings with Protestant churches, especially with Lutheran churches. In October 1999, news of a groundbreaking agreement broke after thirty years of Catholic-Lutheran dialogue on the doctrine of justification. Scholars analyzed the document, hoping it had put an end to a long and difficult separation. We shall first examine the issue of justification by faith and then the matter of whether it is possible for a person to know if he is truly saved.

We might once again consult the older but standard work by Ludwig Ott, a Catholic theologian who represents the traditional sentiments of the Catholic church. Ott writes that "without a special revelation nobody can with certainty of faith know whether or not he has fulfilled all the conditions that are necessary for achieving justification."[2] He also says that the Bible represents justification as the presence of a divine seed in an individual.[3] According to Catholic teaching, achieving justification becomes a difficult life experience: to know that one has a right standing with God, that one is finally just—should we say *safe and secure* in Christ—would necessitate a divine revelation. If this is true, how could anyone ever know that he is just or righteous before God?

These theological facts demonstrate why the "Joint Declaration on the Doctrine of Justification" (JDDJ) provoked serious discussions in Protestant-Evangelical circles. Theologians are still not agreed. Some of them recognize Roman Catholics as sharing the same faith, and they want to cooperate with them. Yet others oppose such fellowship, claiming that nothing has changed. What is the truth of the matter?

---

2. Ott, *Fundamentals of Catholic Dogma*, 262.
3. Ibid., 255.

A few brief paragraphs taken from the JDDJ should be sufficient:

4.3 Justification by Faith and through Grace

25. We confess together that sinners are justified by faith in the saving action of God in Christ. By the action of the Holy Spirit in baptism, they are granted the gift of salvation, which lays the basis for the whole Christian life. They place their trust in God's gracious promise by justifying faith, which includes hope in God and love for him. Such a faith is active in love and thus the Christian cannot and should not remain without works. But whatever in the justified precedes or follows the free gift of faith is neither the basis of justification nor merits it.

26. According to Lutheran understanding, God justifies sinners in faith alone (sola fide). In faith they place their trust wholly in their Creator and Redeemer and thus live in communion with him. God himself effects faith as he brings forth such trust by his creative word. Because God's act is a new creation, it affects all dimensions of the person and leads to a life in hope and love. In the doctrine of "justification by faith alone," a distinction but not a separation is made between justification itself and the renewal of one's way of life that necessarily follows from justification and without which faith does not exist. Thereby the basis is indicated from which the renewal of life proceeds, for it comes forth from the love of God imparted to the person in justification. Justification and renewal are joined in Christ, who is present in faith.

27. The Catholic understanding also sees faith as fundamental in justification. For without faith, no justification can take place. Persons are justified through baptism as hearers of the word and believers in it. The justification of sinners is forgiveness of sins and being made righteous by justifying grace, which makes us children of God. In justification the righteous receive from Christ faith, hope, and love and are thereby taken into communion with him. This new personal relation to God is grounded totally on God's graciousness and remains constantly dependent on the salvific and creative working of this gracious God, who remains true to himself, so that one can rely upon him. Thus justifying

grace never becomes a human possession to which one could appeal over against God. While Catholic teaching emphasizes the renewal of life by justifying grace, this renewal in faith, hope, and love is always dependent on God's unfathomable grace and contributes nothing to justification about which one could boast before God (Rom 3:27).

Perhaps this is not easy to understand. Like most documents, it is written in legalese, the interlocutors using language designed to minimize their differences in order to reach an accord. We shall try to cut to the chase to avoid getting lost in the details. The main point that stands out in a reading of the document is that according to the Catholic point of view, sanctifying grace (called "justifying" grace in the JDDJ) is necessary and is received in baptism. This grace is given to babies as well as to adults. Both the Lutheran and the Catholic churches speak of the importance of faith but baptize babies. This means they must answer the same question that an African bishop, Boniface, put to Augustine: How does one answer those persons who inquire how it is possible for babies to possess faith in order to receive baptism? Second, the Catholic church speaks of the role of the sacrament of baptism as the means by which sanctifying grace is conferred by God. It is not so difficult for these two groups to agree, because they both believe in baptismal regeneration. Here, the reader may wish to review this book's sections on baptism (chapters 4–6). Another question comes up because not all people within a particular denomination are united. The Catholic church faces this hurdle in its dialogues with Protestants of every stripe.

In the USA, the Lutheran Church–Missouri Synod offered this response to a question on the Joint Declaration:

> Rome historically has always taught that we are saved by grace, and grace alone. They emphasize that very strongly. The 16th century Council of Trent makes this point very clear. Thus, there is nothing new on this in the Declaration on this point, even though some Lutherans have made it sound as if Rome's words about grace signal some marvelous breakthrough.

What you probably have not heard is that the JDDJ very carefully avoid [sic] precise definitions of the words grace, faith, sin,
etc. That is no accident. Careful definition of those terms would
have shown how far apart our two churches actually are on the
doctrine of justification.

The problem with Rome's view of justification is that they view it
as a process, whereby we cooperate with God's grace in order to
merit eternal life for ourselves, and even for others (that is a para-
phrase of what the Catechism of the Catholic Church teaches).
They view grace as a sort of "substance" that God infuses into
us that permits us to do those works that are necessary in order
that we might earn more grace. The Bible describes grace as the
loving and favorable disposition of God; in other words, grace
is all about what God is doing and giving.[4]

The Missouri Synod's criticism of the document (third paragraph)
refers to Rome's view that justification is a *process*. Also, according
to Rome, grace is an infused "substance" that enables one to do good
works to earn or merit more grace. In my opinion, this is the heart of
the problem and what we are examining in this chapter and the next.

The Worst of Errors: Salvation by Faith + Works

The apostle Paul, that great expositor of the gospel, wrote to the
Christians in Rome, "Where is boasting then? It is excluded. By what
law? Of works? No, but by the law of faith. Therefore we conclude
that a man is justified by faith apart from the deeds of the law" (Rom.
3:27, 28).

Christians must defend this truth at all costs; they cannot afford
to compromise. Yet someone may say that Paul was speaking of the
Jewish law, which was terminated at Christ's death on the cross, that
church law is different, and that the church has the right to establish
such laws. It is a well-established New Testament principle that it
doesn't matter what law a person wishes to obey, Christians are

---

4. (My italics). The Missouri Synod Lutheran Church's reaction can be found at www.lcms.org/pages
/internal.asp?NavID=2212. The "Joint Declaration" we are discussing is widely available on the Internet.

justified *by faith,* not by works. If we said Paul meant we are not justified by works under the Old Testament law, what would be the difference if we now begin adding other kinds of law or laws for justification? In Romans 10:4, Paul explains, "For Christ is the end of the law for righteousness to everyone who believes." A person is justified by faith in the Lord Jesus. Justification—being made right with God—has nothing to do with any works. It is a spiritual work that God accomplishes through His grace. We are told in Titus 3:5–7 that it is "not by works of righteousness which we have done, but according to His mercy He saved us, through the washing of regeneration and renewing of the Holy Spirit, whom He poured out on us abundantly through Jesus Christ our Savior, that having been justified by His grace we should become heirs according to the hope of eternal life."

Could anything be clearer? This cleansing from sin is God's work; we are justified by His grace, not by any personal works or good deeds. Any thought of salvation by faith plus works would be a violation of God's Word and a sin against God. No wonder Paul introduced his letter to the Galatians in the following manner:

> Grace to you and peace from God the Father and our Lord Jesus Christ, who gave Himself for our sins, that He might deliver us from this present evil age, according to the will of our God and Father, to whom be glory forever and ever. Amen. I marvel that you are turning away so soon from Him who called you in the grace of Christ, to a different gospel, which is not another; but there are some who trouble you and want to pervert the gospel of Christ. But even if we, or an angel from heaven, preach any other gospel to you than what we have preached to you, let him be accursed. As we have said before, so now I say again, if anyone preaches any other gospel to you than what you have received, let him be accursed. (Gal. 1:3–9)

Anyone who strives to save himself by his own works or through his church's works has little faith in the sufficiency of God's work on his behalf. Stop and think for a moment about John 3:16, where we are told, "God so loved the world that He gave His only begotten Son, that whoever believes in Him should not perish but have everlasting life." Do we believe it? God gives, we receive (John 1:12)! This is the gospel message, and there is no better news anywhere. No wonder Christianity spread so fast! The suffering people of the Mediterranean world were overjoyed to learn that a Savior had come into the world.

Faith is the outstretched hand, the means by which we are justified, made right with God. The law was given to make the Israelites conscious of their need for a substitute sacrifice to atone for their sinful disobedience to God. The pagans often led debased and debauched lives, but they also felt the need to make sacrifices and offerings to placate their angry gods. The whole world lies in the Devil's grip and needs a Savior. Galatians 3:22 and Romans 3:10 confirm this. God gave His only Son as an atonement for our sins. Faith receives this fact like a trusting child who joyfully accepts a precious and long-desired present from his loving parents. That no one, Jew or Gentile, can boast of his own works or merits to earn salvation is clear from Romans 3:27–30: "Where is boasting then? It is excluded. By what law? Of works? No, but by the law of faith. Therefore we conclude that a man is justified by faith apart from the deeds of the law. Or is He the God of the Jews only? Is He not also the God of the Gentiles? Yes, of the Gentiles also, since there is one God who will justify the circumcised by faith and the uncircumcised through faith."[5]

This is what the Bible teaches. In the next chapter we will consider the Roman Catholic and Eastern Orthodox systems and what they teach about salvation.

---

5. Romans 3:27 from the NAB (Catholic Bible) is reproduced here below with its footnotes on the passage. Note also that the footnote in HCSB speaks of principle, and the same idea is expressed in the text of the NET (New English Translation).

"What occasion is there then for boasting? ‹1› It is ruled out. On what principle, that of works? No, rather on the principle of faith." ‹2›

(NAB notes, Rom 3:27):

‹1› [27-31] People cannot boast of their own holiness, since it is God's free gift (Romans 3:27), both to the Jew who practices circumcision out of faith and to the Gentile who accepts faith without the Old Testament religious culture symbolized by circumcision (Romans 3:29–30). ‹2› [27] Principle of faith: literally, "law of faith." Paul is fond of wordplay involving the term "law"; cf. Romans 7:21, 23; 8:2. Since "law" in Greek may also connote "custom" or "principle," his readers and hearers would have sensed no contradiction in the use of the term after the negative statement concerning law in Romans 3:20.

CHAPTER 14

The Roman Catholic and Eastern Orthodox Systems

D O ANCIENT CHURCHES actually teach that ecclesiastical rites and practices are necessary for salvation? Is salvation *in* and *through* the church? This is a serious core issue. Do legalism and superstitious teachings confuse salvation with sanctification? And, most importantly, do such teachings undermine the New Testament gospel? Although these issues were touched on in previous chapters, we will now cover them more in depth.

Is Roman Catholicism a works system, another gospel (Gal. 1:6–9)? There are Catholic and Orthodox theologians and apologists who think like Professor Peter Kreeft of Boston College. He believes that eternal life is a gift. Kreeft writes, "Perhaps God allows the Protestant/ Catholic division to persist not only because Protestants have abandoned many precious truths taught by the Church but also because many Catholics have never been taught the most precious truth of all, that salvation is a free gift of grace, accepted by faith."[1]

We could be misled if we did not know that according to official Roman Catholic teaching, mortal sin removes sanctifying grace and

---

1. Peter Kreeft, "Justification by Faith," chap. 44 in *Fundamentals of the Faith, Essays in Christian Apologetics* (San Francisco: Ignatius Press, 1998), 281.

destroys communion with God. According to the church, the Sacrament of Confession (also called Reconciliation) then becomes
necessary to restore grace and communion with God so the person
can avoid Hell. Works, whether sacramental or not, constitute an
integral part of the ancient churches' system for salvation.

In my desire to not misrepresent the belief systems of these
churches, I shall let them explain what they believe. It is easy for misunderstandings to arise between parties involved in serious dialogue.
It happens that people can use the same words but with different
meanings, or else they are not willing to admit what their interlocutor
is really saying. Others strive to synthesize two different views in order
to placate both sides. This is called compromise for the sake of peace.

Peter Kreeft is a Reformed Protestant convert to Catholicism. He
discusses one of the reasons behind his conversion in his comments
on the Catholic-Lutheran dialogue mentioned in chapter 13:

> For one thing, even if the two sides [i.e. Catholic-Lutheran] did
> disagree about the relationship between faith and works, they
> both agreed (1) that faith is absolutely necessary for salvation
> and (2) that we are absolutely commanded by God to do good
> works. Both these two points are unmistakably clear in Scripture.

> For another thing, the terms of the dispute are ambiguous or
> used in two different senses. When terms are ambiguous, the
> two sides may really disagree when they seem to agree because
> they agree only on the word, not the concept. Or the two sides
> may really agree when they seem to disagree because they agree
> on the concept but not the word. The latter holds true here. . . .

> But many Catholics to this day have not learned the Catholic and
> biblical doctrine. They think we are saved by good intentions
> or being nice or sincere or trying a little harder or doing a suf-
> ficient number of good deeds. Over the past twenty-five years I
> have asked hundreds of Catholic college students the question:
> If you should die tonight and God asks you why he should let you
> into heaven, what would you answer? The vast majority of them
> simply do not know the right answer to this, the most important

of all questions, the very essence of Christianity. They usually do not even mention Jesus!

> ... I remember vividly the thrill of discovery when, as a young Protestant at Calvin College, I read Saint Thomas Aquinas and the Council of Trent on justification. I did not find what I had been told I would find, "another gospel" of do-it-yourself salvation by works, but a clear and forceful statement that we can do nothing without God's grace, and that this grace, accepted by faith, is what saves us.[2]

Kreeft says salvation by "God's grace," he does not say "justification by faith alone," which makes all the difference in the world. Justification by *faith alone* was the Reformation cry that shattered Europe's religious unity but brought peace of mind to all believers in the gospel. Of course, Kreeft knows that the Council of Trent condemns anyone who dares to teach justification by *faith alone*. In the Catholic church, works are necessary *in addition to faith* for a person *to achieve* salvation. It is difficult to accept Kreeft's idea of Martin Luther. He says the educated "monk rediscovered a Catholic doctrine in a Catholic book"! If so, what does this say about the doctoral training he received in his church?

The Roman Catholic System

The Western church does not reject either faith or grace. The Catholic church says that these are two infused virtues that must be accompanied by works if a person is to be saved. She teaches that faith and grace are free gifts because one is washed of his sins, justified, and regenerated in (or by) baptism, which infuses faith, grace, and love into the soul. Later on, as a Christian lives his life and commits sins, he loses any just standing before God; he becomes guilt ridden. Grace, the supernatural life that was received in baptism, is lost, and only the Catholic church through the sinner's confession and penance can restore him to grace and communion with God. The

---

2. Ibid., 279, 280, 281.

struggle with sin is a lifelong struggle. A Catholic's (and Orthodox church member's) effort to merit salvation (which seems to me to be a reward for a good life) is called *synergy* because the person has to *cooperate* with God's work of salvation in him. Good works such as fasting, almsgiving, and the sacrament of Penance (also called Confession) are part of his life (cf. *Catechism of the Catholic Church* #1422–24).

During the 1500s, when people were invited to pay hard-earned money to buy indulgences for the reconstruction of St. Peter's Basilica in Rome, they were encouraged by the hope that an indulgence would shorten their time spent in purgatory. Purgatory was the place where, after death, the purging and cleansing of souls from the remaining stains of sin and the punishment due for those sins took place. Indulgences were supposed to remove the temporal punishment that remains after the guilt of sin had been forgiven. It did not matter that these sins had already been forgiven in the sacrament of Confession; satisfaction still had to be made. Indulgences were the Roman Catholic Church's invention to help the souls in purgatory.[3] They are still part of the Catholic church's teaching, although the doctrine has been revised somewhat. According to this teaching, it is possible to apply these benefits to people already dead.[4]

To avoid any beating around the bush, one should read the official documents of the Council of Trent. This so-called Ecumenical Council is important because it took place after the Reformation and because it was called to officially define the Catholic church's position on questions raised by the Reformers. As we are well aware, such documents are arduous to read; the time period and the style of writing are far removed from ours. Nevertheless, it is important to review several quotations from that famous council:

> The Decree Concerning Justification: (Sixth Session; the 13th day of January, 1547).

---

3. The Dominican preacher Tetzel, preached, "As soon as the coin in the basket rings, the soul out of purgatory springs." See, Newman C. Eberhardt, *A Summary of Catholic History,* vol. 2, section 22.

4. #1471 in, *Catechism of the Catholic Church,* and footnote #82 referring to CIC (*Codex Iuris Canonici*), canon 944.

Chapter IV: A brief description of the justification of the sinner and its mode in the state of grace.

In which words is given a brief description of the justification of the sinner, as being a translation from that state in which man is born a child of the first Adam, to the state of grace and of the adoption of the sons of God through the second Adam, Jesus Christ, our Savior. This translation however cannot, since promulgation of the Gospel, be effected except through the laver of regeneration or its desire, as it is written: Unless a man be born again of water and the Holy Ghost, he cannot enter into the kingdom of God.

Chapter XV, by every mortal sin grace is lost, but not faith.

Against the subtle wits of some also, who by pleasing speeches and good words seduce the hearts of the innocent, it must be maintained that the grace of justification once received is lost not only by infidelity, whereby also faith itself is lost, but also by every other mortal sin, though in this case faith is not lost; thus defending the teaching of the divine law which excludes from the kingdom of God not only unbelievers, but also the faithful [who are] fornicators, adulterers, effeminate, liars with mankind, thieves, covetous, drunkards, railers, extortioners, and all others who commit deadly sins, from which with the help of divine grace they can refrain, and on account of which they are cut off from the grace of Christ.

Canon 9. If anyone says that the sinner is justified by faith alone, meaning that nothing else is required to cooperate in order to obtain the grace of justification, and that it is not in any way necessary that he be prepared and disposed by the action of his own will, let him be anathema.

Canon 15. If anyone says that a man who is born again and justified is bound ex fide to believe that he is certainly in the number of the predestined, let him be anathema.

Canon 16. If anyone says that he will for certain, with an absolute and infallible certainty, have that great gift of perseverance even to the end, unless he shall have learned this by a special revelation, let him be anathema.

The chapters cited above state that justification is given in baptism and that grace is lost through mortal sin. The canons list the anathemas, or curses, effective against those holding contrary ideas. In the three canons listed above, condemned are those who claim that justification is by faith alone, that a Christian is elect and predestined to salvation (security of the believer), and that perseverance is guaranteed (again, the eternal security of the believer is condemned).

Of course, Protestants believe that works are a necessary part of the Christian life and indicate a holy walk with our Lord Jesus. The works add nothing to the salvation that we possess as one of Christ's lambs. Christ, the Good Shepherd, tells us, "My sheep hear My voice, and I know them, and they follow Me. And I give them eternal life, and they shall never perish; neither shall anyone snatch them out of My hand" (John 10:27, 28). The works are the fruit of God's Holy Spirit working in us. We who have already been made holy in Christ become ever more holy, more like our Savior, as we allow Him to work out his life in us and through us (Gal. 2:20; Col. 3:11).

This is what differentiates the two theologies, and it certainly is not "hair-splitting." Catholics make works in addition to faith necessary for salvation. They confuse sanctification, which is growth in grace, with salvation, which is God's redemptive work in us. The Catholic church teaches that "baptism confers the grace of justification."[5] The Bible teaches us that salvation, justification, and adoption as God's children are not due to any work of man or a church. Having been born again, God's children are called to grow in grace and obedience to God (godly works) (Eph. 2:8–10).

The Eastern Orthodox System

In the Orthodox church a Christian is encouraged to engage in spiritual *struggle* (Greek, *askesis, askeo,* "to do one's best") to be saved. We derive our English word *asceticism* from this Greek word. Examples of

5. Ott, 354.

the Orthodox teaching on asceticism are found in a four-volume work called the *Philokalia*, which means "love of what is good." This work is a collection of spiritual writings that describe the manner in which Orthodox Christians should live and practice "quietness," or "stillness" ("hesychasm," from the Greek *hesychia*), by praying the Jesus Prayer repeatedly and by imitating the lives of the saints and spiritual church elders. Through certain physical postures and sometimes breathing techniques, a disciple may acquire more quickly the desired goal. The idea is to go beyond words, images, and all mental ideas about God and to allow the prayer to enter the heart. At this point, it is believed, the ascetic experiences and *knows* God, the Unknowable One. The fasting, prayers, and liturgies will enable the Orthodox Christian to unite himself with his Creator. The purpose of Christian theology (knowledge of God) is to experience union with God, to *know Him*. The work of asceticism is chiefly practiced by monks and nuns and is undertaken under the guidance of a spiritual father or mother to avoid delusions that come from within the human heart or from Satan.

Justin Popovitch (d. 1979), a saint of the Serbian Orthodox Church, explains how a person is saved according to that church.

> The members of the Church, by living in it, live in these holy virtues and achieve their salvation, christification, deification and likeness to the God-Man according to the measure of their zeal.
>
> . . . A man enters into Christ through Holy Baptism, becoming christified throughout his life by means of the other holy mysteries [i.e. sacraments] and virtues. . . . All the virtues are essential to man for salvation. To attain salvation, man must strive for the ascesis of faith, love, prayer, fasting and every evangelical virtue. There is no salvation without faith, for without faith it is impossible to please God (Heb. 11:6). In the same way, there is no salvation without love, prayer, fasting, mercy and the other holy virtues. . . .

> Without Holy Baptism, there is no salvation. This is the unalterable dogma of salvation in the Saviour's theanthropic [i.e. God-Man] Church.[6]

With Justin Popovitch there is no beating around the bush; he tells us that "the Orthodox Church does not recognize the existence of other mysteries or sacraments outside of itself, neither does it recognize them as being mysteries, and one cannot receive the sacraments until one comes away from the heretical 'Churches,' that is to say the pseudo-Churches, through repentance to the Orthodox Church of Christ."[7] According to him and the majority of the Orthodox national churches, there is no salvation outside the Orthodox church.

Over time in the Orthodox church, gospel teaching was lost from view as the sacraments grew in importance to finally become the necessary means of salvation, and the church became the dispensing machine of the sacraments. Now we understand why Cyprian of Carthage wrote that there is no salvation outside the church.[8] This is true for both the Eastern Orthodox and the Roman Catholic Churches because in both, the church dispenses the grace necessary to salvation. The Catholic church even speaks of a treasury of merits that she is able to apply to the souls of those in purgatory. Would not these words of Paul to the Galatians apply to those who add to the gospel? "You who are trying to be justified by the law are alienated from Christ; you have fallen from grace!" (Gal 5:4, HCSB). What men and women desire is freedom, yes, but a freedom that is possible only in Jesus Christ.

A Lost Message?

I have not cited, and am not now citing, any church father or other ecclesiastical writer to prove the content of the true faith. I quote them from a purely historical point of view in order to document what a particular segment of the church was teaching at a specific period, because

---

6. Justin Popovitch, *The Orthodox Church and Ecumenism* (Birmingham: Lazarica, 2000), 71–72.

7. Justin Popovitch, *Orthodox Faith and Life in Christ,* trans. Asterios Gerostergios, et al. (Belmont, Mass.: Institute for Byzantine and Modern Greek Studies, 1994), 174.

8. Ott, 313; Cyprian, Ep. 73, 21.

another father or even the same father may hold a different opinion elsewhere. Life teaches us the same lesson; we ourselves change our opinions from time to time because of more learning and a wisdom that is acquired only with age and experience. I begin with Clement. In the following quotation, obvious references to the epistle of James and to the teaching of the apostle Paul on justification are identifiable. In this instance, Clement's teaching is balanced and sound.

His comment is found in his *First Epistle of Clement to the Corinthians* (ca. AD 96):

> Let Us Do Those Things that Please God and Flee from Those He Hates that We May be Blessed
>
> Seeing, therefore, that we are the portion of the Holy One, let us do all those things which pertain to holiness, avoiding all evil-speaking, all abominable and impure embraces, together with all drunkenness, seeking after change, all abominable lusts, detestable adultery, and execrable pride. "For God," saith [the Scripture], "resisteth the proud, but giveth grace to the humble." Let us cleave, then, to those to whom grace has been given by God. Let us clothe ourselves with concord and humility, ever exercising self-control, standing far off from all whispering and evil-speaking, *being justified by our works, and not our words.* For [the Scripture] saith, "He that speaketh much, shall also hear much in answer. And does he that is ready in speech deem himself righteous? Blessed is he that is born of woman, who liveth but a short time: be not given to much speaking." Let our praise be in God, and not of ourselves; for God hateth those that commend themselves. Let testimony to our good deeds be borne by others, as it was in the case of our righteous forefathers. Boldness, and arrogance, and audacity belong to those that are accursed of God; but moderation, humility, and meekness to such as are blessed by Him.
>
> We Are Justified Not By Our Own Works, but By Faith
>
> Whosoever will candidly consider each particular, will recognize the greatness of the gifts which were given by him. For from

him have sprung the priests and all the Levites who minister at the altar of God. From him also [was descended] our Lord Jesus Christ according to the flesh. From him [arose] kings, princes, and rulers of the race of Judah. Nor are his other tribes in small glory, inasmuch as God had promised, "Thy seed shall be as the stars of heaven." All these, therefore, were highly honored, and made great, not for their own sake, or for their own works, or for the righteousness which they wrought, but through the operation of His will. *And we, too, being called by His will in Christ Jesus, are not justified by ourselves, nor by our own wisdom, or understanding, or godliness, or works which we have wrought in holiness of heart; but by that faith through which, from the beginning, Almighty God has justified all men;* to whom be glory for ever and ever. Amen.[9]

When Clement says we are justified by faith, he is faithful to the apostle Paul's teaching. Still, this is not to say that all of those living during his time were just as faithful in maintaining the pure apostolic faith, in this or in any other matter. Has true faith ever been lost? No, for Christ's church depends upon it and is built upon it, but as time passed, the gospel was scarcely heard because of innovators who busied themselves with constructing a religion, and also because once church membership became fashionable, multitudes were entering the church.

Correcting Our Religious Philosophy

We have been studying two conflicting theologies, two different religious philosophies in spite of their both having much in common regarding the Trinity and the deity of Jesus Christ. We have contrasted the ancient churches' teaching on the sacraments, salvation, and tradition with the Holy Scriptures. We were able to distinguish the ancient churches from the Reformation's offspring, and easily so, because we perceived two different ways of professing and living their faith. Many Christians hear words like *Christ, Savior, cross, faith, Bible, apostles,* and *worship,* and they see no differences between denominations. They say, "They all believe in Jesus Christ and teach that He

9. *First Epistle of Clement of Alexandria,* chapters 30 and 32 in Ante-Nicene Fathers 1:13 (my italics).

died on the cross for us." In spite of this, the facts prove that we have been dealing with two different religious systems. It does not matter what someone's priest or favorite theologian says if that man is contradicting the official position of his church. People generally want to be nice, and they like to believe that others sincerely love God. The only difference they detect is that the others' worship services may be more devout or more complicated.

If I were asked to summarize this book in just one statement, I would say, *The faith without priests, temples, and material sacrifices is the true faith. God saves sinners, and a church's works or sacraments add nothing to God's work.*

One faith is, yes, more oriental. It is more mystical and more involved with the spirit world with its visions and dreams and visitations by saints, demons, and angels. It has *many gods* (patron saints), one for every thing and event.[10] In this faith, a person's efforts and actions (works, sacraments, fasting, etc.) supplement what God does, the objective being to maintain a righteous position vis-à-vis God. A parish priest is required to consecrate the Eucharist. If the adherent buys a new car, he asks the priest to bless it. If a couple was married outside the church, they will ask the priest to either marry them in the church or to at least bless their union. If an adherent buys a new home, he should have it blessed. Every year the priest is supposed to visit his parishioners' homes for a house blessing (in some churches, this visit may cost money).[11] If an adherent goes on a trip, he asks the priest to bless the trip. All these ceremonies involve candles, holy water, and prayers to God and to patron saints. Call it simony or what you will, money often changes hands for liturgies (masses), the deceased, and other events. Dispensations or annulments of marriages in the Roman church can involve time and money for church lawyers.

Does the evidence lead us to conclude that the bishops, or leaders, of these ancient liturgical churches borrowed from familiar practices in Judaism, gnosticism, and the pagan religions in the Roman Empire?

---

10. The basic meaning of the word *god* is a deity, a powerful one, and may refer to angels and men.

11. In my last Orthodox parish the charge was $50 for a home blessing. A change of rite to Byzantine Catholic from the Roman Catholic Church (rite) cost me $50.

Did they blend these ingredients together and cook up what became a new stew? This is "religion" in the old sense of the word, "to bind"; but it certainly is not apostolic Christianity. Can a person enjoy peace of mind in such a concoction? Martin Luther is a good example of a sincere Catholic who, although he was a monk with a doctor of theology degree, never enjoyed peace until he realized that the "just shall live by faith."

This is why we must conclude that we are dealing with two kinds of religions, or faith systems: one seeks to follow only the Word of God, but the other depends a lot upon the teachings, or traditions, of men. In one system, people bow only to the Triune God in Heaven and pray to Him alone. In the other, adherents often prefer to ask the Virgin Mary for something because she will surely obtain it from her Son, Who would not refuse His mother. The Scriptures, however, direct us to God: Father, Son, and Holy Spirit. They do not direct us to Mary, Peter, an image of God, or another person, however saintly. Therefore, why would you want to listen to men and disregard God's Word? When religious leaders elevate the Virgin Mary, saints, popes or patriarchs, the "holy elders" of Mount Athos, or the desert fathers of Egypt or Syria to a place of honor, shouldn't we refuse to follow them? A Christian must be obedient to God's infallible Word, not to religious systems that have a form of "godly devotion" but are contrary to truth.[12]

One is a religion of *doing*, but the true religion is a matter of *being*. Scripture says, "We are His [God's] workmanship, created in Christ Jesus" (Eph. 2:10). We are what God makes us. In his excellent book *India's Search for the Unknown Christ,* the Indian evangelist Paul Pillai explains what differentiates the gospel of Jesus from other religions:

> They emphasize that man is what he does. But the gospel of Christ comes from a diametrically opposite premise, which is that action reflects what the man is. It is not the doing that determines, rather it is the being that provides the basis for doing. No man is saved by doing anything. Every one is saved by being. Doing is only the

---

12. Read 1 Timothy 3:1–13 and 2 Thessalonians 2:1–3 for Paul's description of a "falling away" (falling away is a translation of the Greek word from which the word *apostasy* is derived in English).

spontaneous reaction of being. The being matures by personal faith in the universal Redeemer who makes everything new. If any man be in Christ he becomes a new creature.[13]

When a person comes to the end of his rope, he hopefully discovers by God's grace what he has been looking for all his life. God becomes the anchor for his soul, a place of refuge and rest. But according to both Roman Catholicism and Orthodoxy, a person can never know for a certainty that he is saved and going to Heaven; that must remain an open question. Why is this? It is because both systems teach that salvation is a struggle to remain faithful and true to the church where one is *in the process* of being saved!

Here are several more examples of Orthodox spirituality that I held back for this chapter. They are taken almost at random from the *Spiritual Psalter,* which is composed of extracts from the works of Ephraim the Syrian. I beg my evangelical readers to pay close attention:

> Oh Virgin Lady and Mother of God, thou who didst bear Christ our Savior and God in thy womb, I place all my hope on thee; in thee do I trust, for thou art higher than all the powers of heaven. Thou, who are All-Pure, protect me by thine all-powerful prayers.

> Direct my life and lead me on the path indicated by the holy will of thy Son and our God.

> Grant me remission of sins, be to me a refuge, a protection, a defense, and a directress, guiding me along the path to eternal life.

> Do not leave me in the terrible hour of death, O my Lady, but rush to my aid, rescue me from the bitter torments of the demons. For if thou so choosest, thou hast the power to do this, for thou art truly the Mother of God who reignest over all.[14]

> To thee do I run; be kind to me, my all-pure Lady. Take advantage of thy motherly boldness before thy Son and God, and gain for

---

13. K.V. Paul Pillai, *India's Search for the Unknown Christ,* 25.

14. *A Spiritual Psalter or Reflections on God,* excerpted by Bishop Theophan the *Recluse from the Works of our Holy Father Ephraim the Syrian,* translated by Antonina Janda (Liberty, TN: St. John of Kronstadt, 1997), 104.

me forgiveness of my former sins. . . . Remain always with me in
my thoughts, words and deeds, in all the movements of my soul
and body, instructing me, leading me and guiding me, deflecting
from me all hostile powers, and preserving me and providing
thy servant, however worthless, with thy grace in every way.[15]

Directly contradicting such prayers, the apostle Peter tells us that
our Lord Jesus is the shepherd and the bishop of our souls: "For you
were like sheep going astray, but have now returned to the Shepherd
and Overseer [or, "Guardian," HCSB and lexical sources] of your
souls" (1 Pet. 2:25). As stated, there can be only one such Shepherd
and Overseer. Why would you want to exchange Christ the Shepherd
of your soul for a creaturely substitute?

The Orthodox Church: What's the Attraction for Evangelicals?

Why are evangelicals attracted to the Orthodox church? The quick
answer might be that they are tired of experiencing church as a place
of entertainment; they are tired of appeals for money; or they are
disappointed, bored by the services and the preachers. Possibly, the
evangelical is himself an unsaved person, and he just can't wait to get
home to his favorite entertainments or pastimes. The question of union
with Jesus Christ may not appear to be immediate because the evangelical easily answers that he has confessed Jesus as personal Savior;
therefore, he must be saved. Is not that what he was taught? Such
people are still searching for stability, for satisfaction in a church that
does not change with the whims and styles of a particular generation.

Here is a summary of some of the things that appealed to me and my
family. I have first listed four positive ideas, then two negative ones:

- A belief that the Catholic church was founded by Christ and is
  the one apostolic church
- The idea that the early church believed that the ordinances of
  baptism and the Lord's Supper were not just symbols, but were
  truly efficacious means of grace; in other words, that in baptism

15. Ibid., 178–79.

there was a literal washing away of sins and that in the Eucharist, the body and blood of Christ were consumed
- Unity of doctrine and practice throughout the world
- The beauty of liturgical worship and ceremonies like matins and vespers
- Disappointment in evangelicalism, where pragmatism is often paramount and the churches of a city or on a mission field compete with one another
- Personal pressures on a minister or missionary to be productive, to excel in his job

Why is it difficult to win these dear Orthodox people to Christ? If they were evangelicals who converted to Orthodoxy, they already know what you want to tell them, and they reject it for the reasons described. They believe they have found "the true faith." They would not think of going back to sit in a pew to listen to gospel messages and hymns. If they were born into the Orthodox church culture, they are proud of their heritage, their language, and customs, such as Serbian, Russian, Ukrainian, Greek, or Arabic. They have confidence in the antiquity of their faith, and they love the liturgies, especially Pascha (Easter). Their liturgies are complex and very unlike anything the Protestant experiences. The Orthodox consider the typical evangelical church buildings to be without aesthetic beauty, just bare walls where real worship is nonexistent. One priest friend told me, "A protestant church is okay if you can be satisfied with four bare walls and a sermon."

Roman Catholicism: What's the Attraction for Evangelicals?

Why are evangelicals attracted to Roman Catholicism? For the same reasons they are attracted to the Orthodox church, but especially for these reasons:

- Unity of doctrine
- The infallibility of the pope, which means that someone has

the final authority to define the faith for all Christians; he is the "vicar of Christ" and has Christ's authority in the church
- A belief that the church of Rome has remained faithful to the deposit of faith and is the head of all the churches because the pope sits on Peter's throne, continuing his ministry

Many converts to Roman Catholicism have considered joining the Orthodox church, but, although they were attracted to its liturgies, they eventually joined the Roman Catholic Church. They viewed Orthodoxy as too ethnic, too divided into competing jurisdictions, and they were impressed by the Roman church's worldwide unity, centered in the papacy.

Sinners Are Called to Come to Christ

The Lord calls us to look to Him, not to an institution, no matter how sacred one may believe it to be. In the Old Testament, the Lord God called to His people, "Look to Me, and be saved, all you ends of the earth! For I am God, and there is no other" (Isa. 45:22). In the New Testament, God continues to call us to Himself. Consider John 6:40 and 12:44–47:

> And this is the will of Him who sent Me, that everyone who sees the Son and believes in Him may have everlasting life; and I will raise him up at the last day. . . . Then Jesus cried out and said, "He who believes in Me, believes not in Me but in Him who sent Me. And he who sees Me sees Him who sent Me. I have come as a light into the world, that whoever believes in Me should not abide in darkness. And if anyone hears My words and does not believe, I do not judge him; for I did not come to judge the world but to save the world."

Christ invites all who are weary to come to Him (Matt. 11:28–30). Do not ever think of doubting the One Who keeps us safe for eternity. We are His sheep, and the Shepherd protects His own. Is such a wonderful God not worthy of our love and service? The Holy Spirit inspired the apostle Peter's words to the scattered and persecuted

Christians of his day: "To an inheritance incorruptible and undefiled and that does not fade away, reserved in heaven for you, who are kept by the power of God through faith for salvation ready to be revealed in the last time" (1 Pet. 1:4, 5).

And a few verses later in the same chapter, he wrote, "For you know that you were redeemed from your empty way of life inherited from the fathers, not with perishable things, like silver or gold, but with the precious blood of Christ, like that of a lamb without defect or blemish" (1 Pet. 1:18, 19).

"Inherited from the fathers" is a translation of the Greek πατροπαραδότου and refers to traditions handed down from one's fathers. Perhaps we all suffer from the same weakness, that is, a tendency to cling to the teachings or customs we received from our parents. Change does not come easily to us. Every country and region within a country suffers from the same sort of pride. In Spain, one says he is Basque; another says he is Catalan. In France, one is from Normandy or from Provence or Languedoc, and he is proud to speak of his ancestry. In the United States people will say they are from the South or the West or the East. People love their homes, their traditions, and their ways of speaking and doing things. This is natural, but in matters pertaining to the worship of God, we must take great care that we cling only to the truth of God's Word; otherwise, we risk finding ourselves on the broad road that leads to perdition.

Conclusion:
Is History Enough?

THIS BOOK HAS SOUGHT to accurately summarize the teachings of the ancient churches. Their sacraments, theologies, and doctrines of salvation have been scrutinized. If more space has been devoted here to the Roman Catholic Church, it is only because it is more prominent in our part of the world. In the West, the Reformation raised issues that continue to divide Protestants and Catholics. Let us not forget that the Orthodox generally hold all other churches to be either schismatic or heretical. Recognizing the need to address pastors and teachers as well as the general public, I have endeavored to identify the differences without intentionally alienating a reader who may believe otherwise.

I wish readers to know I believe that some of God's children can be found in any of the churches I have criticized; our Lord knows His own. I respect such people because I know they love God with their whole hearts and desire to obey Him. Many of them have given their lives in selfless service to others at home and on mission fields. I do not judge them but leave them to the love and mercy of our Heavenly Father, Who sent His Son to save sinners. God saved me through His wonderful grace in the early 1970s in spite of my imperfections and failings, and I have confidence He will complete the work He began in me (Phil. 1:6).

The Pull of History

A number of evangelical leaders seem to consider the Orthodox church a bastion of orthodoxy, conservative in doctrine. Ministers from the Episcopalian and Anglican churches and other large denominations in America have sought refuge in either the Roman Catholic Church or the Eastern Orthodox Church. Many of them desire to continue serving God as ministers and have been received into the ranks of the clergy of these churches. At times, entire congregations have entered one of these ancient churches. The pull of history is very strong. Although the desire to be *connected* to the apostolic church is not evil, it can be misguided. Jaroslav Pelikan (ex-Lutheran) and Frederica Mathewes-Green (ex-Episcopalian) are well-known personalities whose testimonies as converts to the Orthodox church are both interesting and persuasive. Frank Beckwith's return to the Catholic church is interesting because he was president of the Evangelical Theological Society. In a book such as this, it would be appropriate to review Beckwith's reasoning. He explains,

> However, in January, at the suggestion of a dear friend, I began reading the Early Church Fathers as well as some of the more sophisticated works on justification by Catholic authors. I became convinced that the Early Church is more Catholic than Protestant and that the Catholic view of justification, correctly understood, is biblically and historically defensible. Even though I also believe that the Reformed view is biblically and historically defensible, I think the Catholic view has more explanatory power to account for both all the biblical texts on justification as well as the church's historical understanding of salvation prior to the Reformation all the way back to the ancient church of the first few centuries.

His statement is important to me personally because it sounds quite close to my own thinking in the late 1980s. Now that the reader has read this far, it will be up to him or her to decide whether Dr. Beckwith was justified in his decisions. I think he was attracted by the Roman church's strong stand on morality and its monolithic, authoritative structure in contrast with the disarray often evident in the evangelical world. Although this book has nothing to do with individuals and everything to do with history, doctrine, and the Scriptures, Beckwith's reasoning brings several comments to mind.

Freedom and Bondage

The apostle Paul had scarcely left Galatia after working so hard among its people to bring them to faith in the Lord Jesus Christ, when he heard that the Galatian Christians were in danger of subversion to a false gospel. Keep this important fact in mind. *Already*, the church was under attack! Paul wrote, "I marvel that you are turning away so soon from Him who called you in the grace of Christ, to a different gospel" (Gal. 1:6).

Do the ancient churches preach the same gospel as did the more ancient apostle Paul? This is the question before us all. Beckwith and others have answered with a resounding yes. I, however, do not believe they do. History tells us that these religious groups built empires whose structure was supported by coercion, anathemas, physical threats, and at times executions. Such ecclesiastical empires continue to place their members under religious obligations that are either unnecessary or contrary to the freedom Christians experience when they know the Lord Jesus Christ. The law had a purpose that was good: it taught its subjects that they were in bondage to sin, that they needed a liberator! Every form of false religion tends to place its people under a yoke of bondage. This is why Paul told the Galatians, "For if I build again those things which I destroyed, I make myself a transgressor," and again, "do not be entangled again with a yoke of bondage" (Gal. 2:18; 5:1).

The chief mistake that we who have returned to the ancient churches made is that we took our eyes off our Lord when we fixed them upon organizations. We compared our denomination, fractured and divided, with a seemingly monolithic, ancient group that appeared to have kept the faith. We ignored Paul's words to his child in the faith, Timothy, "O Timothy! Guard what was committed to your trust, avoiding the profane and idle babblings and contradictions of what is falsely called knowledge" (1 Tim. 6:20).

Schaeffer, Gillquist, Beckwith, and the others, myself included, made another mistake: we did not maintain our focus on the apostolic faith of the first century. We looked at the church of the second and third centuries and thought it appeared more "Catholic than Protestant." That idea may be true to some extent, as we have seen, which is why the attraction is so strong. We should have kept our eyes on Christ, the gospel, and the freedom we knew and enjoyed in Him! I pray that someday the others will become aware of this fact. They are not enemies; they have made a mistake; and evangelical Christians must have compassion and love for them.

In spite of the many conversions of evangelicals to either one of the ancient churches, things are not so well in the Orthodox and the Catholic churches. The picture is not as rosy as it appears from the outside. Neither of these churches is monolithic, perfectly united. The Roman church has been plagued by several schisms in the last couple of centuries and by various pressure groups during the twentieth century. These pressure groups represent various social trends in Western civilization, and they are threatening the church's unity. The Orthodox church is not without its schisms, rogue bishops, and splinter groups claiming to be the true church, the "little flock."

The Necessity for True History

History is a great teacher. Lessons can be learned from past mistakes. Examples of bad management can help us to improve our planning or redirect our energies. Religious history is important to Christians because we can learn how the true faith spread, or how evils were corrected in the church, or, yes, what went wrong in the church itself. History does not always present the rosy picture some would like to paint of a humble, infallible church. History informs us that papal infallibility, an idea previously held by many, became dogma around 1870. History informs us that there were warrior popes, incestuous and immoral popes, unfaithful bishops, heretical patriarchs, and schismatic patriarchates (jurisdictions of patriarchs). And these were supposed to be Christians who ruled our Lord's flock in His place. Easterners welcomed Muslims rather than continue to be ruled by Constantinople. Through church history we discover how a papacy in Rome, wishing to justify its independence from the Eastern emperor and to establish the spiritual preeminence of Rome, made use of falsified documents such as the *Donation of Constantine* and the *False Decretals*.[1] We are obliged to admit that in spite of all this corruption, there remained enough of the "yeast" of the Biblical preaching to raise up a remnant of sincere Christians striving to believe and live the gospel in fulfillment of the Lord's promises in Matthew 13, 16, and 29 that He will build His church, that the gates of Hell will not prevail against His church, and that He is always with believers—even to the end of the world.

Back to Bondage

It is evident that history is never enough if truth is absent! We must know apostolic history if we are to find our place in history and, maybe, correct our beliefs, but we need truthful history! Most importantly, we need to know the foundations of Christian history. This is why Christians need to read the Bible every day.

One's acceptance of a church as the voice of God makes anything possible: a man becomes infallible, popes become greater than kings or emperors, a woman is born without original sin, and the earth becomes the center of the universe. Clergy may be forbidden to marry. The laity is told to abstain at times from meats, certain foods, and sex. The laity is also commanded to keep feast days under the threat of mortal sin and being lost, doomed to Hell should one ever overthrow such servitude to man. This is as serious as a religion telling you that you must not accept a blood transfusion to save your life or even give blood to save someone else's life, or a religion that tells you to refuse all medical help because you should have faith that God heals.

In Orthodoxy we returned to legalism, allowing ourselves to be enslaved again to the keeping of days, weeks, seasons, new moons, fasts, "touch nots," and the like (Gal. 4:10, 11; Col. 2:21, 22). This is diametrically opposed to the Bible's teaching that the "just shall live by his faith." Christians must reject ideas that destroy the grace of Christ, Who paid our debt and satisfied the law's requirements. Paul wrote, "I do not set aside the grace of God; for if righteousness comes

1. See Peter E. Prosser, "Church History's Biggest Hoax," *Christian History Magazine* 72 (Fall 2001), 35.

through the law, then Christ died for nothing" (Gal. 2:21, HCSB).

History Can Never Be Enough

If history were enough, we might all be Jews or Buddhists or whatever religion can lay claim to being the most ancient. Clearly, history is not enough. Truth is eternal, but many are the errors or heresies that are ancient. Against those who would quote their ancient history and their church fathers, we appeal to the apostolic documents! We lay hold of the Rock of our salvation (Deut. 32:15; 1 Sam. 2:2; 2 Sam. 22:47; Ps. 18:2), for there is no other name given under Heaven by which people can be saved (Acts 4:12). Salvation is in a person, not an organization. Clearly, the Lord would not build His church upon any other rock than the one that has been laid. Did not the apostle Paul write, "For no other foundation can anyone lay than that which is laid, which is Jesus Christ"? The only one that is unmovable and eternally sure is God's own immutable and unchangeable Son, Christ Jesus the Lord (1 Cor. 3:11; Heb. 13:8; 1 Pet. 2:6). And please, do not forget that salvation is a *finished* work: "[God] who *has saved* us and *called* us with a holy calling, not according to our works, but according to His own purpose and grace which was given to us in Christ Jesus *before* time began" (2 Tim. 1:9; italics added).

The gospel, or good news, is this: Salvation is God's work in us and for us. He gives us eternal life; He enables us to believe; and He makes this a *real* salvation because He keeps His "sheep" safe and secure for eternity (John 17). This is the greatest truth we can learn from history!

Appendix: A Few Remaining Questions

AN ARGUMENT FOR the authority and infallibility of the Catholic church is often repeated in the form of this statement: "The Catholic Church is the Mother of the Bible. Her members wrote the New Testament, and her bishops and councils decided which books should be included in the canon of Holy Scripture." Catholics tell us that without the church, Protestants wouldn't have a Bible at all. The point seems well taken and may be reasonable at first glance. We would, therefore, not be remiss in spending a few moments to parry this sword thrust. Perhaps many Protestants have never heard this objection to their existence as "separated brethren." I used similar arguments in conferences when speaking for the Catholic church. Since then, I learned I needed to refocus and take a longer view of matters. I am grateful to a pastor friend who reminded me of this. So, take a deep breath, stand back, and get a little more perspective on the matter. In fact, why not consult the inspired record itself?

The Worshiper

For two thousand years before Christ, and for two thousand years after Him, God did not reject His children for the failings of some, even when the faithful seemed vastly outnumbered. During the Exodus period in Israelite history, a "mixed multitude" accompanied the Israelites who left Egypt under Moses' leadership (Exod. 12:38). This assorted group benefited from its association with the "church" of that day (Acts 7:38, Gr. *ecclesia*). They escaped Egypt and eventually crossed the Jordan with the Israelites. At the time of the Exodus, the Israelites were not even circumcised in obedience to the covenant

God had made with their forefather Abraham (Gen. 17:7–14). Under the leadership of Nehemiah during the post-exilic period, we read that many strangers were among those who inhabited the land: "So it was, when they had heard the Law, that they separated all the mixed multitude from Israel" (Neh. 13:3). The apostle Paul mentions a remnant of only seven thousand in all of Israel who refused to bend the knee to Baal (Rom. 11:4). Is there a lesson here for us? Should it not remind us of Jesus' parables concerning the New Testament people of God and what would transpire in the visible church after His return to Heaven? The parables in Matthew describe God's rule among men during the period when Christ sits at the right hand of the Father before His return for judgment:

> Again, the kingdom of heaven is like unto a net, that was cast into the sea, and gathered of every kind, which, when it was full, they drew to shore, and sat down and gathered the good into vessels, but cast the bad away. So shall it be at the end of the world: the angels shall come forth and sever the wicked from among the just, and shall cast them into the furnace of fire; there shall be wailing and gnashing of teeth. Jesus saith unto them, Have ye understood all these things? They say unto him, Yea, Lord. (Matt. 13:47–51)

Although our Lord is the head of His church, on earth things are not perfect. In spite of strict requirements of faith, baptism, and discipleship for membership in the visible church, weeds appear in the church. A massive cleanup will be necessary at Christ's second coming. This is what the Lord revealed in His parables in Matthew 13. According to the apostle Paul, the true Jew or worshiper of the Lord is one who has circumcision of the heart (Rom. 2:28, 29). The same holds true for baptism today. It is an outward form like circumcision, but it does not guarantee that someone is a real or true Christian, a child of God. The inward washing of the Holy Spirit is what cleanses and qualifies a person for spiritual work; without this, all the going through the motions will avail nothing. On another occasion, Paul wrote to the Philippians, "For we are the circumcision, who worship

God in the Spirit, rejoice in Christ Jesus, and have no confidence in the flesh" (Phil. 3:3).

The New Testament Canon

With these truths firmly in mind, we turn to the matter of the New Testament canon. But first, some history.

Old Testament Prophets

We begin with a question: How was an Israelite to know whether an Old Testament prophet was directed by God to declare His will to the Israelites? The answer is found in Deuteronomy 13 and 18:

> If there arises among you a prophet or a dreamer of dreams, and he gives you a sign or a wonder, and the sign or the wonder comes to pass, of which he spoke to you, saying, "Let us go after other gods"—which you have not known—"and let us serve them," you shall not listen to the words of that prophet or that dreamer of dreams, for the LORD your God is testing you to know whether you love the LORD your God with all your heart and with all your soul. You shall walk after the LORD your God and fear Him, and keep His commandments and obey His voice; you shall serve Him and hold fast to Him. But that prophet or that dreamer of dreams shall be put to death, because he has spoken in order to turn **you** away from the LORD your God, who brought you out of the land of Egypt and redeemed you from the house of bondage, to entice you from the way in which the LORD your God commanded you to walk. So you shall put away the evil from your midst. (Deut. 13:1–5)

> But the prophet who presumes to speak a word in My name, which I have not commanded him to speak, or who speaks in the name of other gods, that prophet shall die. And if you say in your heart, "How shall we know the word which the LORD has not spoken?"—when a prophet speaks in the name of the LORD, if the thing does not happen or come to pass, that **is** the thing which the LORD has not spoken; the prophet has spoken it presumptuously; you shall not be afraid of him. (Deut. 18:20–22)

Concerning the Old Testament prophets whom God had not sent, Jeremiah, speaking on behalf of the Lord, said, "Therefore thus says the LORD concerning the prophets who prophesy in My name, whom I did not send, and who say, 'Sword and famine shall not be in this land'—'By sword and famine those prophets shall be consumed'" (Jer. 14:15). Regarding those prophets who were recognized by the people, we read in 1 Samuel 9:9 and following verses that the people went specifically to consult those prophets concerning God's will. Today we have the benefit of immediate access to an authoritative collection of inspired, canonical books, but such collections were compiled at a relatively late date.

Apostles and Their Companions

Why would these same principles not apply to the matter of inspired writings belonging to the New Testament era? How would this work? It seems that the prophets who said they spoke on behalf of God were judged by their words—whether they were sound, whether they were in harmony with God's will, and whether they came to pass. The basic meaning of a prophet is one who declares or reveals the mind of God. There were also prophets and inspired writers in New Testament times. The writers of the New Testament books were either apostles or companions of the apostles. Luke accompanied Paul on His voyages, and tradition says that Mark was an interpreter of Peter. Tradition also says that Mark founded the church in Alexandria, although this is not confirmed by any factual information. The other writers, James and Jude, were disciples of Jesus Christ and active in the Jerusalem church. The writers and their letters were known to the early church because they were written before the close of the first century. Those writings were circulated among the churches and read each Lord's Day in their assemblies. As said above, they were authoritative because the writers were apostles or their companions.

True, other early writings were circulated and read for a time during Christian worship services. These were not numerous, and soon enough the church decided to stop this practice because they contained material that was not as edifying as the apostolic writings. For a time there was some hesitation about the book of Revelation, also called the Apocalypse. Yet if we look closely, we discover that Revelation demonstrates a dependency upon the Old Testament writings, to which it alludes some four hundred times. Revelation develops themes found in the book of Genesis, such as the woman, the seed, the serpent, the tree of life, a lamb, judgment, and death. Themes from the book of Exodus are the tabernacle, the sacrificial lamb, the altar, the brass laver, the high priest and other priests, and the Holy of Holies. We should not forget to mention allusions to the writings of the prophets Ezekiel and Daniel. Revelation is a beautiful and majestic book filled with visions and signs wherein God's plan is perfectly fulfilled to His glory and for the happiness of redeemed mankind. If it had not been for the exaggerations of the Montanist sect, the book would not have fallen out of favor for a time in some areas.

Christian Literature

Just as the *Apocrypha,* also called the *Deuterocanonicals,* was known to the Jews and its books were read in the synagogues, especially outside of Palestine, so other early writings from the second century were considered profitable to be read in the Christian synagogue or worship services. The Septuagint (LXX) was in wide use in the early church. In any case, apocryphal books, whether belonging to the LXX or to the period following the New Testament writings, were not recognized as possessing authority to settle doctrine. When the gnostic heresy became widespread and a danger to the early church, the question of the canonical New Testament books became more important, because the gnostics appealed to their own writings as corrections to the Christian writings. If one compares such "fairy tales" with the New Testament writings, the gnostic writings pale from the comparison. Their writings were quickly rejected as non-canonical or heretical. Due to the gnostic and other heretical sects that sprung up, Christians felt the need to draw up their own lists of recognized books. Eventually twenty-seven books were accepted as apostolic and canonical in contrast to other books that could be read as profitable but not equal in value to the canonical books. In time the bishops formally proclaimed that the books in the latter group should no longer be read in public. Although Christians everywhere knew which books were most important, this explains why there were different lists at different times and locations.

When the Christians gathered for worship, they read or sang the psalms and hymns they knew; they read the Prophets, the Pentateuch, and the Wisdom literature; and they found Christ everywhere in those writings. They read the apostles' letters and the Gospels they had received. It did not take long before these writings gained equal status with the Old Testament canon. Tertullian was apparently the first to use the term *New Testament*. It is asking too much to expect us to believe that God's scattered and persecuted flock had to wait indefinitely for a decision by a pope or a council to know which writings were sacred and trustworthy. Sirach, a deuterocanonical book also known as Ecclesiasticus (i.e., Church Book), although read in the church from early times, was admitted *definitively* into the Roman Catholic catalog of inspired books only at the Council of Trent.[1]

Then there is the matter of the Vulgate Bible. When Pope Sixtus V authorized a new edition of the Latin Vulgate Bible (1590), he threatened with excommunication anyone who would seek to modify it. Shortly thereafter it was extensively modified by order of Pope Clement VIII. It would appear that the argument that Protestants are indebted to the Roman Catholic Church's decisions concerning both the canon and the text of Scripture is very weak.

Ratifications of the Canon

Simon J. Kistemaker, a professor at the Reformed Seminary in Oviedo, Florida, in an address delivered in 1976 to the Evangelical Theological Society at their twenty-eighth annual meeting, spoke

---

1. Emil Osty and Joseph Trinquet, trans. "Introduction to the Book of Ecclesiasticus," *La Bible Osty* (Paris: Editions du Seuil, 1973), 1419.

The comment from the original French follows. «Bien que très apprécié des rabbins et cité souvent par eux, il n'a jamais été admis dans le canon juif. Après quelques hésitations, il est entré définitivement dans le catalogue des livres inspirés (concile de Trente). Les Églises protestantes le rangent parmi les Apocryphes.»

on the development of the New Testament canon and explained its acceptance in the following manner. "The Church did not create the canon. The Church merely ratified decisions that had already been reached by believers individually and by congregations collectively. . . . The individual believers meeting in worship had accepted these books and had acknowledged that they came from God."[2]

The Muratorian Canon (ca. AD 180) gives a listing of the Gospels, thirteen Epistles, and the Revelation. The epistle to the Hebrews is traditionally listed as belonging to the apostle Paul and is quoted in Clement of Rome (AD 90–110). There was some hesitation over the epistle to the Hebrews in the East. The "dominical Scriptures" read in the churches are listed in Eusebius's *Ecclesiastical History*. The Council of Laodicea (AD 363) listed all the New Testament books except the Apocalypse. Athanasius, in his thirty-ninth Paschal Letter (AD 367), listed all the New Testament books we know as canonical, as well as the Didache and the Shepherd, which were considered worthy to be read as had been the custom.[3]

It is not my intention to cover ground that has been covered by excellent writers in this specialized area. The goal is simply to answer in a commonsense manner a few questions that others have asked me. The bibliography provides several references for anyone especially interested in the canon of the Bible.[4]

Concerning the church councils and their decisions relative to the Biblical canon, New Testament scholar F. F. Bruce comments, "They did not impose any innovation on the churches; they simply endorsed what had become the general consensus of the churches of the west and of the greater part of the east."[5] Patristic scholar John Chryssavgis says that in the Eastern church, official recognition of a *closed* canon took longer: "In the New Testament, it was the book of Revelation that caused the most controversy, but no one after the sixth century

2. Simon Kistemaker, "The Canon of the New Testament," *Journal of the Evangelical Theological Society* 20, no. 1 (March 1977): 13.

3. F. F. Bruce, *The Canon of Scripture* (Downers Grove, IL: IVP Academic, 1988), 208–09.

4. Ibid. Compare Brook Foss Westcott, "Introduction," *A General Survey of the History of the Canon of the New Testament*, 6th ed. (Grand Rapids: Baker Book, 1980), 1–12 and chapter 3 of Kelly, *Early Christian Doctrine*.

5 Ibid., 97.

expressed any doubts concerning its canonicity. Nonetheless, up until the twelfth century, there was no 'closed' Canon clearly defined in Byzantium."[6]

To those who put the opening question to me, my short and simple response is this: If a pope is infallible when making decisions formally, *ex cathedra*, why, say around AD 150 or even 250, didn't he define the New Testament canon (or even the Old Testament canon) because the New Testament Scriptures were the "rule of faith" for the early church?[7] Christians recognized God's superintendence of the writings that were read and commented on in the churches, and the church simply recognized that they are what they are, inspired Holy Scripture.

Successionist Belief: A Proof of Apostolicity?

After the second century of the church, apostolic succession was pointed to as a guarantee that the truth was held by Christian believers. Doubters or heretics were told to search the lists of bishops ordained in a direct line of succession from the apostles. The bishops or pastors of the churches in the line of succession to the apostles came to be thought of as the conservators and guarantors of the apostolic faith. This was Irenaeus's argument in his writings against the heretical gnostics, who quoted their own writings as proof of their peculiar doctrines. This was also the beginning of the promotion of a teaching called tradition. In this way, true Christians answered those who wouldn't acknowledge canonical proofs as support for correct doctrine. Let us not forget what we said concerning Tradition. *The early church considered the gospel as the tradition received from the apostles.* Orthodox priest and scholar Georges Florovsky wrote,

> Tradition was not, according to St. Vincent, an independent instance, nor was it a complementary source of faith. "Ecclesiastical understanding" could not add anything to the Scripture.

6. John Chryssavgis, *The Way of the Fathers: Exploring the Patristic Mind*, ANALECTA VLATADON, 62 (Thessaloniki: Patriarchal Institute for Patristic Studies, 1998), 64.

7. Ibid., 18. F. F. Bruce cites Thomas Aquinas, who stated, "Canonical scripture alone is the rule of faith," in *On the Gospel of St. John*, lesson 6 on John 21.

> But it was the only means to ascertain and to disclose the true meaning of Scripture. *Tradition was actually "Scripture rightly understood."* Tradition was, in fact, the authentic interpretation of Scripture. And in this sense it was co-extensive with Scripture. And Scripture was for St. Vincent the only, primary and ultimate, canon of Christian truth (Commonitorium, cap. II, cf. cap. XXVIII).[8]

What does this have to do with us? Successionist belief has played an important role in the conversion of many evangelicals who believe that history is enough. What can we say to them? First, it is apparent that such history is not enough. Why? Because if we compare the teachings of those who say they are in the line of apostolic succession and empowered to celebrate baptisms, consecrate the Eucharist, and forgive sins, we find that many of their doctrines are definitely not apostolic, as we have discovered throughout the various chapters of this book. Their teachings are not part of the "deposit of faith." With true succession there must also be correct belief, not superstitions or late ideas such as transubstantiation, the worship of images, the immaculate conception of Mary, the infallibility of the pope, or the idea that Christians, Jews, and Muslims worship the same God.

Personal Questions

A few years ago I drew up a list of questions as I mused upon my spiritual situation. I used my personal difficulties to challenge others, for I was also playing the role of devil's advocate. I wanted answers to my questions. Receiving very little help, I decided to conduct my own investigation. Now the reader knows what I found. Admittedly, I have confronted and answered these questions in different ways in the past, but I believe personal experience, continuous study, and daily Bible reading over the years are good teachers, and I have benefited greatly from them.

These are the questions I considered:

---

8. Florovsky, *Collected Works of George Florovsky*, 74 (my italics).

1. Did the Holy Spirit lead the church unto all truth, as promised?
2. Did Jesus remain with His church, keeping it as He had promised?
3. If the first Christians were "once saved, always saved," how would it have been possible for the church as a whole to lose saving gospel truth (James 1:18)?
4. Did the world have to wait for Luther and Calvin to recover the gospel from Scripture and set up gospel churches?
5. Is it credible to maintain that the Catholic church preserved the gospel until the 1500s?
6. Can evangelicals, especially Reformed Christians, honestly claim Augustine, Athanasius, and Thomas Aquinas as part of their heritage as spiritual ancestors?
7. Can a church baptize and commune (administer Communion to) members if it has rejected the gospel or distorted it by including works as necessary for salvation, and should evangelical churches receive baptisms from such denominations and groups?

Questions 1 and 2

1. Did the Holy Spirit lead the church unto all truth, as promised?
2. Did Jesus remain with His church, keeping it as He had promised?

I am obliged to respond with a strong yes to these two simple questions. Further, never in my life from the moment of my conversion to Christ and my baptism have I believed otherwise. God fulfills His Word, even if at times we don't understand the manner in which He accomplishes it. Through the Holy Spirit, the Third Person of the Trinity, Jesus was always with His church, which is His body.[9] Of course there are people who believe that God is bound to only one organization, to one particular group or denomination. Nevertheless, the Spirit of God is free from such earthly ideas and moves wheresoever He wishes. Miracles of conversion occur everywhere in the world,

9. John 14:16, 17, 26; 15:26; 16:13, 14; Eph. 1:23; 3:19.

and I might add, in spite of personal unfaithfulness. India, China, Africa, and everywhere else—the Sovereign King of the universe moves to find and fill men's hearts with His love.

Question 3

3. If the first Christians were "once saved, always saved," how would it have been possible for the church as a whole to lose saving gospel truth (James 1:18)?

For this question we must ask what is meant by "the first Christians"? Do we mean every member of the apostolic church of Corinth, or Jerusalem, etc.? Do we mean all who took the name of Jesus upon themselves in water baptism? How about all those who were brought up in the church and made a profession of faith and adopted the religion of their parents? Someone from the ancient churches might look at question 3 and reply, "They didn't lose the gospel because the church has an uninterrupted, continuous history. The truth as the 'deposit of faith' was transmitted from one generation to the next as tradition." On the other hand, if we acknowledge that the true church is composed of God's children and that God promises He will never allow Satan to rob Him of what is His, we can imagine that should a church or group become unfaithful, God still remains faithful to His children and to His Word (2 Tim. 2:13). God's Word is alive and is a powerful instrument to bring His elect to true faith in Jesus (1 Pet. 1:23). If a church contaminates the purity of the gospel by binding unnecessary burdens on its members, that group is unfaithful to the Lord Jesus, Who freed us of such law-keeping. God carries out His work of grace in an individual's heart. It is possible that it may not even be by means of reading the written Word, but through the hearing of portions of it in some far-off desert, jungle, or prison.

Question 4

4. Did the world have to wait for Luther and Calvin to recover the gospel from Scripture and set up gospel churches?

From all that has been said, it is evident that we are under obliga-tion to love people who may be members of a questionable religious group, especially when there is evidence that they know Jesus Christ and love Him. We are called to love people, not false doctrines. Such was the situation at the time of the Reformation. The Reformation brought clarity to the pulpit and exposed superstitious practices. True, it did lead to a breakup of the visible unity of an earthly church ruled by the hierarchy. The Reformation sought to rid the church of useless works and dogmas that clouded the gospel and brought it into disrepute. There were now two camps: those who wished to main-tain tradition (the status quo) and those who hungered after Jesus Christ and the truth that frees a soul of its burdens. Many did choose to remain in the Roman church or even returned to it later; thus, we cannot say that all of God's children went "outside the camp" (Heb. 13:13). God knows and judges the heart, and we should respect this.

During the Middle Ages a number of reformers and groups spoke out against Rome's doctrines and abuses long before the Reformation of the sixteenth century. They may have held some errors, but they were seeking to live an evangelical life free of traditions and supersti-tions. Their lives were constantly threatened, and some of them were tortured and put to death for their "free thinking." They translated and wrote down gospel portions that they distributed door to door. These evangelists often traveled under the guise of being vendors and merchants. When they felt safe to leave the tracts with people, they did. Men's hearts were touched by the gospel truth long before the Reformation. The God of all grace has always been at work (1 Pet. 5:10). The company of true believers, whose names are written down in Heaven, continued to increase through the ages after the apostles fell asleep in death. Working secretly like yeast, the lump was being raised. If we agree on this, question 4 has been answered.

Question 5

5. Is it credible to maintain that the Catholic church preserved the gospel until the 1500s?

To answer this question, we are only looking at Europe because of the history of the Reformation. We know that during the Dark Ages, monks copied and translated the Scriptures and that the Gospels were read during the Mass. The Scriptures were studied in monasteries and theological schools. Theology was one of the main departments of university studies during the Middle Ages. Consequently, although many church rules and unscriptural beliefs were added to the true deposit of faith, no one should doubt that the gospel was preserved, although it may not have been preached clearly from the pulpit and understood by illiterate and superstitious serfs. Years ago, I read that during the Dark Ages many priests barely knew enough Latin to say the Mass.

Question 6

6. Can evangelicals, especially Reformed Christians, honestly claim Augustine, Athanasius, and Thomas Aquinas as part of their heritage as spiritual ancestors?

It seems the question might also be put this way: Should we not take the good where we find it and leave the bad? In many instances, men such as Augustine, Athanasius, and Thomas Aquinas studied and preached God's Word and demonstrated a love for God, neighbor, and the church. A number of the ancient writers suffered persecution and banishment for their faith. John Chrysostom immediately comes to mind, as well as Ignatius of Antioch, who was mentioned in earlier chapters. In any anthology of such writings, we will find portions that offer real enjoyment and instruction, although other ideas would be better ignored. In fact, I have such an anthology in my library; it is compiled and edited by David Otis Fuller (a Baptist). His acknowledgments page lists men like Drs. Criswell, Culbertson, Edman, and Walvoord, all well-known evangelicals who endorsed Mr. Fuller's anthology of evangelical writings.[10] The ancient authors were part of the "church visible," and God alone knows where they stood in

---

10. David Otis Fuller, ed., *A Treasury of Evangelical Writings, Valiant for the Truth* (Grand Rapids: Kregel, 1974).

relation to Him and the church whose "names are written in heaven" (Luke 10:20). I willingly admit that Augustine, Athanasius, Aquinas, and others are part of our Christian heritage. Yet I do not feel an obligation to claim them as spiritual ancestors. They wrote as men of their times. I am grateful for the good they preached, but as a Christian I have the liberty to reject what is not in harmony with the apostolic faith. For these reasons, we do not crown them as "saints," but leave such "fathers" to God's great and final judgment.

For example, when the mighty Augustine of Hippo teaches that the baptism of the Donatists (a schismatic body) is valid baptism because Christ is the true baptizer, consequently, the minister's personal piety does not play a major role; he is already speaking in terms of Roman juridical authority. He is laying a foundation for the Roman church's later declaration that anyone can baptize in an emergency. All that is required is that the person baptizing should have the right intention, pour water on the individual, and repeat the formula for baptism, in which case even a Muslim could administer baptism.[11]

Question 7

7. Can a church baptize and commune (administer Communion to) members if it has rejected the gospel or distorted it by including works as necessary for salvation, and should evangelical churches receive baptisms from such denominations and groups?

This question will undoubtedly be rather difficult for many denominations to resolve. In fact, the Orthodox church itself is not united on the matter of the reception of baptisms from other churches. The actual practice of the spiritual guides of Mount Athos or the national church in Greece will differ from that of the Greek Orthodox Archdiocese in America and of the Orthodox Church of America. The bishops, following the decisions of the former Standing Conference of Orthodox Bishops (SCOBA), have made rulings on baptism, but they are not always followed by every single priest in

---

11. *Catechism of the Catholic Church*, #1234. Cf. J. N. D. Kelly, *Early Christian Doctrines*, 412, 415, 424–25.

their jurisdictions. In other words, uniformity does not exist among the Orthodox people in America. Some parishes follow practices known as strictness and others follow economy, and many parishes follow *both* according to the local pastoral situation. In the Russian Orthodox Church Outside Russia (ROCOR), reunited with the Russian Patriarchate in May 2007, the practice is uneven depending on the diocese. ROCOR was not a member of SCOBA, but we can expect that future discussions on these issues will be held due to ROCOR's reunification with Mother Russia.

Uniformity does not exist among Baptist churches, because they practice a congregational style of church government. Reformed churches answer this question one way and independent evangelical churches another way. One might read with some benefit Wayne Grudem's discussion on baptism in his *Systematic Theology*.[12] Grudem's calm discussion could serve as a starting point for a church interested in reviewing its practices. Landmark Baptist Churches reject "alien baptisms"; this means that to become a member of one of their churches, a person must have received baptism in a Landmark or Landmark-type Baptist church. This question needs attention. Was Augustine's answer to Donatism (that their baptism was valid) correct?

True, I have placed this discussion in the context of the Western church, but I am sure that most of what has been written applies equally to the Eastern church. Sharing my personal thoughts will, I hope, prove helpful to those who are going through the same thought processes. Perhaps they have or will come up with different answers. I believe my answers are in line with history, and more importantly, with Biblical principles. Let us keep in mind that history is not enough; truth must always be present.

The Packaging of the Services

The Orthodox packaging is good; the services are bright, colorful, melodious, and powerful. If a person were to compare them with the

---

12. Wayne Grudem, *Systematic Theology: An Introduction to Biblical Doctrine* (Grand Rapids: Zondervan, 1994; Leicester, England: IVP, 2000), 982–84.

typical evangelical package one sees on a Sunday morning, he might say the latter is quite plain, like a cardboard box. The fact is that the evangelical liturgy does not draw much attention to itself, often being rather intellectual with appeals to Scripture, reason, and logic, accompanied by a number of anecdotes to maintain interest. This is why the attendees are seen taking notes, turning pages, and standing for a prayer or a hymn, and why they sometimes nod off or dream about the afternoon's lunch plans. In other churches the services may be extremely emotional, music blasting, accompanied by vigorous and oftentimes great singing, lots of shouting, clapping, and body movement. I must admit with all truthfulness that I mostly enjoyed the Orthodox services (not always), although the standing can be physically challenging at times. I love to listen to a beautiful choir from Russia or Bulgaria or Greece, but if someone does not understand the language, how can he agree with everything that is sung?

Liturgy can be beautiful, but could it also be included in the passage where Paul speaks of a "tickling" of the ears, something that pleases the flesh?[13] Why do we go to church? Do we go there to sing or to pray, "Most holy Theotokos, save us"? Are we saved? Have we been saved? *What* or *who* saves us? If there is no "salvation in any other, for there is no other name under heaven given among men by which we must be saved," why invoke Mary (Acts 4:12)? Should we assemble with others to listen forty times to "Lord, have mercy"? Has He had mercy on us, or are we still lost in our sins and looking for mercy? We need to face these issues squarely. I pray for my loved ones in these churches. I petition God on their behalf that by His grace we could agree together with Ignatius of Antioch: "But to me the official record is Jesus Christ; the inviolable record is His Cross and His death and His Resurrection and the faith of which He is the Author. These are the

---

13. Wayne Grudem, *Systematic Theology: An Introduction to Biblical Doctrine* (Grand Rapids: Zondervan, 1994; Leicester, England: IVP, 2000), 982–84.

"For a time will be when they will not endure sound doctrine, but according to their own lusts, they will heap up to themselves teachers tickling the ear," Jay P. Green Sr., trans. "2 Timothy 4:3," *Literal Translation of the Holy Bible* (Shallotte, NC: Sovereign Grace Publishers, 2001).

things which, thanks to your prayer, I want to be my justification."[14]

I appeal to my evangelical Protestant friends to consider all that has been written here before entering either the Orthodox church or the Catholic church. If you love the Lord Jesus Christ and have entrusted your life to Him, do not go where glory and veneration are given to creatures, no matter how much you enjoy their liturgy or how moving you find the lives of the saints and fathers. Give yourself completely to the Lord Jesus Christ, the only Savior, and trust Him completely. He does save to the uttermost (Heb. 7:25).

14. Ignatius of Antioch, *To the Philadelphians* (paragraph 8).

Subject Index

Scripture Index